MODERN GOTHIC

The Inventive Furniture of
Kimbel and Cabus, 1863–82

MODERN GOTHIC

The Inventive Furniture of Kimbel and Cabus, 1863–82

Edited by Barbara Veith and Medill Higgins Harvey

Brooklyn Museum   **HIRMER**

CONTENT

FOREWORD

Modern Gothic: The Inventive Furniture of Kimbel and Cabus, 1863–82 is the first museum exhibition and publication to chronicle the history of the influential and enterprising partnership of Anton Kimbel (1822–1895) and Joseph Cabus (1824–1898). As directors of a leading cabinetmaking and decorating firm in post-Civil War New York City, theirs is an inspiring story of immigrant success. Sons of German and French cabinetmaking families, both came to the United States seeking opportunity, demonstrated talent and tenacity, and worked in the upper echelons of the burgeoning New York City cabinetmaking industry. By the time they joined forces in 1863, Kimbel and Cabus were seasoned professionals, well-versed in adapting to stylistic change. Together, they created a panoply of furniture forms in a variety of styles and price points "within reach of all" to satisfy a broad range of customers. Their prescient embrace of the progressive British Modern Gothic style in the early 1870s, then nascent in the United States, attracted an equally forward-looking clientele. Kimbel and Cabus fluidly combined British and Continental European design sources, both medieval and contemporaneous, to fashion bold Modern Gothic forms emblematic of the creativity and inclusiveness of the United States during the late nineteenth century. The firm's

critically acclaimed Modern Gothic display at the 1876 Centennial Exhibition in Philadelphia catapulted them into the national spotlight and, for a while, rendered their names synonymous with the style.

With arresting, clean lines, which at times appear protomodern, and rich surface decoration, Kimbel and Cabus's eclectic furniture forms retain their powerful visual impact to this day. Intrigued by these striking characteristics, the late Dr. Barry R. Harwood, curator of decorative arts at the Brooklyn Museum from 1988 to 2018, assembled the preeminent institutional collection of Kimbel and Cabus's work. Barry's passionate interest in late nineteenth-century American furniture, of which Kimbel and Cabus's work is exemplary, is documented by his thoughtful accessions that shaped our Decorative Arts collection, his focused thematic installations, and, most notably, his 1997 exhibition and publication, *The Furniture of George Hunzinger: Invention and Innovation in Nineteenth-Century America*. A long-planned monographic study of Kimbel and Cabus, for which Barbara Veith joined him as curatorial research assistant, was to be his final project. Sadly, Barry passed away in 2018 before he could complete it. We committed to seeing it through as a tribute to Barry, who had been at the museum for thirty years, and because of our shared appreciation of Kimbel and Cabus's distinctive work.

We are grateful that Barbara Veith assumed the mantle as guest curator of this show, advised by Alice Cooney Frelinghuysen, Anthony W. and Lulu C. Wang Curator of American Decorative Arts, and Medill Higgins Harvey, Ruth Bigelow Wriston Associate Curator of American Decorative Arts and manager, The Henry R. Luce Center for the Study of American Art, both at the Metropolitan Museum of Art. Barbara partnered with co-author Medill to complete the exhibition catalogue in Barry's memory. With this publication, they present new scholarship drawn from myriad primary sources and provide fresh insight into the renowned yet little-explored Kimbel and Cabus partnership. In tandem with *Design: 1880 to Now*, our reinterpreted and renovated installation of the fourth-floor decorative arts galleries, the Kimbel and Cabus exhibition and publication marks an exciting new chapter for the Brooklyn Museum.

We thank authors Max Donnelly, curator of nineteenth-century furniture at the Victoria and Albert Museum, London; Alice Cooney Frelinghuysen, Anthony W. and Lulu C. Wang Curator of American Decorative Arts at the Metropolitan Museum of Art, New York; and Dr. Melitta Jonas, art historian, Berlin for their illuminating contributions to the publication, which provide broad context as well as specific insights that enrich our understanding of Barbara and Medill's research.

Special thanks to the lenders and institutions whose generous support and enthusiastic participation, not to mention flexibility and adaptability, have made this exhibition possible. Together, we have overcome both large and small challenges during an extraordinary year.

And finally, our deepest and most sincere gratitude goes to Deedee and Barrie Wigmore for their constant encouragement, insightful counsel, and generous leadership support of the exhibition and publication. As enthusiasts and scholars of nineteenth-century furniture, the Wigmores have long advocated for the realization of this significant project. And it is thanks to their exemplary and essential championing of late nineteenth-century decorative arts scholarship, exhibitions, and publications that we have been able to make this important exhibition happen.

Anne Pasternak
Shelby White and Leon Levy Director
Brooklyn Museum

"RICH AND TASTEFUL ENOUGH": KIMBEL AND CABUS IN THE NEW YORK FURNITURE TRADE

Alice Cooney Frelinghuysen

At the 1876 Centennial Exhibition in Philadelphia, the partnership of Anton Kimbel and Joseph Cabus displayed an entire room setting of furniture of their own design and fabrication; one critic heralded it as "rich and tasteful enough to rank it among the very best of the American exhibits in household art."[1] The furnishings and woodwork were all in the new Gothic style that had already gained traction abroad, and it signaled the firm's emergence to prominence as an important player among several flourishing New York furniture-makers catering to a burgeoning upwardly mobile, artistically minded clientele.

In the preceding decades the cabinetmaking trade in New York had seen huge improvements in efficiency, technology, and marketing, and a greater influx of skilled immigrant labor than ever before, setting the stage for this generation of premier furniture and decorating firms. By the middle of the nineteenth century, New York had established itself as the nation's leading city for high-end furniture-making. As one foreign traveler observed in 1850: "The Americans begin to make

gorgeous articles of furniture now,"[2] a statement that would resonate even more deeply a quarter of a century later.

If the residences of New York City's social elite were richly furnished in the antebellum years, this decorative extravagance was no match for the striving that occurred at the top of the social order in the post-Civil War era: the grandest houses in the city's history were erected along Fifth and Madison Avenues, and their owners sought to fit them out with furnishings both luxurious and distinctive. Kimbel and Cabus joined the ranks of such prestigious cabinetmaking firms as Herter Brothers, Leon Marcotte, Pottier and Stymus, and George A. Schastey, who supplied this new and avid market. Through determination, hard work, and, undoubtedly, exploitation, their clients amassed fortunes the likes of which the country had never seen before; they were also often adventurous in their tastes, and gave the designers unusual freedom to produce inventive and original furnishings. Most of the firms' principals and skilled craftspeople had arrived among the legions of workers fleeing political unrest and economic hardship in Europe. Many were immigrants from Germany and France who had trained in their home countries, bringing their craft and designs to their adopted nation where they reinterpreted them for eager patrons used to taking risks.

Kimbel and Cabus were important players on this stage. It is instructive to consider their enterprise in comparison with Herter Brothers. On the surface, the two firms had much in common. Anton Kimbel came from Mainz, Germany, and his partner, Joseph Cabus, from Calmoutier, France. The brothers Gustav and Christian Herter hailed from Stuttgart. The Kimbel and Cabus partnership commenced in 1863, and the Herter brothers joined up just a year later. Both firms' careers were bolstered by the 1876 Centennial Exhibition, with their heydays lasting only until the early 1880s. The Kimbel and Cabus partnership ceased in 1882; Christian Herter died in 1883, thirteen years after Gustav had withdrawn from their firm. The two enterprises produced a wide range of high-quality furnishings, working in a variety of woods. Both businesses dealt with labor strife and a fluctuating workforce, yet were able to achieve remarkable success in a favorable consumer market. The influence of British design reform was undeniable in their work, and each used it as a springboard for developing their own individual aesthetics. The influence of the work of Edward William Godwin is evident in some of Herter Brothers' work; Kimbel and Cabus directly appropriated British forms based on Bruce James Talbert's published Gothic designs, replicated designs by Christopher Dresser in its printed paper appliqués, and even incorporated British tiles as ornamentation (fig. 1). They also drew significant inspiration from the work of German architect Edwin Oppler.

There are many parallels between the two firms, but there are also many differences. For one, Herter Brothers primarily produced finely crafted, luxurious furnishings tailored to specifically commissioned interiors, while Kimbel and Cabus marketed their innovative work individually to like-minded customers. The Herters often employed the most opulent materials—rosewood, mother-of-pearl, and intricate marquetry—while Kimbel and Cabus relied on more modest embellishments, such as elaborate nickel-plated hardware or applied paper panels mimicking more expensive inlay or tiles. Both were poised to meet the demands of a newly affluent consumer base. While firms like Herter Brothers catered to some of the nation's wealthiest individuals, Kimbel and Cabus produced work at a wider range of grades, selling to a broader community of the increasingly upwardly mobile middle class—a clientele that was arguably more progressive in their thinking, as demonstrated by the firm's avant-garde designs. The city's dynamic and complex cabinetmaking trade employed many skilled and specialized craftspeople, and likely there was a certain amount of undocumented mobility of workers between shops as commissions were received; they may even have served as anonymous subcontractors for larger firms. Thus, New York City during the 1870s and 1880s provided a fertile ground in which diverse approaches could flourish, and Kimbel and Cabus's forward-looking designs found a ready market.

The in-depth study of the firm and work of Kimbel and Cabus that follows adds to a growing body of scholarship on the major cabinetmaking firms working during arguably the city's most original epoch. The Metropolitan Museum of Art's landmark 1970 exhibition *Nineteenth-Century America: Furniture and Other Decorative Arts* was among the first to devote serious attention to the much-neglected field of decorative arts made during the second half of the nineteenth century. The museum identified and exhibited works by Herter Brothers, Leon Marcotte, Alexander Roux, and others, sparking interest in the field. At that time the work of Kimbel and Cabus was virtually unknown, and was not among the firms represented. Just over a decade and a half later, however, the Metropolitan featured three important works of Kimbel and Cabus in *In Pursuit of Beauty: Americans and the Aesthetic Movement*, devoting a substantive discussion to them in the accompanying publication. Several serious studies of nineteenth-century cabinetmakers, principally from New York, have been made since then. These include *Herter Brothers: Furniture and Interiors for a Gilded Age* (Metropolitan Museum of Art, 1994); the publication accompanying the exhibition *The Furniture of George Hunzinger: Invention and Innovation in Nineteenth-Century America* (Brooklyn Museum, 1997); and the work of

George A. Schastey in *Artistic Furniture of the Gilded Age* (Metropolitan Museum of Art, 2016). The Hunzinger study was the work of Barry R. Harwood, curator of decorative arts at the Brooklyn Museum, whose long-time dream was to add this study on Kimbel and Cabus to the canon. His untimely death prevented him from seeing this wish come to fruition, but he deserves credit both for his pursuit of the subject and for the insights he shared with Barbara Veith, the curator of the current exhibition, who is fulfilling Harwood's important legacy along with her co-author Medill Higgins Harvey. This work on Kimbel and Cabus significantly addresses a long-standing gap in the scholarship, introducing the firm and its work in all its scope, while also accounting for and celebrating its innovative designs and marketing practices.

1   [George Titus Ferris], *Gems of the Centennial Exhibition: Consisting of Illustrated Descriptions of Objects of an Artistic Character, In the Exhibits of the United States, Great Britain, France* [. . .] (New York: D. Appleton, 1877), p. 140. For succinct discussions of the New York furniture-making trade during the nineteenth century, see Catherine Hoover Voorsanger, "'Gorgeous Articles of Furni-

ture': Cabinetmaking in the Empire City," in *Art and the Empire City: New York, 1825– 1861*, eds. Catherine Hoover Voorsanger and John K. Howat (New York: Metropolitan Museum of Art, 2000), pp. 287–325; and see Catherine Hoover Voorsanger, "From the Bowery to Broadway: The Herter Brothers and the New York Furniture Trade," in Katherine S. Howe, Alice Cooney Frelinghuysen, and Catherine Hoover

Voorsanger, *Herter Brothers: Furniture and Interiors for a Gilded Age* (New York: Harry N. Abrams in association with the Museum of Fine Arts, Houston, 1994), pp. 56–77.

2   Thomas Mooney, *Nine Years in America . . . in a Series of Letters to his Cousin, Patrick Mooney, a Farmer in Ireland* (Dublin: James McGlathan, 1950), p. 150.

POETIC AND PRACTICAL: GOTHIC FOR THE MODERN HOME

Max Donnelly

"Mr. Ruskin has eloquently described to us the poetry of mediæval art; Pugin and other writers have shown its practical advantages."

Charles Locke Eastlake, *Hints on Household Taste*[1]

As the designer and tastemaker Charles Locke Eastlake (1836–1906) noted in the subtitle of his *History of the Gothic Revival* (1872), the Gothic style had "lingered in England during the last two centuries."[2] In the later eighteenth century interest was rekindled by antiquaries and patrons including Horace Walpole (1717–1797) and in the early nineteenth century it was increasingly the subject of scholarly study, notably by the architect Thomas Rickman (1776–1841).[3] What had begun as a domestic and landscape garden phenomenon, and later spread to ecclesiastical architecture, became a fashionable style for domestic buildings, furniture, and furnishings during the Regency period. Its monastic associations made it particularly suitable for libraries and studies, and examples can be found among the hand-colored plates of *The Repository of Arts* published by the German-born Rudolph Ackermann (1764–1834).[4]

At the brink of the next phase in the development of the Gothic Revival, the style became synonymous with moral virtue and social reform—largely through the writings of the architect-designer A. W. N. Pugin (1812–1852). An ardent Roman Catholic convert, Pugin published his provocative book *Contrasts* in 1836, its plates illustrating the difference between an idealized medieval past and the perceived squalor and social disarray of his present.[5] His publications, along with designs for the furniture and interiors of Charles Barry's new Palace of Westminster (constructed from 1840), and for the objects in the Medieval Court at the Great Exhibition in London in 1851, sealed Pugin's reputation as an interior design reformer. Pugin's furniture (fig. 2) came to reflect his "great rules for design": that "convenience, construction, or propriety" should govern the design of buildings, and that "all ornament should consist of enrichment of the essential construction of the building."[6]

FIG. 1 Unknown photographer, "Pericles" sideboard designed by Bruce James Talbert (British, 1838–1881), at the Paris *Exposition Universelle*, 1867. Victoria and Albert Museum, 52485

FIG. 2 A. W. N. Pugin (British, 1812–1852). Table, 1852–53. Oak, carved and chamfered (beveled) decoration. Victoria and Albert Museum, W.26-1972

FIG. 3 William Burges (British, 1827–1881). Design for a painted cabinet, ca. 1860. Pencil, watercolor, gouache on paper. Victoria and Albert Museum, 8829:5

Pugin died, prematurely, just as *The Stones of Venice* (1851–53) was being published, written by Britain's foremost art critic and champion of the Pre-Raphaelite Brotherhood, John Ruskin (1819–1900). Ruskin's compelling prose in his chapter "On the Nature of Gothic" reinforced the style's credentials by pitting the nobility of the "workman" against dehumanizing mechanization. Ruskin inspired a whole generation of Gothic Revival architects, many of whom, including George Edmund Street (1824–1881), studied Gothic architecture in continental Europe. By the late 1850s, the annual Architectural Association exhibitions in London were showcasing a new revival: painted medieval-style furniture designed by the architect William Burges (1827–1881), the painting executed by artists of the Pre-Raphaelite school. Burges continued to design many such pieces, including some for himself (fig. 3).[7]

These developments were set before a wider international audience at the Medieval Court of the London International Exhibition in 1862, organized by the Ecclesiological Society. Showing a preference for the massive forms of early Gothic, the furniture on display included several elaborately painted pieces designed by Burges and constructed by the London firm Harland and Fisher, and painted furniture designed by Philip Webb (1831–1915) and others for the recently founded firm of Morris, Marshall, Faulkner and Company. The architect John Pollard Seddon (1827–1906) displayed pieces of furniture and two organ cases made by his family's cabinetmaking firm. In Seddon's furniture, constructional details were emphasized; painted and inlaid decoration were analogous to the structural polychromy— whereby construction materials were used to color buildings—with which he and other Gothic Revival architects were experimenting.

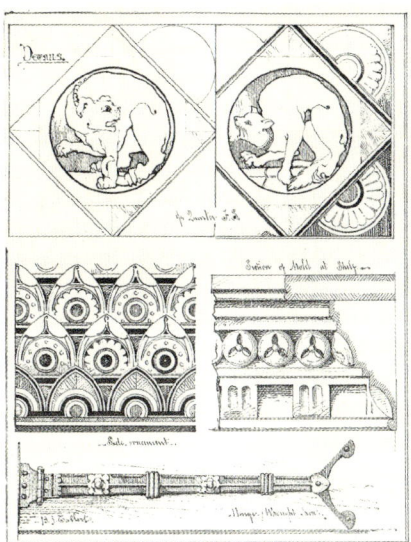

FIG. 4 Bruce James Talbert, *Gothic Forms Applied to Furniture, Metal Work and Decoration for Domestic Purposes* (Birmingham: S. Birbeck; London: the author, 1867–68), plate 12

In the Medieval Court the Ecclesiological Society hoped to demonstrate, in the words of its president, Alexander Beresford Hope (1820–1887), "the further development of that type of art in which we have confidence, and which, though called mediæval, is still modern and progressive [. . .] we find that there are many things which make mediæval art the most serviceable to the present nineteenth century."[8] While many critics did not concur with this view, the structural ingenuity of an ebonized and painted armchair designed for Morris, Marshall, Faulkner and Company by Webb did excite the interest of rising designer Christopher Dresser (1834–1904).[9] Meanwhile, the display of Cox and Son, which exhibited church furniture in the Medieval Court, unashamedly illustrated how modern technology could be harnessed to the Gothic cause: its exhibits included a reredos made by steam-powered carving machines, one of which could be seen in operation in the Machine Galleries in the Western Annexe of the exhibition.

Throughout the 1860s, architects such as Street, Richard Norman Shaw (1831–1912), and Edward William Godwin (1833–1886) developed the "reformed" Gothic style which Pugin had pioneered, designing bold structural furniture for commissions such as Godwin's Northampton Town Hall and Dromore Castle, Ireland, the latter singled out for praise by Eastlake.[10] At the same time, more ambitious cabinetmakers increasingly engaged architects and independent designers—a new profession—for special commissions and exhibitions. Two of the most successful designers, both based in London, were Charles Bevan (ca. 1815–1891) and Bruce James Talbert (1838–1881). Bevan, a designer and cabinetmaker who was influenced by Seddon, designed furniture with bold geometric inlays for the Leeds cabinetmaker Marsh and Jones, commissioned by the mill owner Titus Salt Jr. (including a grand piano illustrated in the *Building News* in 1867).[11] Talbert, a Scot who had trained as a carver and then an architect before becoming a designer of furniture, metalwork, textiles, and wallpaper, supplied designs to cabinetmakers including Gillow and Company in Lancaster and, like Bevan, to the Manchester firm of James Lamb. In thriving mercantile centers this vigorous Reformed Gothic seemed to encapsulate the energy and drive of the industrialists who commissioned it. In 1867 the style received international publicity at the Paris *Exposition Universelle*, where Talbert's gargantuan "Pericles" sideboard formed the centerpiece of Holland and Sons' display (fig. 1),[12] winning a silver medal.

In June 1867, while the Pericles sideboard was being shown in Paris, the *Building News* published a letter from an unnamed cabinetmaker, who wrote that "A great deal is said and done for Gothic architecture, but little in favour of Gothic furniture. Could you inform me, Mr. Editor, where I could get any good Gothic designs for domestic furniture, or with whom I could communicate in London on the

FIG. 5 Bruce James Talbert, *Gothic Forms Applied to Furniture, Metal Work and Decoration for Domestic Purposes* (Birmingham: S. Birbeck; London: the author, 1867–68), plate 21

subject?"[13] The editor's reply provides a revealing snapshot of the contemporary state of play, singling out the "well-known Gothic furniture makers" Bevan, Seddon, and Harland and Fisher, as well as authorities in the field, Burges, Godwin, "Dr. Dresser," and Talbert, who "is publishing a useful work on the subject." Talbert's *Gothic Forms*, published in two parts (1867–68) was evidently timely.[14] Echoing Pugin, Talbert pointed out that "the best isolated efforts of the Architectural Profession can do little to render this class of furniture popular, until the cabinet-maker and his workmen take some interest in their work." He called for a "more severe treatment of outline," espousing

the virtues of using straight wood, which was economical and structurally stronger, and describing traditional methods of construction as practical and "honest." For decoration he advised that carving should be restrained (although "there still remains a fair field for the display of flowing forms in the panels and ornamental incisions"[15]), that metalwork could be decorative but should always serve a purpose, and that enameled or painted decoration could be used to introduce color.

Talbert's illustrations included a wide range of furniture types, sometimes accompanied by diagrams showing constructional techniques (fig. 4) and metalwork. Also depicted were imaginary interiors showing furniture in integrated settings, in harmony with fireplaces, paneling, stained glass, and portières (fig. 5), appealing to cabinetmakers and prospective clients alike. Although this was not received uncritically, one British reviewer thought that "in many instances of his design we have been agreeably surprised by the fertility of his invention and the appreciation of sound, honest workmanship which is embodied in his taste . . . The truth is that in the present day we do not want *monumental* furniture, i.e., furniture of which the features are derived from the rood screens and church stalls of a bygone age . . . we must work in the spirit rather than in the letter of mediæval art." The reviewer concluded that "His designs do not, perhaps, represent the most refined development of mediæval art, but no better ones, as far as we know, have yet been published."[16]

Almost simultaneous with Talbert's publication was *Hints on Household Taste* (first published 1868) by Eastlake. The culmination of several articles published in *The Queen* and *The London Review* (1864–66), the book was what would now be termed a "lifestyle manual" for the middle classes who wanted "art" furnishings and hints on everything from furniture to crockery and clothes and beards. Eastlake's lively text was at once authoritative and humorous and occasionally provocative—"The British public are, as a body, utterly incapable of distinguishing good from bad design, and have not time to enquire into principles"—but accessible and never preachy.[17] Echoing Ruskin's dismay at the separation of art from manufacture, although not rejecting "modern science" in production *per se*, Eastlake advocated functionalism and, while claiming no affiliation to a particular style, illustrated his book with pieces of furniture,

FIG. 6 Charles Locke Eastlake, *Hints on Household Taste* (Boston: J. R. Osgood, 1872), p. 219

FIG. 7 Unknown, Chest of Drawers, ca. 1875. Walnut, metal, 37 ¾ × 49 ⁵⁄₁₆ × 22 ¼ in. (95.9 × 125.3 × 56.5 cm). Brooklyn Museum, Modernism Benefit Fund, 2013.36

GOTHIC FURNITURE.

Master George (on the arrival of the new cabinet). "Oɪ, Pᴀ! ᴅᴏ ʟᴇᴛ ᴍᴇ Hᴀᴠᴇ ɪᴛ ғᴏʀ ᴀ Rᴀʙʙɪᴛ-Hᴜᴛᴄʜ!"

FIG. 8 Charles Keene, "Gothic Furniture," *Punch* 49 (1865): 195. Lincoln Financial Foundation Collection, Allen County Public Library, Fort Wayne, Indiana

many designed by him, in a simplified medieval or "Old English" style (fig. 6). In Britain and the United States, cabinetmakers produced their own versions of Eastlake-designed furniture, some closely based on the illustrations in *Hints* (fig. 7). In describing his design for this chest of drawers, Eastlake directed his readers' attention to the fact that the slightly projecting sides gave, as well as the appearance of greater stability, "an opportunity to introduce a little decoration in the way of mouldings or carved work to relieve the rigid box-shaped appearance."[18] Such details were clearly necessary: a few years earlier an illustration in *Punch* likened the radical plainness of similar designs to a rabbit hutch (fig. 8), and some years later the designer John Moyr Smith (1839–1912) wrote that furniture designed by Eastlake was "in construction too much like that of a packing-case."[19]

Hints was such a success, however, that by 1872, when the first U.S. edition appeared, Americans' familiarity with the British editions

(three by then) allowed its editor, the author and critic Charles Callahan Perkins (1823–1886), to introduce it as "an old acquaintance in a new dress."[20] In a perceptive assessment of this edition in the *North American Review*, an unnamed writer echoed British reservations by stating that "Any one who feels tempted to appropriate Mr. Eastlake's designs would, in our opinion, do better by consulting a volume of designs for furniture of a similar character by Mr. Talbert."[21] When the U.S. edition of Talbert's *Gothic Forms* was reviewed in the same periodical the following year, a writer (perhaps the same one) observed that: "Mr. Talbert has met the work in an entirely different spirit from Pugin. Recognizing modern needs and such good modern usages as obtain in the joiner's trade in our day, he has simply applied to them picturesque forms and pure Gothic detail without mimicking the work of past ages . . . But Mr. Eastlake's book on household taste, although healthy and refreshing in its arguments, is illustrated with designs which to most of us seem uncouth, heavy, and ugly. Mr. Talbert's designs are the reverse of all this, and explain Mr. Eastlake's text of the first-mentioned book in a manner much more attractive to most people than his own drawings [. . .] What brings the Gothic style home to most people is its freedom and picturesqueness, its ready adaptation to modern forms and requirements."[22] The reviewer also noted that architects had already bought or were buying the British edition of Talbert, although regretted the fact that, despite the U.S. edition being reproduced by the more econo-

mical heliotype process, it was still unaffordable to draftsmen.[23] Nevertheless, Talbert's style was swiftly assimilated by many leading cabinet-makers in the United States in the 1870s, including Herter Brothers and Kimbel and Cabus in New York.

In his introduction to *Hints*, Perkins argued that "we are in many ways the most inventive people upon earth" and described how native U.S. plants could be used as a starting-point for ornament.[24] In advocating this, Perkins was effectively paraphrasing the writings of the abovementioned Christopher Dresser, designer, theorist, and botanist. Like Talbert a Scot by birth, Dresser was a product of the London Government School of Design, founded to improve the standards of British industrial designers; he can be considered an heir to his mentor, Owen Jones. Several U.S. art periodicals, including the *Art Amateur*, publicized Dresser's comments on household decoration and design and a series of articles which appeared in the British *Technical Educator* (1871–72) and collectively as *Principles of Decorative Design* (1873) were clearly known to U.S. manufacturers, for a conical sugar bowl illustrated by Dresser appears on a Kimbel and Cabus trade card (see p. 36, fig. 1).[25] Commenting on Eastlake's *Hints*, Dresser wrote that "I think Mr. Eastlake right in many views, yet wrong in others, but I cannot help regarding him somewhat as an apostle of ugliness, as he appears to me to despise finish and refinement." He branded one armchair illustrated by Eastlake as "defective in the highest degree."[26] Talbert's *Gothic Forms* was "very excellent" and "well worthy of the most careful consideration and study," but although Dresser admired the "simplicity of the structure" of a Talbert sideboard (fig. 9) he thought Talbert also "not always right."[27]

FIG. 9 Christopher Dresser, "Principles of Design–X. Art Furniture," in *The Technical Educator: An Encyclopedia of Technical Education*, vol. 1 (London: Cassell, Petter and Galpin, 1872), p. 377, illus. Getty Research Institute

As in Britain, Dresser's work as an ornamentalist was more widely felt in the United States. In furniture his advocacy of stylized natural forms—of a type also popularized by English architect and illustrator James K. Colling (1816–1905), whose work was likewise published in the United States[28]—manifested itself in the kind of incised or inlaid ornament that he, Eastlake, and Talbert all advocated in place of carving. In his lavishly illustrated

Studies in Design (1874–76), Dresser provided further models for cabinetmakers and designers (figs. 10 and 11), including Celtic-inspired "Grotesque 'powderings,' suitable for the wall ornaments of a smoking-room,"[29] two of which were used as models for printed panels ornamenting Kimbel and Cabus furniture (fig. 12).

FIG. 10 Christopher Dresser, *Studies in Design* (London: Cassell, Petter and Galpin, 1874–76), plate XX

FIG. 11 Christopher Dresser, *Studies in Design* (London: Cassell, Petter and Galpin, 1874–76), plate VI

FIG. 12 Desk, ca. 1875. Walnut, nickel silver, printed paper, 73 × 39 ¼ × 19 in. (185.42 × 99.7 × 48.26 cm). Milwaukee Art Museum, Purchase, by exchange, M1999.205

Dresser's influence is clear in the published designs and work of the Liverpool-born stained-glass artist Charles Booth (1844–1893), active in New York and New Jersey, in the buildings and furniture designed in Philadelphia by the architect Frank Furness (1839–1912), and in the work of cabinetmaker Daniel Pabst (1826–1910), who executed many of Furness's designs. Dresser himself visited and delivered lectures at Furness's splendid new Pennsylvania Academy of the Fine Arts in 1876. Likewise, English medieval-themed transfer-printed earthenware tiles designed by Dresser's one-time assistant John Moyr Smith are found on British "art"

furniture, from chairs to cabinets, and were also incorporated by U.S. makers of Modern Gothic furniture, including Kimbel and Cabus; other designs depicting medieval musicians that appear on English tiles likewise served as models for printed patterns for Kimbel and Cabus furniture.[30]

In the 1870s, "art" furniture makers, such as the newly founded London firm of Collinson and Lock, experimented with the "Queen Anne" style, so-called because it transformed eighteenth-century forms of architecture and decorative design through combination with other features, for example intricately turned elements and

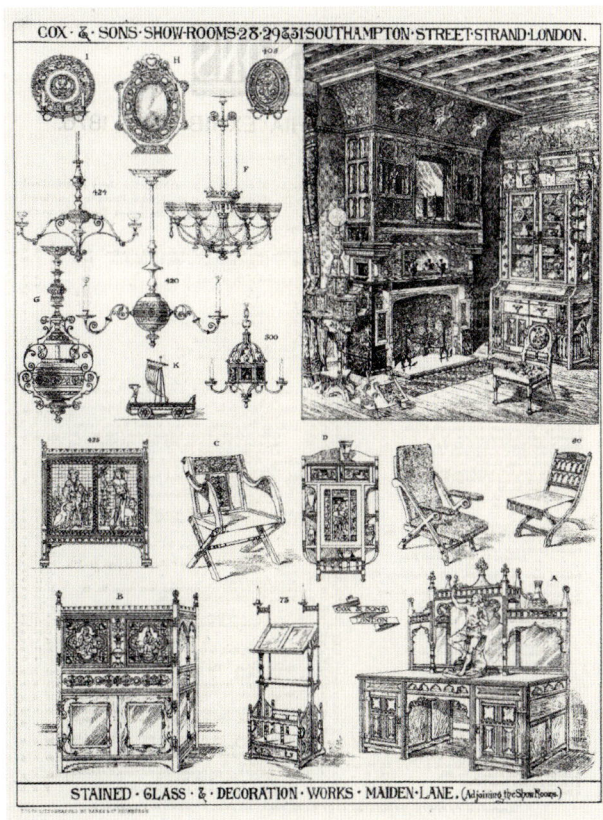

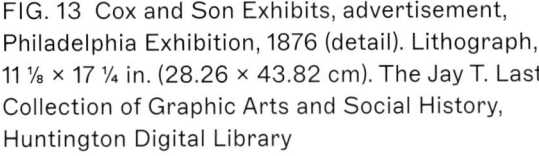

FIG. 13 Cox and Son Exhibits, advertisement, Philadelphia Exhibition, 1876 (detail). Lithograph, 11 ⅛ × 17 ¼ in. (28.26 × 43.82 cm). The Jay T. Last Collection of Graphic Arts and Social History, Huntington Digital Library

FIG. 14 Cox and Son (1838–about 1936), Sideboard, ca. 1872. Ebonized wood, mirror glass, brass, paint, gold leaf, 77 ¼ × 72 × 20 ¼ in. (196.3 × 182.8 × 51.4 cm). National Gallery of Victoria, Melbourne. Purchased, 1975

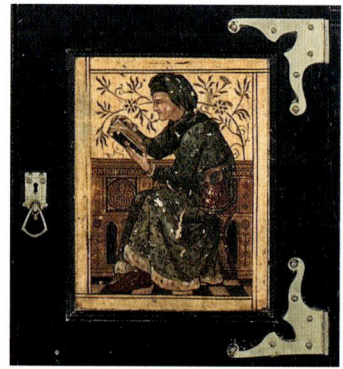

FIG. 15 Chair (detail), ca. 1875. Ebonized cherry, gilding, paper, modern textile, 35 × 20 ¼ × 24 ½ in. (88.9 × 51.43 × 61.59 cm). The Metropolitan Museum of Art, Promised Gift of Barrie A. and Deedee Wigmore, L.2019.66.30

FIG. 16 Cox and Son, Sideboard (detail), ca. 1872. Ebonized wood, mirror glass, brass, paint, gold leaf, 77 ¼ × 72 × 20 ¼ in. (196.3 × 182.8 × 51.4 cm). National Gallery of Victoria, Melbourne. Purchased, 1975

spindled galleries. Gothic forms were often subtly integrated into Queen Anne and "art" furniture, such as an ebonized and painted cabinet designed by the architect Thomas Edward Collcutt (1840–1924) and exhibited by Collinson and Lock at the London International Exhibition in 1871.[31] Talbert's *Examples of Ancient & Modern Furniture, Metal Work, Tapestries, Decorations* (London 1876, Boston 1877) showed his progression toward this lighter style, as did the designs of his pupil, Henry William Batley (1846–1932). Cox and Son was one of a number of firms which began to branch out into home decor in the 1870s, employing architects and freelance designers such as Talbert and Moyr Smith as well as artists such as Charles Rossiter (1827–1897; figs. 13 and 14), whose designs, like those of Dresser and possibly also Talbert, were adapted by Kimbel and Cabus for printed panels (figs. 15 and 16). The fact that Rossiter, who had worked with Burges on some of the earliest painted medieval furniture and interiors in Britain the 1850s and 1860s, was now designing for a new manufacturer of "art" furniture which boasted a branch in Boston, and was one of the British exhibitors of Gothic Revival furniture at the Philadelphia Centennial Exhibition of 1876, is a neat illustration of the Anglo-American dialogue between makers of "Reformed" or "Modern" Gothic furniture in the 1870s.

I am grateful to Clarissa Ward, Megan Aldrich, Martin P. Levy, Sarah Medlam, and Marc Fecker for their advice and assistance in researching and writing this essay.

1   Charles Locke Eastlake, *Hints on Household Taste in Furniture, Upholstery and Other Details*, second British edition (London: Longmans, Green, 1869), p. 35; in the first British edition (London: Longmans, Green, 1868), p. 35, Eastlake wrote that Ruskin "has ably brought before us the poetry of Mediæval art."

2   Charles Locke Eastlake, *A History of the Gothic Revival: An attempt to show how the taste for mediaeval architecture, which lingered in England during the two last centuries, has since been encouraged and developed* (London: Longmans, Green, 1872).

3   Thomas Rickman, *An Attempt to Discriminate the Styles of English Architecture, from the Conquest to the Reformation; preceded by a sketch of the Grecian and Roman Orders, with Notices of Nearly Five Hundred English Buildings* (London: Longman, Hurst, Rees, Orme, and Brown, 1817).

4   Rudolph Ackermann, *The Repository of Arts, Literature, Commerce, Manufactures, Fashions and Politics* (London: the author, 1809–29).

5   A. W. N. Pugin, *Contrasts, or, A parallel between the noble edifices of the fourteenth and fifteenth centuries, and similar buildings of the present day; shewing the present decay of taste: accompanied by appropriate text* (Alderbury: the author, 1836).

6   A. W. N. Pugin, *The True Principles of Pointed or Christian Architecture* (London: John Weale, 1841), p. 1.

7   Matthew Williams, "Gorgeously Arrayed in Blue and Gold," *Country Life* 192, no. 10 (March 5, 1998): 56–59.

8   *Ecclesiologist* 149 (April 1862): 229.

9   Christopher Dresser, *Development of Ornamental Art in the International Exhibition* (London: Day and Son, 1862), p. 82.

10   Eastlake 1872 (as in note 2), p. 359.

11   *Building News* 14 (March 1, 1867): 160–61. The grand piano is at Lotherton Hall, Leeds.

12   Collection of the Metropolitan Museum of Art, New York.

13   *Building News* 14 (June 7, 1867): 400.

14   Bruce James Talbert, *Gothic Forms Applied to Furniture, Metal Work and Decoration for Domestic Purposes* (Birmingham: S. Birbeck; London: the author, 1867–68).

15   Ibid., pp. 4–5.

16   "Mediæval Furniture," *Building News* 14 (July 12, 1867): 483.

17   Eastlake 1868 (as in note 1), p. 106.

18   Ibid., p. 192.

19   John Moyr Smith, *Ornamental Interiors, Ancient and Modern* (London: Crosby Lockwood, 1887), p. 54.

20   Charles Callahan Perkins, Editor's Preface to Charles Locke Eastlake's *Hints on Household Taste in Furniture, Upholstery and Other Details*, second U.S. edition (Boston: J. R. Osgood, 1874), p. v.

21   *North American Review* 116, no. 238 (January 1873): 206.

22   *North American Review* 118, no. 242 (January 1874): 205–6, 210.

23   Ibid., 209.

24   Perkins 1874 (as in note 20), p. xiv.

25   Christopher Dresser, *Principles of Decorative Design* (London: Cassell, Petter, and Galpin, 1873), p. 139, fig. 149.

26   Ibid., p. 52, note; p. 53.

27   Ibid., pp. 56, 58.

28   James K. Colling, *Art Foliage, for Sculpture and Decoration* (Boston: J. R. Osgood, 1873).

29   Christopher Dresser, *Studies in Design* (London: Cassell, Petter and Galpin, 1874–76), caption to plate VI. This plate illustrated the fact that "The sense of humour finds expression in grotesque forms"; ibid., p. 4.

30   The tiles designed by Moyr Smith were manufactured in Stoke-on-Trent by Minton, Hollins and Co. and Minton and Co., while some examples of the medieval-musician tiles were manufactured by Minton and Co.

31   Two other versions of the cabinet were exhibited by Collinson and Lock at the Vienna *Weltausstellung* (1873) and the Philadelphia Centennial Exhibition (1876), respectively.

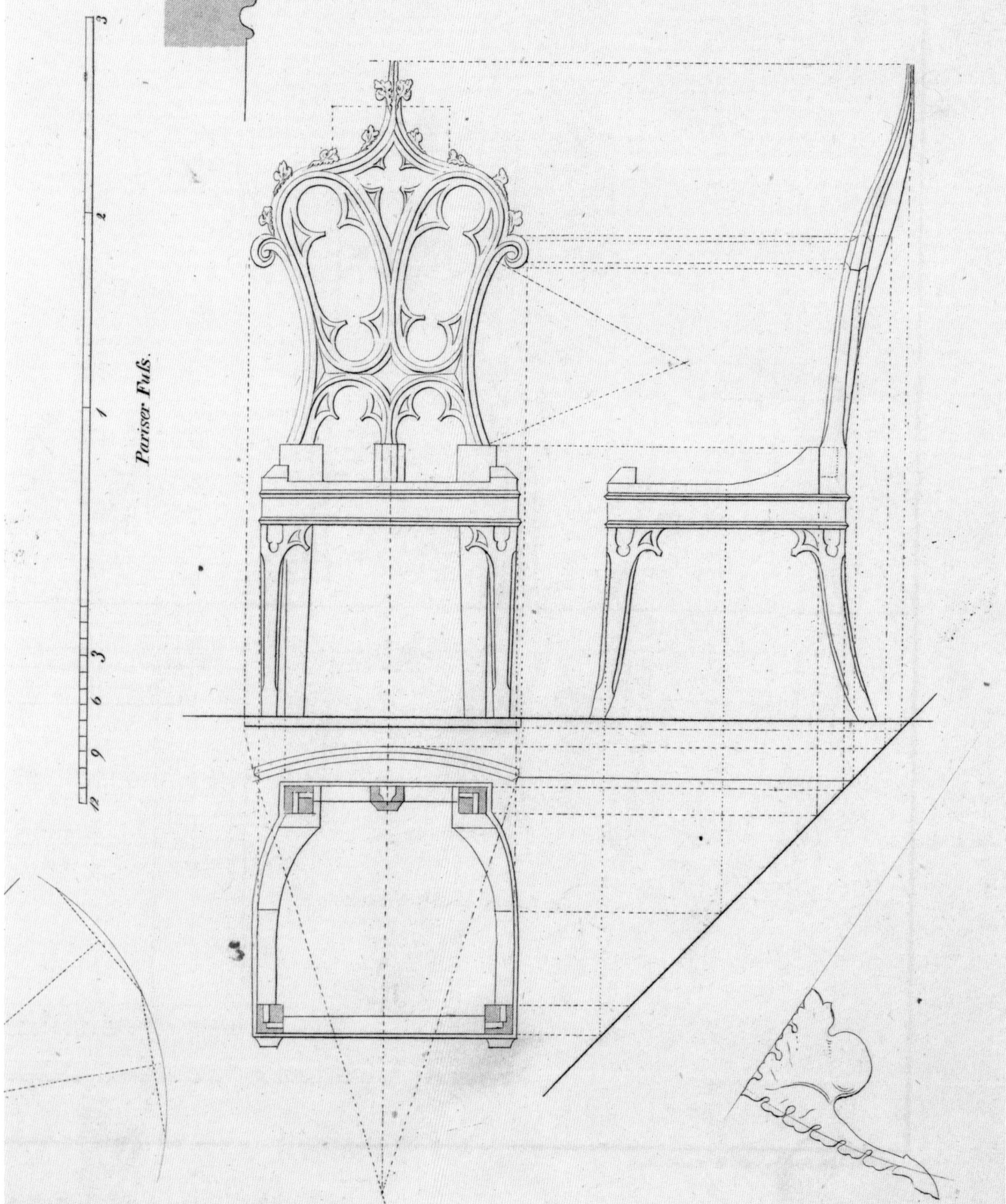

Pariser Fuſs.

THE KIMBEL DYNASTY: A FINE TRADITION OF CABINETMAKERS

Melitta Jonas

For several generations, from the late eighteenth century to the twentieth century, the Kimbel cabinetmakers formed one of Europe's leading dynasties for crafting furniture and complete interior fittings of the highest quality. All male members of the family practiced the trade at the preeminent handicraft companies in Germany, Austria, England, France, and the United States. As we will see, they gained an international reputation through important master works and participation in large exhibitions.

The cabinetmaker Sebastian Kimbel (ca. 1762–unknown) immigrated to Mainz around 1784 from Kaub am Rhein (fig. 3). Because the name Kimbel is very common in Kaub, it is reasonable to assume that this is where the family originated—even if it is no longer verifiable. In the memoirs of Sebastian's grandsons, it is said that their grandfather came to the school in Mainz as a *Pedell*, the late Middle High German term for school caretaker, through the mediation of a canon of the archbishopric estates in Rheingau.[1] In Mainz, Sebastian founded the Kimbel workshop. His son Wilhelm (1786–1869; fig. 2) was taught the

trade and became a cabinetmaker and draftsman, and he in turn taught the craft to his eldest son, Anton (1822–1895), who apprenticed in his workshop in the early 1840s.

Mainz was an important center of furniture production at the time Sebastian Kimbel arrived. By the eighteenth century, during the Baroque and Rococo periods, it was already established as a major source of outstanding works by highly skilled cabinetmakers. Into the first half of the nineteenth century, it remained a principal center for furniture production by traditional artisans. According to the scholar Heidrun Zinnkann, two political events had a decisive impact on the production of the cabinetmakers in Mainz: the French occupation of the city in 1792, and the revolution of 1848.[2]

Though closely bound to the rich tradition of cabinetmaking in Mainz, Wilhelm Kimbel realized that the future of the trade would come from a collaboration between designers and craftspeople. He saw this as an advantage, resulting in clear specialization and thus an increase in quality. In the foreword of *Role models for manufacturers and craftsmen*,

FIG. 2 Wilhelm Kimbel (1786–1869). Henrietta Mehlbach Richardson's Kimbel Family Collection, courtesy of Elizabeth Richardson Elisher

published by the Prussian Trade Institute beginning in 1821 and edited by Karl Friedrich Schinkel (1781–1841), the institute's director Christian Peter Wilhelm Beuth (1781–1853) gave the instruction that furniture manufacturers and craftspeople should "not be tempted to compose themselves, but to imitate them [designs provided] diligently, faithfully and with taste."[3] This recommendation, which reflected a new but enduring attitude, suggested that carpenters or goldsmiths should rely on the work of individuals who specialize in design. At this point the artisan (a term that would not appear until the end of the century) ranked far below the free artist in status; after the concept of collaboration between designers and

craftspeople gained ground, the latter's social status would improve.[4]

Wilhelm had moved the Kimbel workshop to Langgasse Street in 1815 together with his brother Martin (b. 1797, year of death unknown), who appears to have worked there only very briefly.[5] After Napoleon's defeat in Germany in 1813, the Congress of Vienna redrew the map of Europe and created the constitutionally weak German Confederation in 1815. Because Germany was not cohesive politically, it could not meaningfully participate in international trade and industrial progress, which was led by England and France; it thus lost its ties to international developments in craftsmanship. Craftspeople and manufacturers were unable to keep up to date on the latest developments in the field. The fact that Germany did not have a robust system of training for industrial designers and craftspeople further isolated it and limited its economic growth. But to become free from dependence on foreign markets, it needed a strong economy that would ensure sales of its products at home. Moreover, it became clear that the traditional German guild system hindered Germany's ability to participate in the international markets for goods, and must therefore be dismantled.

In England, where more liberal attitudes prevailed, the power of the craft guilds had already diminished in the eighteenth century, while in France they had been abolished in 1791, after the revolution.[6] Long-established, the guild system limited the number of masters in a city to ensure they always had enough work, but it also promoted conservatism. Although it ensured that the quality of products remained high, the system's operating rules, which had hardly changed since the Middle Ages, were restrictive and strictly controlled. Until 1830, traditional German guild rules forbade anyone to set up a workshop of more members than the master himself and up to two journeymen and two apprentices. No master could encroach the

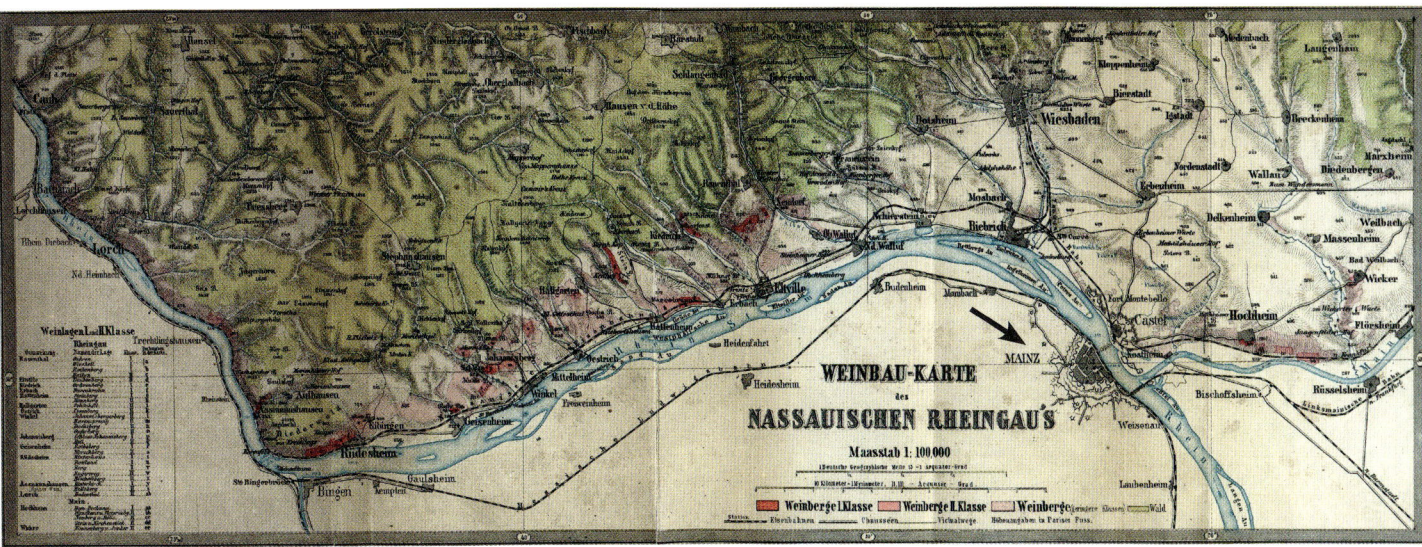

FIG. 3 Rheingau Wine Official Classification of 1867. The classification was the basis for taxation of wineries after the annexation of the Duchy of Nassau by the Kingdom of Prussia in 1866.

specialties of other guilds. For example, a carpenter was limited to making furniture that did not contain carved parts, turned parts, extensive ironwork, or cast supports, and was not allowed to embellish them with paint. If he wanted such parts or decorations, he had to obtain them from a sculptor, lathe operator, locksmith, founder, or painter, then bring them into his workshop and assemble them into a finished piece of furniture. Small, highly specialized master craftsmen's shops such as Wilhelm Kimbel's, that were distinguished for producing very fine pieces of furniture, maintained this demarcation between the various handicrafts.[7]

Under the guild system, the training of cabinetmakers was both highly intensive and comprehensive. They were required to spend several years as journeymen, learning skills through placements in multiple shops. Yet before 1830 German cabinetmakers received little to no training in drawing, and the skills they were allowed to master were limited; as a result they rarely developed new styles. By the middle of the nineteenth century, however, they would regularly travel abroad to study and work. Indeed, it had become common for fine cabinetmakers, like the Kimbels, to apprentice in France or England, where they would master new skills and develop their draftsmanship before returning home a few years later. Drawing became recognized as the foundation of all the arts, and patrons and state institutions began sponsoring the establishment of schools teaching geometry and perspective as well as drawing from flowers, figures, and other objects from nature. Would-be architects—whom we would today call designers—thus learned to give expression to their ideas.[8]

WILHELM KIMBEL (1786–1869)

Between 1815 and roughly 1830, the neo-Gothic (also known as Gothic revival) was promoted in Germany as an anti-French, national style. It seemed appropriate given the prevailing spirit

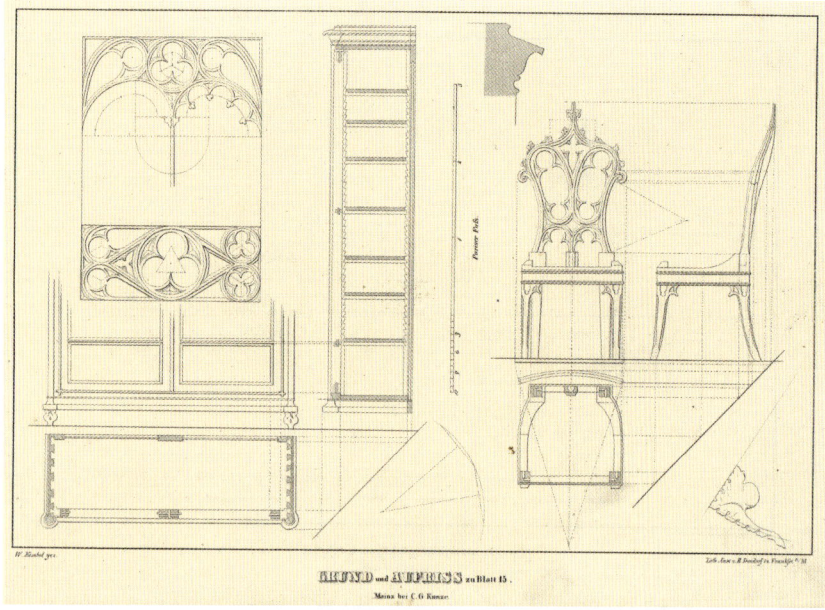

FIG. 4 Wilhelm Kimbel, *Journal für Möbelschreiner* (*Journal for Cabinet Makers*) (1835/37): pl. 15. Kunstbibliothek, Staatliche Museen, Berlin, L 79 u kl R (Rara)

following the Wars of Liberation against Napoleon. Accordingly, the first furniture to be produced in Wilhelm Kimbel's workshop was neo-Gothic in style. Soon, however, owing to influences from France and England and under the pressure of competition fostered by inter-regional exhibitions, German furniture makers had to expand their offerings beyond the neo-Gothic. Baroque- and Rococo-revival forms and ornaments from France began to reappear alongside the Gothic and neoclassical.

Wilhelm began receiving instruction in geometry, perspective drawing, and shading in 1828. With the rise of large-scale operations geared above all toward special orders, draftsmen who could create designs that realized a client's wishes were essential. In 1835, as historical styles were revived and multiple furniture types appeared, Wilhelm started producing a trade publication, the *Journal für Möbelschreiner und Tapezierer* (*Journal for Furniture Makers and Upholsterers*). These

so-called Kimbel Journals, published in Mainz until 1842 in four issues, were the first and best of their kind in Mainz, among the most important in Germany, and in demand even beyond Germany's borders, with "far-reaching influence on the masters of his time."[9] What made them unusual were their construction diagrams drawn to scale—doubtless inspired by technical drawings from England—that Wilhelm's apprentices and journeymen could follow precisely (figs. 1 and 4).

Indicative of the impact of influences from France and England and the pressure of competition to which they were exposed through exhibitions, the 1838 Kimbel Journal contains not only Gothic designs but also proposals in the style of Louis XVI, the Baroque, and the Renaissance. The contents stimulated cabinet-makers' imaginations and provided them with exemplary designs. By this time it had already become commonplace for workshops such as Kimbel's to introduce a broad variety of styles, and the celebration of originality further encouraged a breadth of design. During the 1840s, in both England and Germany, there was a great interest in stylistic pluralism. Furniture forms in Germany were emancipated from the restrictions of prior styles: Gothic was mixed with Rococo and forms inspired by nature, and figural carving took the place of marquetry—the art, dominated by a few makers, of applying pieces of veneer to create patterns or pictures. The catalogue of the first "world exhibition," or World's Fair, held in London in 1851, shows these developments in German furniture-making.[10]

ANTON KIMBEL (1822–1895)

Anton Kimbel's experience with the styles of the so-called Second Rococo had a lasting effect; in New York in the 1850s to 1860s, one of the things he would be known for was the Rococo-revival style (fig. 5).[11]

Like his father, Anton created detailed drawings; Anton's nephew Wilhelm Kimbel (1868–1965) would do likewise decades later: in the latter's workshop books we also find scale drawings to be followed by his coworkers. After training at his father's workshop, in 1839 the young Anton apprenticed at the leading Cologne firm of Heinrich Pallenberg (1802–1884), founded in 1824, before going abroad for further training.[12] At some point, in the years before the revolution of 1848, he went to Brussels, then worked in Paris for Alexandre-Georges Fourdinois (1799–1871) and Desiré Guilmard (1810–ca. 1885), before finally perfecting his skills under Nerkin in St. Petersburg.[13]

Particularly important for Anton was his training under Fourdinois, one of the nineteenth century's most famous French cabinetmakers, who had founded Fourdinois et Fossey with Jules Fossey in 1835. When Anton was working there, they participated with great success in the 1844 *Exposition des produits de l'industrie française*, in the Champs Elysées, submitting Renaissance

FIG. 5 Anton Kimbel (1822–1895). Henrietta Mehlbach Richardson's Kimbel Family Collection, courtesy of Elizabeth Richardson Elisher

cabinets carved of walnut, oak, and pear wood. Critics at the time, however, urged the show's participants to switch to "progressive" serial production, for France had not yet followed the trend to industrialization.[14] Anton's journeyman years abroad had been sponsored by his godfather and uncle, Philipp Anton Bembé (1799–1861), a man closely associated with Wilhelm Kimbel through both kinship and commercial dealings, and the son of Martin Bembé (1768–1813).

The Bembé furniture and upholstery shop in Mainz was among the most well-respected firms in central Germany. As a third-generation upholsterer, Philipp Anton Bembé had opened the store in the 1830s to sell the furniture his firm produced, and in 1840 he established a parquet floor manufactory that has survived to this day. The decoration of the Wiesbaden city palace that same year was one of his largest commissions; it was stipulated that the furniture was not to be Rococo in style, so the result was a naive, hybrid style typical of the Late Biedermeier (the period after 1848). The enterprising and financially successful Bembé helped make the Kimbel workshop a thriving concern by buying its furniture. But in the late 1840s there was a falling out between Bembé and Wilhelm, which ultimately led to the demise of the Kimbel firm in Mainz.[15]

In the revolutionary year of 1848, twenty-six-year-old Anton Kimbel emigrated to New York, where until 1854 he worked as a furniture designer in the workshop of the well-known cabinetmaker and interior designer Charles A. Baudouine (1808–1895), best known for pieces in the Rococo-revival style. Coincidentally, also in 1848, the young German cabinetmaker and wood sculptor Gustav Herter (1830–1898) left his home in Württemberg and moved to New York. There, in 1864, he and his brother Christian founded the firm Herter Brothers, which soon became known for luxury furnishings. There are remarkable parallels between the histories of that firm and that of Anton and his younger brother Martin.[16]

At some point after 1851, Anton returned to Germany with some three hundred furniture designs.[17] In 1854, with the ongoing support of Philipp Anton Bembé, he established the firm Bembé and Kimbel in New York. Just as Bembé's father Martin had helped Anton's father Wilhelm in Mainz, Bembé financed the undertaking, apparently without ever visiting New York himself.[18] Thanks to Anton's thorough knowledge of European styles and ornament, especially the Rococo, and his ability to fabricate fine furniture for a discriminating North American clientele, the firm flourished.

Among Bembé and Kimbel's commissions was the creation of 131 armchairs after designs by the architect Thomas Ustick Walter for the House of Representatives in the United States Capitol. Upon Anton Bembé's death in 1861, Anton Kimbel was required to repay the Bembé family the considerable start-up capital, but he was eventually able to reignite his own business and expand it.[19]

KIMBEL AND CABUS (1863–1882)

By 1863, with the French-born cabinetmaker Joseph Cabus (1824–1898), Anton Kimbel founded the firm Kimbel and Cabus in New York. Its presentation of furnishings in the Modern Gothic style at the Centennial Exposition in Philadelphia in 1876 brought it greater recognition and an increasing number of commissions.[20] The Modern Gothic style developed in opposition to the ornate excesses of earlier Rococo and Renaissance revival styles. Modern Gothic furniture displayed clean lines, angular forms, striking ebonized surfaces enriched with gilt decoration, many times inset with tiles and featuring bold strap-hinges and hardware.

While training in his father's workshop, Anton was involved in the design and creation of mainly neo-Gothic furniture. He was undoubtedly familiar with the work of German architect Conrad Wilhelm Hase (1818–1902), the founder of the Hanover school of architecture, and his student Edwin Oppler (1831–1880). Their neo-Gothic designs for buildings and furniture of medieval inspiration are characterized by rendering structure and materials visible to the viewer. Anton's later designs manifest intriguing references to the furniture and interiors of Marienburg Castle (1857–67) in Schulenburg,

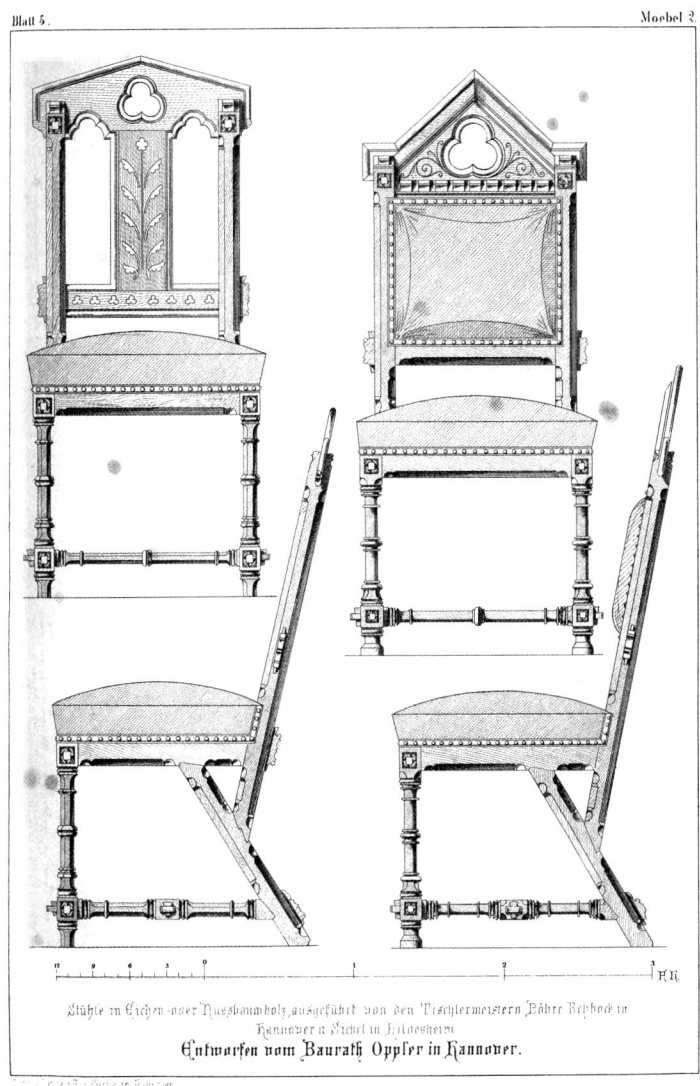

Blatt 5.   Moebel 2.

Stühle in Eichen- oder Nußbaumholz, ausgeführt von den Tischlermeistern Böhte Beyhod in Hannover u. Sichel in Hildesheim
Entworfen vom Baurath Oppler in Hannover.

FIG. 6 Edwin Oppler, *Die Kunst im Gewerbe* (*Industrial Art*) 1, issue 1 (1872): pl. 5, fig. 2

begun by Hase in 1857 and completed by Oppler after 1864, as well as Villa Cahn in Bonn, built by Oppler between 1868 and 1870. Most notable is Oppler's distinctive design for the hind legs of both arm and side chairs, which Anton incorporated into his own chair designs (fig. 6 and see pp. 112–13, 121, 125).[21] As editor of the design journal *Die Kunst im Gewerbe* (*Industrial Art*) from 1872 to 1878, Oppler promoted his

own designs and those of others, as well as medieval furniture and designs as sources of inspiration. Along with furniture in the Gothic taste, Kimbel and Cabus produced pieces in the so-called Anglo-Japanese style, which was popular from 1851 to 1900, and took inspiration from what was then seen as the "exotic" decorative arts and cultures of Japan and China.

MARTIN KIMBEL (1835–1921)

Around 1852 Anton's brother Martin (1835–1921), Wilhelm Kimbel's third son, also moved to New York (fig. 7). He first worked with Anton, then established the firm Laun and Kimbel with Jahn Laun in 1856.[22] In a diary from 1939 kept by Martin's son Wilhelm Kimbel, we read: "He founded a workshop J. Laun and Kimbel in New York, which thanks to his ingenuity achieved rapid success. I remember the design for President Abraham Lincoln's salon car executed by his firm, that alone the sign of its swift rise."[23]

Upon the outbreak of the Civil War (1861–64), Martin joined a Union Army artillery regiment as a volunteer.[24] Around 1862/63 he deserted and returned to Europe, first to London, where according to his son's diary he again took up his old trade as draftsman: "He published a small lithographed pamphlet on 'modern furniture.' I know this booklet. It contained a number of pieces, all of them in the neo-Grecian style popular at the time."[25] From London he returned to Mainz, planning to join his father's workshop, but his stepmother prevented it. In any case he apparently stayed in Mainz long enough to publish his first pattern book in 1864, *Model- und Musterbuch für Schreiner* (*Model and Pattern Book for Cabinetmakers*). He then proceeded to Cologne and, like his older brother Anton, went to work for the firm of Heinrich Pallenberg. In 1866 he moved to Breslau, where he first served as the artistic director of the firm Bauer Brothers.[26] A year later he founded his own eponymous firm in

FIG. 7 Martin Kimbel (1835–1921). Henrietta Mehlbach Richardson's Kimbel Family Collection, courtesy of Elizabeth Richardson Elisher

FIG. 8 Wilhelm Kimbel (1868–1965) and wife. Henrietta Mehlbach Richardson's Kimbel Family Collection, courtesy of Elizabeth Richardson Elisher

Breslau.[27] In 1872 Martin made a name for himself as a reformer in the applied arts with a second book of patterns, *Der decorative Ausbau, dargestellt und gezeichnet zur Benutzung für Malerei, Holz- und Steinhauerei, Decoration etc.* (*Decorative Furnishing, Pictured and Drawn to Scale for Use in Painting, Wood and Stone Sculpture, Designing, etc.*).

WILHELM KIMBEL (1868–1965)

In 1897 Martin's second son, Wilhelm (1868–1965),[28] who established the firm Kimbel and Friederichsen in Berlin, was named

cabinetmaker and designer to Kaiser Wilhelm II. By around 1900, he was the owner and artistic director of one of Berlin's leading furniture stores (fig. 8).[29] As a young boy he had been diligently trained in drawing by his father; at fourteen he began his apprenticeship and training as a cabinetmaker and draftsman with well-known German architects and interior designers in Hamburg (Christian Böckenkröger), Dresden (Herrmann and Söhne), and Bayreuth (Firma Eysser). For a time, he returned to his father's workshop in Breslau, before going on to Berlin (Cremer and Wolffenstein) and Cologne (Heinrich Pallenberg).

From 1889 to 1894 he sojourned in the United States, where he worked in his uncle Anton's firm, A. Kimbel and Sons, Furniture and Interior Decoration, for three months before working at Herter Brothers. At the end of his career, reflecting back on his life, he judged his time in the United States to have been most important for his development: "All in all these years I was fortunate enough to live and work in the United States played a decisive role in my artistic work."[30]

Wilhelm's designs largely ignored the more fashionable stylistic and artistic approaches of his time, Jugendstil and Art Deco. His furniture, all of the highest quality, documents the persistence of historical trends up into the 1930s, and provides an interesting commentary on the conservatism of his patrons, predominantly from aristocratic and upper-middle-class circles in Germany.[31] The degree to which Wilhelm was influenced by the styles of his father Martin and his uncle Anton is clear from both the numerous surviving examples of his own works and from over sixty thousand surviving design drawings. The albums of photos of his commissioned work are indexed by style—Gothic, Renaissance, Baroque, Louis XVI, Rococo, Adam, Biedermeier, and Empire— each preceded by the adjective "modern" to indicate their adaptation to modern trends.[32] There are also occasional designs for neo-Gothic and Japanese-influenced pieces of the kind he had come to know at his uncle Anton's in New York.

Wilhelm's son Martin (1905–1996) carried on the family tradition, in 1938 establishing in Berlin the new firm Kimbel and Sponer with Hermann Sponer, which he had to abandon at the end of World War II. In the early 1950s, he founded the firm Kimbel and Company in Wuppertal, which survived until 1973.

The works of Kimbel and Cabus provide both stylistic and technical evidence of the years each spent learning and teaching in a range of workshops either in Europe or in those run by European immigrants in New York City. They brought these lessons and approaches to the work they created together, which in turn exerted a significant influence on their peers and on later cabinetmakers in both Europe and the United States.

1   Heidrun Zinnkann, *Mainzer Möbelschreiner der ersten Hälfte des 19. Jahrhunderts* (Frankfurt am Main: Historischen Museums, 1985), p. 152.

2   Ibid., p. 10.

3   Christian Peter Wilhelm Beuth, "Foreword," in *Role models for manufacturers and craftsmen*, ed. Karl Friedrich Schinkel (Prussian Trade Institute, 1821).

4   Melitta Jonas, "'Vorbilder für Fabrikanten und Handwerker,' Karl Friedrich Schinkels Einfluss auf das Kunstgewerbe," *Weltkunst* 23 (December 1, 1992): 3508-511.

5   Zinnkann 1985 (as in note 1), p. 152 n. 669.

6   Jonas 1992 (as in note 4): 3508.

7   Hans Ottomeyer, "Germany," in Katherine S. Howe, Alice Cooney Frelinghuysen, and Catherine Hoover Voorsanger, *Herter Brothers: Furniture and Interiors for a Gilded Age* (New York: Harry N. Abrams, in association with the Museum of Fine Arts, Houston, 1994), p. 15.

8   Ibid., p. 22; Jonas 1992 (as in note 4).

9   Barbara Mundt, in *Der Traum vom Glück, Die Kunst des Historismus in Europa, 24. Europarat Ausstellung*, vol. 2 (Vienna: Christian Brandstätter Verlag, 1996), p. 426, cat. 8.19; Georg Himmelheber, "Klassizismus, Historismus, Jugendstil," in Heinrich Kreisel, *Die Kunst des deutschen Möbels*, vol. 1 (Munich: C. H. Beck, 1973), p. 106.

10   Barbaba Mundt, *Historismus. Kunstgewerbe zwischen Biedermeier und Jugendstil* (Munich: Keyser, 1981), p. 95.

11   Joanna Banham, "Rococo Revival," in *Encyclopedia of Interior Design* (London: Routledge, 1997), p. 1078.

12   In Cologne, then belonging to Prussia, the Pallenberg furniture firm dominated the market. In 1861 Heinrich Pallenberg took in his sons Jakob (1831–1900) and Franz (1834–1882) as partners, and the firm continued to be operated by his descendants until 1932. Pallenberg produced entire interiors complete with paneling and furnishings, and participated with great success in London's 1851 World's Fair.

13   Zinnkann 1985 (as in note 1), p. 157.

14   *Catalogue Exposition des produits de l'industrie francaise, Paris,* vol. 3, *Rapport Du Jury Central* (Paris: Fain et Thunot, 1844); Mundt 1981 (as in note 9), p. 102.

15   In 1865, Kimbel's youngest son Jean took over the workshop, but was unable to build up the business again. Zinnkann 1985 (as in note 1), p. 156.

16   Katherine S. Howe and Alice Cooney Frelinghuysen, "Introduction," in *Herter Brothers* 1994 (as in note 7), p. 13; Ottomeyer 1994 (as in note 7), p. 27.

17   Zinnkann 1985 (as in note 1), p. 157 n. 714.

18   Ottomeyer 1994 (as in note 7), p. 27.

19   Thanks to its solid business footing, the firm survived as a family business into the twentieth century. See Zinnkann 1985 (as in note 1), p. 183.

20   See Peter Thornton, *Authentic Décor: The Domestic Interior 1620–1920* (London: Viking, 1984), p. 337, no. 448.

21   I thank Wayne Mason for this reference. See "Journey of an Architect in the North-West of Europe. V," *American Architect and Building News* (February 24, 1877): 63–64; and the website of the Schloss-Marienburg at https://www.schloss-marienburg.de/en/history.

22   Zinnkann 1985 (as in note 1), p. 218 n. 713.

23   W. Kimbel Papers, Kunstbibliothek, Staatliche Museen, Berlin, Stiftung Preussischer Kulturbesitz, inv. 1996.24, Tagebuch Wilhelm Kimbels, Rheinsberg 1939, unpaginated.

24   Ibid.

25   Ibid.

26   Ibid.

27   Ulrich Thieme and Felix Becker, eds. *Allgemeines Lexikon der bildenden Künstler von der Antike bis zur Gegenwart*, vol. 19, ed. Hans Vollmer (1992: Leipzig: E. A. Seeman, 1927), pp. 309–10.

28   Melitta Jonas, formerly Schmidt, "Wilhelm Kimbel und die Kunsttischlerei Kimbel und Friederichsen, Studien zum Firmennachlass, Text- und Bildband" (master's thesis, Technische Universität Berlin, 1987), p. 9: "I can still see the old, cozy apartment at Margarethenstrasse 7–9 in my mind's eye. My father is seated at a table making a drawing for his great work 'Der decorative Ausbau.'"

29   Melitta Jonas, "Wilhelm Kimbel. Ein Historist in der Moderne," in Christian Juranek, Ulrich Feldhahn, and Melitta Jonas, *Art Déco, Kunst des Historismus?* (Wernigerode: Edition Schloss Wernigerode, 2019), pp. 77–89.

30   Jonas 1987 (as in note 28), p. 16 n. 110.

31   Jonas 2019 (as in note 29), p. 84.

32   W. Kimbel Papers (as in note 23). Eleven commissioned albums with the names of private clients from the years 1898–1910 and 1913–24, as well as display pieces from the years 1901–11.

KIMBEL & CABUS,

**7 & 9
East 20th St.**

New York.

Cabinet Manufacturers and Decorators.

KIMBEL AND CABUS: ECLECTIC CABINETMAKERS AND DECORATORS

Barbara Veith and Medill Higgins Harvey

This essay traces the timeless immigrant success story of Anton Kimbel (1822–1895) and Joseph Cabus (1824–1898), the design team who pioneered an inventive take on Modern Gothic furniture forms and thereby defined a significant aesthetic in the United States. Immigrant sons of German and French families, they embodied an entrepreneurial spirit. Over the course of a remarkable partnership of nearly twenty years, Kimbel and Cabus employed artistic talent, technical expertise, business acumen, and ambitious marketing practices to create a leading cabinetmaking and decorating firm of post-Civil War New York City. The firm reached its zenith with a critically acclaimed display of Modern Gothic furniture at the 1876 Centennial Exhibition in Philadelphia, attracting a wealth of eager clients, inspiring imitators, and securing their position as leading arbiters of progressive taste and "artistic" interiors.

In architecture, Gothic pertains to the style of building, especially of cathedrals, characterized by pointed arches and associated with the period from the twelfth through the sixteenth centuries in Western Europe.[1] Revived interest in the Gothic era flourished in Britain through successive waves during the late eighteenth and early nineteenth centuries, as architects sought a national source of design inspiration in contrast to the prevailing Greco-Roman classicism. Initially, fanciful aspects of Gothic architecture were incorporated into building, interior, and furniture designs.[2] Then, beginning in the 1830s under architect A. W. N. Pugin (1812–1852), and further promoted by a second generation of architects and designers during the 1860s, a new version of the Gothic revival emerged, known as the Modern or Reform Gothic. Rejecting industrialization, progressive architects and designers such as Bruce James Talbert (1838–1881; fig. 2) and Charles Locke Eastlake (1836–1906) drew inspiration from a romanticized vision of the medieval guild system and advocated a return to handcraft, revealed construction, clean lines, and restrained decoration. Their influential publications—Talbert's *Gothic Forms Applied to Furniture, Metal Work and Decoration for Domestic Purposes* (1867) and Eastlake's *Hints on Household Taste in Furniture, Upholstery and*

FIG. 1 Kimbel and Cabus trade card (detail), ca. 1875. 4 ⅞ × 3 ⅜ in. (12.4 × 8.6 cm). Collection of Susan W. Paine

Other Details (1868)—provided Modern Gothic furniture designs and advice on home decor that shaped public taste. Christopher Dresser (1834–1904) was another important British designer and theorist of the time who advocated for the use of conventionalized or abstracted botanical decorative motifs on unostentatious Modern Gothic forms. In the United States, critics Clarence Cook (1828–1900), writing for *Scribner's Monthly*, and Harriet Prescott Spofford (1835–1921), writing for *Harper's Bazar* (the spelling would change to *Harper's Bazaar* in 1930) and *Harper's New Monthly Magazine*, disseminated Talbert's and Eastlake's ideas, interpreting them for an eager North American audience. Their respective collected essays were eventually published as Cook's *The House Beautiful: Essays on Beds and Tables, Stools and Candlesticks* (1878) and Spofford's *Art Decoration Applied to Furniture* (1878), which offered consumers comprehensive home decorating advice in single volumes.

During the 1870s, due to increasing prosperity following the Civil War, a much larger percentage of the U.S. population had the time and resources for artistic and leisure pursuits. Those with progressive taste cultivated an interest in home decor modeled on the recommendations of Talbert, Eastlake, Cook, and Spofford. Major exhibitions such as the 1876 Centennial Exhibition in Philadelphia introduced Americans to British design reform and the Aesthetic Movement, which advocated that art be integrated in all aspects of life. Newly established department stores offered an abundance of products to well-to-do customers striving to craft an identity through material goods. As is still the case, in such circles what you displayed in your home said something about your knowledge and position in the world. Consumers filled their houses with artistic furniture, ceramics and glass, metalwork, textiles, and wallpaper in the latest styles.

FIG. 2 Bruce James Talbert (British, 1838–1881). Cabinet, ca. 1870. Cherry, oak; veneers of thuya, ebony, walnut, and rosewood, 85 ⅞ × 24 ⅜ × 44 ¼ in. (218.1 × 61.9 × 112.4 cm). Museum of Fine Arts, Boston, John Wheelock Elliot and John Morse Elliot Fund and Arthur Tracy Cabot Fund, 1997.188

In New York City, Kimbel and Cabus were early advocates of these modern design reform ideals, at least with respect to aesthetic sensibilities, if not entirely in practice. They synthesized British and Continental European design sources to produce a diversity of Modern

FIG. 3 Anton Kimbel (1822–1895). Henrietta Mehlbach Richardson's Kimbel Family Collection, courtesy of Elizabeth Richardson Elisher

of the burgeoning middle class. To satisfy a flourishing market they worked in a vast range of styles as well as Modern Gothic, and executed not only domestic interiors but also commissions for churches and other public spaces. This exhibition and publication draw on primary sources such as censuses, credit reports, city directories, ephemera, newspapers, periodicals, and photographs to present illuminating new research that traces the firm's business history, marketing practices, furniture forms, clientele, and commissions.

ANTON KIMBEL (1822–1895)

The first of eleven children, Anton Kimbel was born on August 28, 1822 to the prosperous cabinetmaker Wilhelm Kimbel (1786–1869) and Margarethe Bembé Kimbel (1796–1875) in Mainz, Rhineland-Palatinate, now Germany (fig. 3).[3] Wilhelm trained in Vienna and Paris before opening his shop in Mainz in 1815.[4] A skilled draftsman who was uncompromising about his craft, Wilhelm exhibited bi-annually at craft fairs in Frankfurt, where his furniture garnered favor with the regional aristocracy. He forged an auspicious business relationship in Frankfurt with the esteemed decorating and furniture-making Bembé family, a bond further strengthened by his marriage to Margarethe in 1821. Margarethe's brother Philipp Anton Bembé (1799–1861) directed a successful furniture-making and upholstery business in Mainz from 1825.[5] He specialized in creating fully decorated and furnished interiors in a variety of styles for noble patrons, eventually earning the title *Hoflieferant*, purveyor to the court.[6] Anton Kimbel grew up in this tight-knit community of cabinetmakers, decorators, and upholsterers, apprenticing in the workshops of his father and uncle. Bembé recognized the talent of his nephew and godson, financed his education, and facilitated connections for him with renowned cabinetmaking firms across

Gothic furniture forms that combined bold, clean lines with arresting surface decoration drawn from a vast ornamental vocabulary. They used elements of their designs and decorative schemes interchangeably to produce an almost infinite variation of wares at multiple price points for a broad range of customers. Unlike some of their competitors, such as Herter Brothers and Pottier and Stymus, who catered to the robber-barons and most elite echelons of society, Kimbel and Cabus appealed to doctors, merchants, stockbrokers, and other members

Europe and then in the United States. While training, Anton worked in Cologne with Pallenberg; in Brussels; in Paris with Alexandre-Georges Fourdinois and designer and publisher Desiré Guilmard; and in Saint Petersburg with Nerkin.[7] These formative experiences presaged success for the twenty-six-year-old Anton embarking on the ship *Zurich* from the French port of Le Havre to begin the next chapter of his career in New York City.[8]

When Anton Kimbel arrived on September 15, 1848, he stepped off the boat into a city teeming with immigrants from all over the world. He was one of nearly 1.5 million Germans who immigrated to the United States between 1843 and the start of the Civil War in 1861.[9] The influx rendered New York City home to the third-largest German-speaking community in the world after Vienna and Berlin. These immigrants were fleeing famine, resulting from poor harvests and a pernicious potato rot, as well as economic turmoil caused by the political strife sweeping Europe. In the German states, the March Revolution of 1848 erupted in the south and west, regions densely populated by artisans and craftsmen.[10] Steady work was elusive during these tumultuous times, and hardship motivated many to seek better prospects in the United States. With the opening of the Erie Canal in 1824 and the ensuing increase in trade, New York City surpassed Philadelphia and other port cities to become the nation's mercantile and cultural capital. As the center of cabinet and furniture making in the country, the city was a beacon of opportunity for enterprising German craftspeople who excelled in this sector of trade.[11] Many settled in Manhattan in the German-American neighborhood known as "Kleindeutschland," or "Little Germany."[12] Bounded by 14th Street on the north, Division Street on the south, the East River on the east, and 3rd Avenue and the Bowery to the west, Kleindeutschland encompassed a multitude of tailors, shoemakers,

bakers, and furniture-makers, as well as grocers and peddlers.[13] The recollections of German cabinetmaker Ernest Hagen (1830–1913), who immigrated to New York with his family in 1844 and later worked with German cabinetmakers Krieg and Dohrmann at 106 Norfolk Street, provide a vivid insight into the neighborhood work environment.[14] Hagen describes "cabinet maker shops, saw mills and marble mills everywhere." Journeyman cabinetmakers worked in small shops of two to six men and specialized in a single furniture type, such as box sofas or

FIG. 4 Charles A. Baudouine (American, 1808–1895). Armchair, ca. 1852. Rosewood, ash, modern upholstery, 37 ⅜ × 23 ⅝ × 24 in. (94.9 × 60 × 60.9 cm). Munson-Williams-Proctor Arts Institute, Proctor Collection, PC. 423.5

bureaus. Completing work by hand using tools and workbenches that they supplied themselves, these craftsmen were paid by the piece. The small shops supplied larger firms across the city that sent furniture West, South, and to the West Indies. In 1853 Hagen left his Norfolk Street employer to work for several shops on Broadway, the locus of the elite furniture businesses, ultimately securing a position with Charles A. Baudouine's cabinetmaking establishment at 335 Broadway and Anthony Street. During his two years with Baudouine, Hagen undoubtedly became acquainted with the firm's principal designer, Anton Kimbel.[15]

The circumstances that led to Kimbel's engagement as a designer for Baudouine between 1848 and 1854 are not certain, but it is likely that his uncle (Philipp) Anton Bembé facilitated the initial connection.[16] A leading firm of the day, Baudouine's establishment employed nearly two hundred people, including cabinetmakers, carvers, varnishers, and upholsterers.[17] From his showrooms, described in 1852 as one of the city's greatest attractions, Baudouine offered his own furniture in all the fashionable European styles—from Rococo revival (fig. 4) to Renaissance revival—and sold imported French furniture, upholstery coverings, hardware, and trimmings.[18] Along with French competitors Ringuet-LePrince and Leon Marcotte, Baudouine offered not only cabinetmaking but also an interior-decorating service—a concept familiar to Kimbel through his prior experience with Bembé in Mainz, but then only nascent in New York City. Although Baudouine's firm did not participate in the Exhibition of the Industry of All Nations of 1853, also known as the New York Crystal Palace, an 1876 article in the *American Cabinet Maker, Upholsterer and Furniture Reporter* reflecting upon designers active during the exhibition suggests Kimbel's participation and offers evidence of early regard for his artistic skill. The author identifies Kimbel and esteemed

FIG. 5 Pauline Blank Kimbel (1822–1862), right. Henrietta Mehlbach Richardson's Kimbel Family Collection, courtesy of Elizabeth Richardson Elisher

cabinetmaker, carver, and sculptors Gustav Herter, Ernst Plassmann, and Joseph Bailly as the "only four designers of any note in all Manhattan Island" at that time. Kimbel "contributed a dignity to chisel, gouge and saw that has resulted in the permanent establishment of household art in America . . . [and] gave evidence of his future prominence in some choice work which is remembered to this day with much pleasure."[19]

At some point during his first few years in New York City, Kimbel married Mainz-born Pauline Blank (1822–1862; fig. 5), and they had five children together between 1852 and 1861: Francis, Anthony, Henry, Elizabeth, and Pauline.[20] Kimbel is first listed in the *New York City Directory* in 1854 living and working at 56 Walker Street in lower Manhattan with "furniture" as his profession.[21] By the time

FIG. 6 "A Parlor View in a New York Dwelling House." *Gleason's Pictorial Drawing-Room Companion* 7, no. 19 (November 11, 1854): 300. American Antiquarian Society, Periodicals, Worcester, Massachusetts

Baudouine closed shop in May 1854, Kimbel had established a reputation as a noted cabinetmaker in the city.[22] On February 7, 1854, the partnership of "Bembé and Kimbel, Furniture and Upholstery" commenced in "commodious warerooms" at 56 Walker Street.[23] Bembé, who remained in Europe, provided the critical capital of 30,000 guilders, or *Gulden*; weekly announcements in the *New York Daily Times* throughout that September proclaim the firm to be "in regular communication with A. Bembé's well-known Furniture and Upholstery manufactories in Paris and Mayence [Mainz], so extensively patronized by the wealthy aristocracy" and that the latest European styles were reproduced in the shop.[24] The November

FIG. 7 Bembé and Kimbel, Armchair used in the U.S. House of Representatives, 1857–73. Leather, oak, wood, 40 ½ × 26 × 23 ½ in. (102.87 × 66.04 × 59.69 cm). From the Collections of The Henry Ford, 68.127.1

issue of *Gleason's Pictorial Drawing-Room Companion* illustrates an opulent New York parlor designed by Mr. Kimbel of Bembé and Kimbel replete with étagère, center table, sofa, chairs, and plant stand displaying the curvilinear lines characteristic of the French Rococo revival style (fig. 6).[25] The accompanying text describes the dwelling as "magnificent" and sumptuous, and goes on to state that "the furniture represented in the engraving . . . is not altogether French in design." Kimbel is credited for "his unique styles [that] appear to be American modifications of those now in vogue abroad." "Bembe A. & A. Kimbel" is listed as a furniture business at 56 Walker Street in the 1855 *New York City Directory*.[26] An entry in the New York State Census that same year attests to Kimbel's growing prosperity, describing him as a landowner residing in a brick residence valued at $16,000 with his wife, two sons, and two female servants.[27]

By 1857 the firm had moved uptown to a new location at 928 Broadway between 21st and 22nd Streets, in the heart of the fashionable Ladies' Mile shopping district, where they would remain until 1862.[28] R. G. Dun and Company credit reports for 1857 reflect Bembé and Kimbel's continued growth, describing the business as worth $25,000 to $30,000, Kimbel to be "of good charac[ter] & bus[iness] ability," and that they "have been prompt in their paym[en]ts & good houses cr[edit] them for mod[est] am[oun]t."[29] That year the firm secured a commission of national importance: to produce 131 oak chairs to a design created by Thomas Ustick Walter (1804–1887), architect of the United States Capitol extension from 1851–65, for the House of Representatives (fig. 7). Robust in scale and ornament, the chairs are embellished with carved classical and foliate Renaissance revival details. In early August, Bembé and Kimbel sent sample chairs and desks to Washington, D.C. for inspection by Quartermaster General Montgomery C. Meigs.[30] After comparing Bembé and Kimbel's samples with those made by rival firm Doe, Hazelton Company of Boston, Meigs deemed Bembé and Kimbel's chairs superior and their prices less expensive, although their desks not as good. Determined to secure the commission, Kimbel traveled to Washington, D.C. to meet Meigs in person on August 19th and "make a bargain for the chairs." Meigs clearly found him compelling, for an order was placed for half of the 262 chairs required. Later that month Meigs contracted the Hammitt Desk Manufacturing Company of Philadelphia to complete the other half of the chair order. Doe, Hazelton Company fulfilled the order for the desks. Given the numbers required, firms who produced larger volumes of furniture were better suited to meet the demand. Unlike Hammitt and Doe, Hazleton, Kimbel and Cabus made work on a singular basis. Fulfilling this prominent commission required them to scale up their workforce and reflected their ambition to further their success and reputation.

Credit reports show that Bembé and Kimbel flourished during the next few years. They are repeatedly described as being in good credit and doing a "good profitable bus[iness] with a good class of customers," and that its capital held steady at $20,000.[31] The reports underline that the financial security of the firm depended on Bembé, however, who is consistently identified as the senior partner, worth $200,000, while Kimbel is characterized as not having much means.[32] By 1858 Kimbel and his growing family had moved to a new home address at 87 1/2 West 26th Street.[33] The U.S. Federal Census for 1860 identifies thirty-eight-year-old Kimbel as "Master Cabinetmaker" with a personal estate valued at $500. In addition to Kimbel, his family, three servants of German origin, his thirty-year-old cousin Charles [Carl] Bembé, Anton Bembé's son, a clerk, resides at the same address.[34] By 1861, the city directory lists an additional address for Bembé and Kimbel, presumably their factory, on East 22nd

Street, and Kimbel and family now reside at 146 East 23rd Street, between 3rd and 4th Avenues.[35] Family history recalls "a well-ordered household, a most comfortable home, the social center of a group of people of good standing and education" and the loyal friendships of prominent individuals such as a physician named Dr. Niergrad and a Mr. and Mrs. Sattig, wealthy importers of Rhenish and French wines.[36]

Tragically, on March 3, 1861, after more than twelve years of increasing prosperity and success, Kimbel experienced a dramatic reversal of fortune with the sudden death of his uncle Anton Bembé.[37] By this time, his cousin Carl Bembé, a silent partner in Bembé and Kimbel, had become the second manager. Upon Anton's death the partnership was dissolved, and Carl required Kimbel to repay the money that his uncle had invested in the firm on his behalf. This sizeable financial demand, insurmountable for Kimbel at the outbreak of the Civil War, required swift action. He auctioned off the firm's stock and sold his house to repay his cousin for his share in the business. Carl continued the firm under the Bembé name at the same address.[38] Amid the upheaval, Kimbel's wife Pauline gave birth to their fifth child.[39] The family of seven moved to a "little room in a second class boarding house on Third Avenue," where Pauline contracted typhoid and died on April 13, 1862.[40] Widowed and practically destitute, Kimbel sent his five children, one a mere infant, to live with his mother and mother-in-law in Germany before contracting typhoid himself. Family letters recollect him overhearing his "watchers" planning to distribute his possessions among themselves as he lay feverish in the sick room, but Kimbel miraculously recovered and re-established himself—a testament to his strength of will, talent, and business acumen. While working as a draughtsman for a former competitor, he befriended Simon Gerber, a Swiss man "of education and refinement," who came to New York City to open a branch of his family's

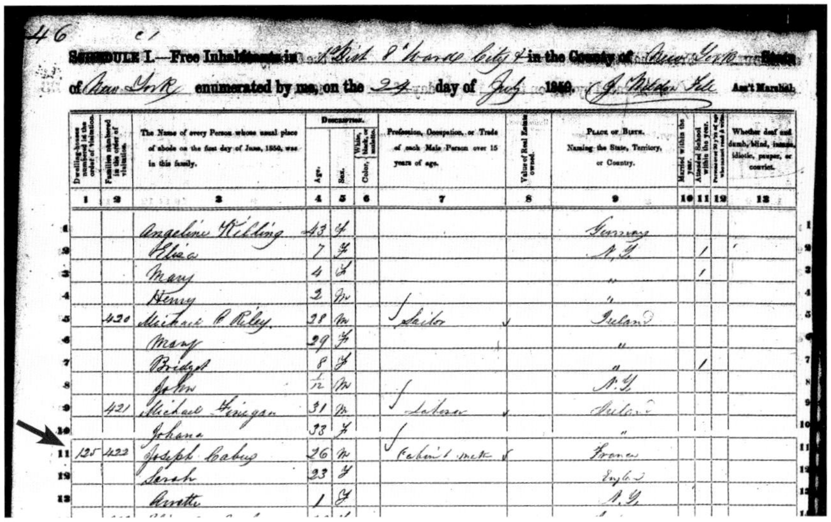

FIG. 8 Seventh Census of the United States, 1850. Records of the Bureau of the Census, National Archives, Washington, D.C.

wholesale cheese house.[41] Gerber's offer of $6,000 in financial support enabled Kimbel to commence business anew, this time in partnership with Joseph Cabus, a neighboring furniture maker at 924 Broadway.

JOSEPH CABUS (1824–1898)

Joseph Cabus, about whom less is known, was born June 15, 1824, in Calmoutier, France, to Claude and Annette Cabus.[42] As an eight-year-old, Joseph set sail with his parents and two younger brothers from Le Havre on the ship *Louise*, arriving in New York City on April 8, 1833. Passenger records identify father Claude and his young sons as farmers. Although the circumstances that motivated the family to cross the Atlantic are not known, they may have resulted from the anti-monarchical revolutions that convulsed France during the second quarter of the nineteenth century. It was also a time in which countless citizens moved from rural regions to urban centers in search of opportunity in an increasingly industrialized world.[43] Some, like the Cabus family, made the decision to try their luck in the United States. Claude Cabus is first listed in the *New York City Directory* in 1838 as a cabinetmaker at 138 Centre (Centre Street) in lower Manhattan, and at 226 Centre the following year.[44] He may have adopted this profession upon arriving in New York, or he might have already become experienced in cabinetmaking—farmers often needed to cultivate multiple talents. Surviving records suggest that Joseph spent his formative years apprenticing with his father. The Federal Census for 1840 documents Claude residing with his wife, three sons, daughter, and an older female, and it indicates that two family members, probably Claude and sixteen-year-old Joseph, work in manufacturing and trade.[45] Joseph is first listed in the *New York City Directory* of 1850 as a cabinetmaker working at 37 Grand (Street), an address he shared with his father.[46] The Federal Census for 1850 and Joseph's naturalization record from 1851 provide further insight into his young adult life: he, his English-born wife Sarah Sangster, and their one-year-old daughter Annette lived in "Gowannes, Long Island," a region of Western Brooklyn (fig. 8).[47]

Joseph continued to be listed as a cabinetmaker in the 1852 and 1853 city directories at different addresses on Wooster Street.[48]

The New York State Census for 1855 offers the earliest evidence of Cabus's association with renowned French-born cabinetmaker Alexander Roux, for whom he worked for a number of years.[49] The census indicates that Joseph and Sarah Cabus, along with Annette and her younger siblings Sarah, William, and Joseph, occupied the same brick residence as Roux, his four children, housekeeper, and cook, suggesting a mutually supportive relationship not unusual in nineteenth-century immigrant communities. Having arrived in the United States during the 1830s, Roux was directing one of the preeminent cabinetmaking firms in New York City by the mid-1850s.[50] A participant in the 1853 New York Crystal Palace exhibition, Roux's firm was awarded a bronze medal and special notice for an elaborately carved black walnut sideboard. A surviving version of this imposing form in French Renaissance style features elaborate naturalistic carving depicting all manner of fish, fowl, fruit, and game among foliate scrolls, demonstrating the virtuosity of Roux's craftspeople (fig. 9). Its sumptuous visual feast alludes to the dining rituals of affluent individuals who purchased such elite objects for their homes. Ernest Hagen, in his above-mentioned reminiscences about New York City cabinetmaking, describes Roux as "the next best to Baudouine" though he also found Roux's style "rather better than Baudouine's."[51] Hagen describes Roux's work as "generally lighter in character, running off in the Louis XVI style," which suggests a striking contrast to the richly carved Renaissance-style sideboard and indicates that Roux's workers were well-versed in a range of fashionable French revival styles. Located at 479 Broadway and 46 and 43 Mercer Street, Roux's firm employed 120 men.[52] He owned $20,000 in real estate, $3,000 in machinery, and $30,000 in raw materials, and

FIG. 9 Alexander Roux (American, born France, 1813–1886). Sideboard, ca. 1853. Black walnut, pine, 92 ¾ × 71 ¾ × 25 ⅝ in. (235.6 × 182.2 × 65.1 cm). The Metropolitan Museum of Art, Purchase, Friends of the American Wing Fund and David Schwartz Foundation Inc. Gift, 1993, 1993.168

his annual production was worth $144,000, making his cabinetmaking firm one of the city's largest. Beginning in 1851, Roux lived at 41 Mercer Street, next door to his business, in the dwelling that he would share with the Cabus family in 1855.[53] City directory listings for 1857–60 confirm Cabus's employment with Roux.[54] Cabus became foreman and oversaw the production of myriad furniture forms in rosewood, oak, and walnut, thus earning appointment to partner in 1858.[55] Credit reports from December 14, 1858, indicate that Roux, with a "reputed w[orth] of $75,000" was the dominant partner and that Cabus had "a sm[all] int[erest] in the bus[iness]" but "not much means." Between 1856 and 1860 Cabus and his wife welcomed three more children into their family—Alexander, Theresa, and Frank—and by 1861 they had moved to 73 Greene Street.[56] For reasons unknown, the short-lived partnership between Roux and Cabus had ended by January 1860 and both men continued business independently.[57] The Civil War caused a significant contraction in the cabinetmaking business, and many firms ceased operations during this period. Civil War Draft Registration records indicate that Cabus served as member of the 55th New

York Volunteer Infantry, otherwise known as the Gardes De Lafayette.[58] Active beginning August 28, 1861, this Union Army regiment consisted primarily of French immigrants and ceased to exist on December 21, 1862, when it was consolidated with the 38th New York Infantry. Although nothing further is known about Cabus's military service in 1862, he demonstrated remarkable tenacity that year, re-establishing his furniture-making business uptown at 924 Broadway, next to Bembé and Kimbel at 928 Broadway (fig. 10).[59]

A. KIMBEL AND J. CABUS (1863–1882): FORGING A PARTNERSHIP

The conversations that motivated Anton Kimbel and Joseph Cabus to join forces can only be imagined. Perhaps they met as neighbors on Broadway as Kimbel was liquidating furniture stock to settle affairs with his cousin Carl Bembé. Perhaps, as seasoned professionals in the upper echelons of the New York City cabinetmaking industry, they were already acquainted. We have descriptions of the two men from their passport applications: Kimbel, aged forty, was five feet, eleven inches tall with black and grey hair and blue eyes, and Cabus, aged thirty-nine, was five feet, eight and a half inches tall, with thin hair, blue eyes, a moustache, and beard.[60] Their synergistic partnership was defined by artistic talent and technical expertise, fortified by an established professional network in both the United States and Europe. In addition, after years of designing and creating furniture and interiors for style-conscious consumers, Kimbel and Cabus were attuned to the ebb and flow of changing taste. Their adaptability and creativity augured success.

According to family history, Kimbel and Cabus commenced as a "small factory supplying other dealers with high class furniture."[61] The firm is first listed in the 1863 city directory as "Kimbel A. & J. Cabus, cabinetmakers"

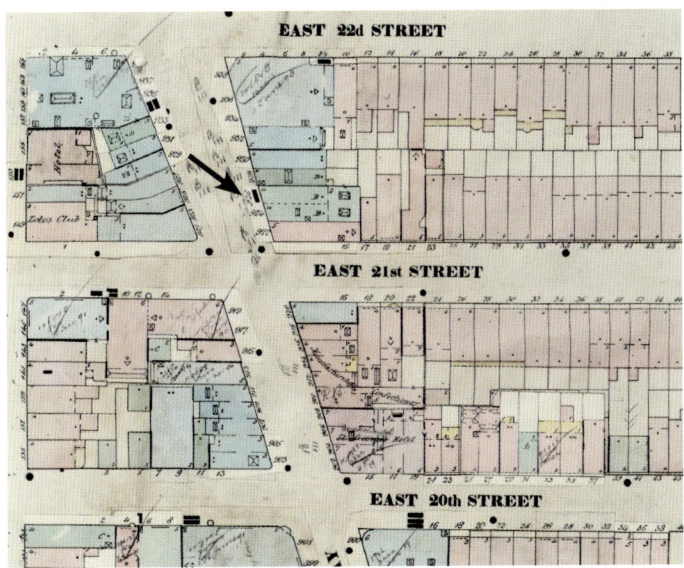

FIG. 10 Map bounded by West 22nd Street, East 22nd Street, Fourth Avenue, Union Place, East 17th Street, Broadway, East 18th Street, West 18th Street, Sixth Avenue; Including West 21st Street, East 21st Street, West 20th Street, East 20th Street, West 19th Street, East 19th Street, Fifth Avenue. From Perris and Browne, *Insurance Maps of the City of New York* (New York: Perris and Browne, 1868), plate 48 (detail). Lionel Pincus and Princess Firyal Map Division, Atlases of New York City, The New York Public Library

Furniture.

AT REDUCED PRICES.

FURNITURE,

Rich, Decorated & Plain.

KIMBEL & CABUS,

928 Broadway.

Our Stock is very large and well assorted. We use none but the

BEST

WELL-SEASONED

WOODS,

And WARRANT all our Work.

Owing to the dull times, we offer our present Assortment of

ROSEWOOD, BLACK WALNUT,

PARLOR, LIBRARY,

DINING ROOM & BEDROOM

Furniture

AT PRICES WITHIN THE REACH OF ALL.

FIG. 11 Advertisement, *New York Observer and Chronicle* (May 14, 1868): 160

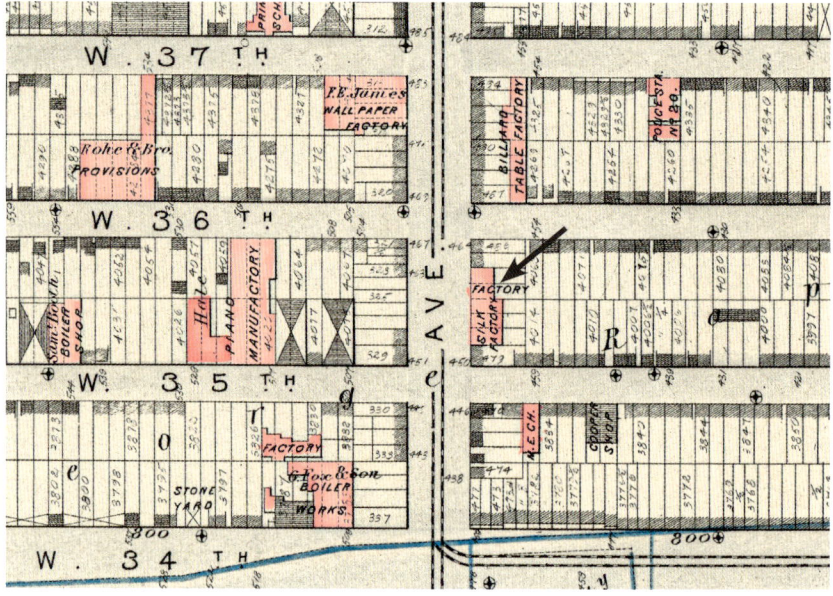

FIG. 12 Map [Bounded by W. 38th Street, Sixth Avenue, W. 26th Street and (Hudson River) Twelfth Avenue.] From G. W. Bromley, *Atlas of the Entire City of New York. Complete in One Volume. From Actual Surveys and Official Records* (New York: G. W. Bromley and E. Robinson, 1879), plate 14 (detail). Lionel Pincus and Princess Firyal Map Divison, Atlases of New York City, The New York Public Library

(hereafter referred to as Kimbel and Cabus) at 924 Broadway, Cabus's former address.[62] A credit report from February 1863 describes Kimbel as "a reliab[le] man" who "attends to his bus[iness] closely" and Cabus as "a good mechanic" and that the two will "no doubt succeed & do well."[63] In April of the same year the partners advertised in the *New York Herald* that they had steam power and well-lit manufacturing rooms for rent at a second address, 111 East 18th Street.[64] Attesting to the firm's progress, an April 1866 credit report states that they "Do a good Bus[iness] [are] In good standing, and considered good for all they want."[65] As the firm flourished, so too did Kimbel's personal life: he married again, to English-born Mary Ann Saunders (1838–1898), and had two more children, Richard and Laura.[66] From 1865 until 1868 the Kimbels resided on

East 20th Street, near the business.[67] Cabus and family resided at 27 17th Street in Brooklyn.[68]

Information about Kimbel and Cabus's early partnership is scarce, and there are no documented examples of their work from this period. Slivers of insight gleaned from extant records such as newspaper accounts, city directories, and census records reveal an ambitious enterprise under development. The 1867 city directory locates Kimbel and Cabus at 928 Broadway, the address of Kimbel's cousin Carl Bembé and the former quarters of Bembé and Kimbel, corroborating family history that Bembé foundered and Kimbel came to his aid, buying the business.[69] Kimbel and Cabus also moved the factory to 136 East 18th Street.[70] Within four years, the firm grew from a small business serving larger concerns to entrepreneurial "Cabinet Makers and Decorators," as they identified themselves nationally in advertisements in the *Chicago Tribune* between September and November 1867. They touted their location at 928 and 930 Broadway as being "Two squares below [the] Fifth-av. Hotel," which was a luxurious six-story hub of political and social activity in New York City that offered accommodation for eight hundred guests, had private bathrooms, fireplaces in each bedroom, steam-powered elevators, and a staff of four hundred.[71] According to Kimbel and Cabus's advertisements, their business produced "the most elaborate and Plain Drawing-room, Library, Bed and Dining room suites; Wooden Mantels, Looking-Glasses, and Decorations in general," and they also provided room designs and estimates if supplied with a diagram. Regular advertisements from at least May 1868 through May 1869 document the firm's strategy to attract a broad range of customers by offering wares at varied price points.[72] A *New York Observer* notice announced a "very large and well assorted" stock of "rich, decorated & plain" furniture offered "at reduced prices," "within the

reach of all" (fig. 11). They used the "best, well-seasoned woods," including rosewood and black walnut, and warrant all their work. Positive credit reports from this time indicate that they were "doing fair bus[iness]," could "hold their c[usto]m[e]rs," and that they were "honest reliable men, [who] enjoy a good reputation and stand well."[73] By 1868 Kimbel and Cabus moved their factory to a new location on Tenth Avenue, ultimately securing 458 and 460 Tenth Avenue between West 35th and 36th Streets by 1869, which would remain the factory address for the duration of their partnership (fig. 12).[74]

Data from the Federal Census of 1870 offers insight into Kimbel and Cabus's personal lives and relative prosperity. Kimbel, now a U.S. citizen, is listed as a cabinetmaker with a personal estate valued at $10,000—a considerable increase from the $500 value in 1860—and real estate valued at $50,000.[75] He reunited with the younger three of his five children from his first marriage: Henry, a clerk, and Lizzie and Pauline, both at school. He resided with them, his second wife Mary, their son Richard, and two Irish female servants at 337 West 32nd Street, which was halfway between the factory and the showroom, and would be his home address for the remainder of his life. His merchant and professional neighbors included a fruit dealer, a meat market purveyor, a tobacco importer, a judge, a law student, and a mason builder, some American, some British, and others of Continental European origin. In comparison, Joseph, who continued to live in Brooklyn and is also listed as a cabinetmaker, had a personal estate valued at $1500 and real estate valued at $10,000.[76] He, his wife Sarah, their daughters Annette and Sarah, and sons Joseph Jr. (an upholsterer's apprentice), Alex and Frank (both at school), resided at 27 17th Street. Their neighbors included schoolteachers, clerks, seamstresses, a printer, carpenters, a laborer, and a huckster (salesman), all predominantly

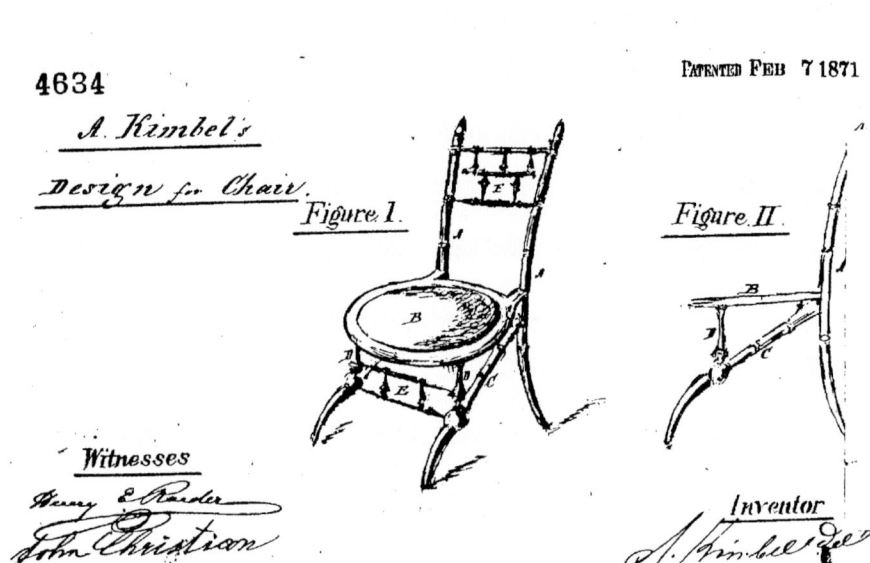

FIG. 13 Anton Kimbel (German, 1822–1895), Design patent for a chair, design
no. 4634, February 7, 1871. United States Patent Office

American and British-born. Within four years, however, Cabus and his family would move to 343 West 30th Street in Manhattan, two blocks south of Kimbel, and this too would remain Cabus's home address for the rest of his life.[77]

Kimbel and Cabus followed an upward trajectory, as documented by the Dun reports for 1870 and 1871, which state that this "well estab[lishe]d firm" did "a first class & profitable" business now worth $40,000 to $50,000.[78] On February 7, 1871, Kimbel registered two chair design patents, numbers 4634 and 4635, with the U.S. Patent Office (fig. 13).[79] The patents elucidate design improvements for two similar chairs that display outward-curving continuous back stiles and legs and down-turned diagonal front legs, attached to the back stiles under the seat. Additional stretchers secure the front legs to each other and to the front underside of the

seat. Kimbel's patents protected his iterations of the diagonal front leg, a defining characteristic of Kimbel and Cabus's seating furniture, and demonstrate his focus on innovation.

Nearly a decade of partnership and financial growth did not completely insulate the firm from the labor strikes that rocked New York City for two months during the spring of 1872. Beginning in May, workers, rallied by organizers from the newly formed National Labor Union and global network of Eight-Hour Leagues, demanded improved work conditions, better salaries, and a reduction of the workday from the standard ten hours to the eight prescribed by state law. Although union efforts to universally realize these demands would continue for years to come, workers in the building trades succeeded in securing a shorter day and celebrated with a parade through the city in

June.[80] The *Cabinet Maker* reported that many New York City cabinetmaking firms joined together to resist the strikers.[81] According to its article, "acceding to the demands would drive manufacturing to other localities, to the injury of workman, as well as of the employer; while submission on the part of latter to the dictation of outside parties, irresponsible and intangible 'leagues,' 'unions,' . . . would be at the expense of self-respect." A professional organization for manufacturers was established in opposition to the unions, the Furniture Board of Trade, chaired by a man named George Brown. Concerned that the local Eight-Hour League was exaggerating its successes, Brown canvassed 181 New York City cabinetmakers to document each firm's employees, the number of men working ten versus eight hours, and whether workers were on strike or discharged.[82] His report for the *Cabinet Maker* provides the earliest insight into the Kimbel and Cabus workforce. Compared to larger firms such as Pottier and Stymus, which employed 320 men, Herter Brothers' 162 men, or Alexander Roux's establishment which employed 150, Kimbel and Cabus was a small enterprise. Of its seventy-seven male employees, forty worked ten-hour days; thirty-seven men, nearly half of the work force, were on strike. None were working eight-hour days or had been discharged. German cabinetmakers and woodcarvers were known to be well-organized union members and at times radical labor agitators.[83] Although nothing further is known about Kimbel and Cabus's

FURNITURE.

A. KIMBEL & J. CABUS, FURNITURE MANUFAC-
turers and Decorators, will remove from 928 and
930 Broadway, to their spacious warerooms, Nos. 7 and 9
East Twentieth street, opposite Lord & Taylor's.

FIG. 14 Advertisement. *New York Herald* (July 27, 1873): 9.

employees, it is likely that the striking workers were German.

Despite the upheaval of 1872, all evidence suggests Kimbel and Cabus were thriving in 1873. For example, the Dun reports for the year state that they were "doing a large business and thought to be making money," they could manufacture "a fine class of furniture and get good prices," and that they were estimated to be worth $100,000, more than double their worth just three years prior.[84] As further evidence of their development, between July and September 1873 Kimbel and Cabus advertised regularly in the *New York Daily Tribune*, the *New York Tribune*, the *New York Herald*, and the *New York Times* about moving to new "spacious Ware-rooms, 7 and 9 East Twentieth-st., opposite Lord and Taylor" (fig. 14).[85] Founded in 1826 as a downtown dry goods shop on Catherine Street, the renowned retailer Lord and Taylor moved successively uptown following the northward expansion of the fashionable shopping district. In 1872 they relocated to the first iron-frame building in New York City, at Broadway and 20th Street. By pointing out their proximity to Lord and Taylor, Kimbel and Cabus aligned themselves with progress, prosperity, and fashion.

The first Kimbel and Cabus commission for which documentation survives, the Fifth Avenue Presbyterian Church, is also one of their most significant public efforts. Built between 1873 and 1875 under the direction of the charismatic Reverend John Hall, other church leaders, and innovative German architect Carl Pfeiffer, Kimbel and Cabus designed and created the interior woodwork for the newly constructed building at Fifth Avenue and 55th Street in Manhattan. Formed in lower Manhattan in 1808 as the Presbyterian Church in Cedar Street, the congregation had gradually moved further uptown in 1836 and 1852, amending their name in accordance with each new address. Church membership burgeoned after Reverend Hall's installation in 1867, for his "powerful preaching and wise churchmanship . . . made the Fifth Avenue Presbyterian Church one of the great religious powers in the city."[86] Plans were initiated and land purchased to build a new Gothic revival style edifice of New Jersey red sandstone at the relatively undeveloped intersection of Fifth Avenue and 55th Street (fig. 15).[87] The cornerstone was laid on June 9, 1873, and within two years a two-towered church with the tallest steeple in the city was complete.[88] Reporting on the dedication on May 9, 1875, the *Brooklyn Union* announces that "the new structure . . . surpasses in the completeness and elegance of its arrangements any other in the city devoted to ecclesiastical purposes. Its

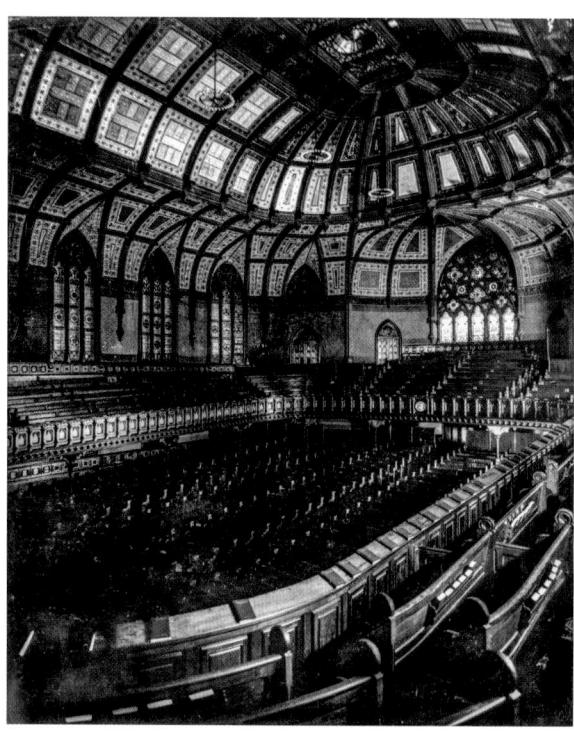

FIG. 16 Interior, Fifth Avenue Presbyterian Church, Fifth Avenue and 55th Street, New York City, ca. 1875. Courtesy of Fifth Avenue Presbyterian Church, Fifth Avenue and 55th Street, New York City

FIG. 15 Fifth Avenue Presbyterian Church, Fifth Avenue and 55th Street, New York City, undated (ca. 1882–1919). Glass negative, 5 × 7 in. (12.7 × 17.78 cm). New York Historical Society, Robert L. Bracklow photograph collection, 1882–1918 (bulk 1896–1905), nyhs_pr-008_66000_2103

cost completed will not be far from $1,000,000."[89] Although Pfeiffer's church exterior evoked the grandeur of Gothic cathedrals, his interior incorporated thoroughly modern engineering features with respect to acoustics and comfort (fig. 16). The main space, designed to seat two thousand worshippers, has no sharp curves or angles or obstructing columns. Both the inclined ground floor and gallery feature pews arranged in concentric curves that permit a direct view of the minister. The pulpit is centrally located below the choir gallery and a monumental organ. Pfeiffer's design considered light sources, both sunlight and gas, and incorporated pews equipped with hearing tubes connected to the pulpit for hearing-impaired congregants. Most ingenious was Pfeiffer's heating and cooling system, which consisted of wooden louvers that opened under the pews and permitted warm air

FIG. 17 Armchair, ca. 1875. Wood, 38 ¾ × 23 ¾ × 24 in. (98.4 × 60.3 × 61 cm). Courtesy of Fifth Avenue Presbyterian Church, Fifth Avenue and 55th Street, New York City

to rise from basement steam pipes in winter or for ice-cooled air to be blown upwards by fans during summer. Although original carpenter, mason, and stone-cutter specifications are found in the church archives, records of Kimbel and Cabus's work are not known to be extant. The church's building committee minutes from 1873 to 1875 do document the evolution of Kimbel and Cabus's bids, however, as well as the decision to hire them in November 1873.[90] The minutes record Kimbel and Cabus's first bid to create 116 pews for the main floor, sixty-three pews for the gallery, the gallery front, and pulpit at a total cost of $29,187.[91] Due to a modification in pew design, the proposed price rose to $30,287 by July 1873.[92] The December 1875 minutes enumerate Kimbel and Cabus's charges as including the original contract fee plus additional expenses for the organ case, carving numbers into the pews, raising the gallery,

carving panels at the back of the pulpit, and other items, altogether totaling $37,720.50. Among the additional expenses, a listing for "Furniture for ministers & trustees room," indicates that some of the armchairs and a table in the chancel were designed by Kimbel and Cabus (fig. 17). One of the armchairs appears to be an adaptation of German architect Edwin Oppler's chair designs for Marienburg Castle, a form which Kimbel and Cabus would continue to utilize (see pp. 112–13, 120–21).[93] According to the *American Architect and Building News*, Kimbel and Cabus designed and made "all the pews, gallery-fronts, organ-case, and . . . interior joiner's work . . . of the best ash wood and polished."[94] Throughout the church, architectural elements display a striking combination of stylized low relief carving including quatrefoils, linen fold panels, and bands of geometric designs combined with more sculptural, naturalistic vegetal carving that animate the interior and became favored motifs in many of Kimbel and Cabus's progressive furniture designs.

The way they engaged with this commission signals Kimbel and Cabus's embrace of the Modern Gothic style, which progressive British architects and designers such as Pugin had proselytized as the antidote to industrialization, urging a return to the medieval guild system, handcraft, and restrained decoration, beginning in the 1830s. A second wave of interest had followed during the 1860s, when British reformers Talbert and Eastlake promoted Modern Gothic design reform ideals through seminal publications.[95] Kimbel and Cabus developed a distinctive take on Modern Gothic sensibilities, creating bold forms that frequently synthesize Talbert's and Eastlake's recommendations with Continental design sources, especially the work of Oppler.[96] Carved roaring lion masks and owls, angled legs, a dynamic interplay of carved abstract botanical and geometric ornament, and richly varied surface

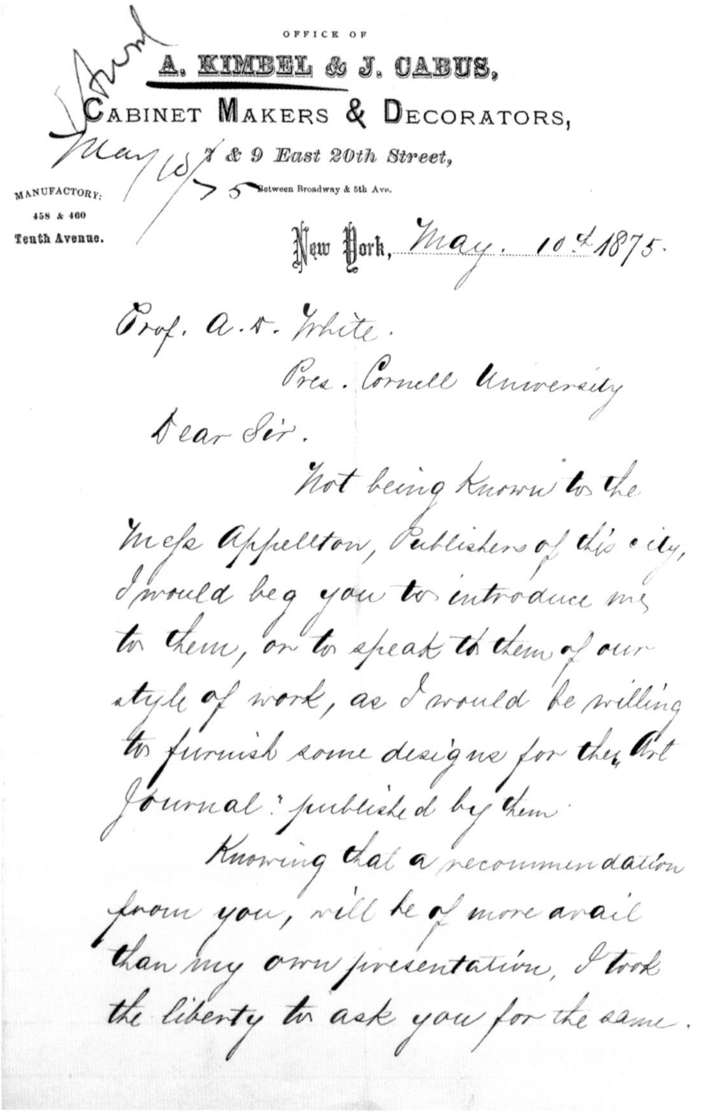

OFFICE OF
A. KIMBEL & J. CABUS,
CABINET MAKERS & DECORATORS,
7 & 9 East 20th Street,
MANUFACTORY:
458 & 460
Tenth Avenue.
Between Broadway & 5th Ave.

New York, May. 10th 1875.

Prof. A. D. White.
    Pres. Cornell University
Dear Sir.

        Not being known to the Mess Appleton, Publishers of this city, I would beg you to introduce me to them, or to speak to them of our style of work, as I would be willing to furnish some designs for their Art Journal, published by them.

        Knowing that a recommendation from you, will be of more avail than my own presentation, I took the liberty to ask you for the same.

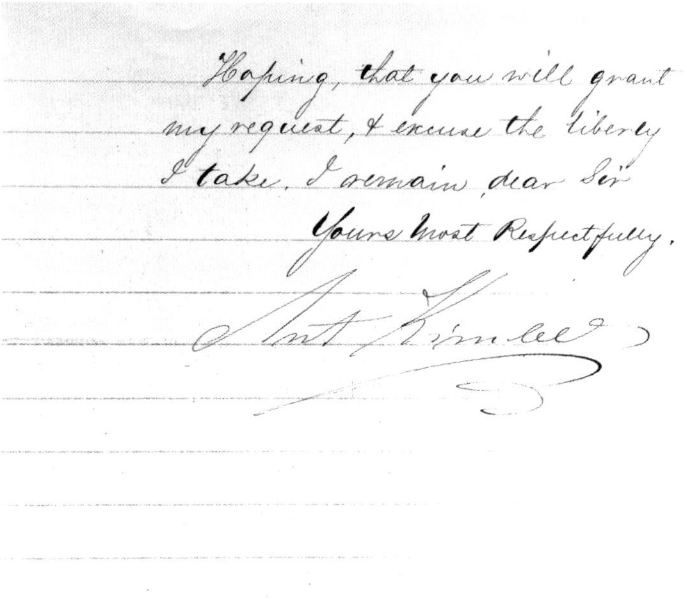

Hoping, that you will grant my request, & excuse the liberty I take. I remain, dear Sir

Yours most Respectfully.

FIG. 18 Letter from Anton Kimbel, New York, NY, to Andrew Dickson White, Ithaca, New York, May 10, 1875. Andrew Dickson White (American, 1832–1918) papers. Volume/Box: 19, Folder 4. Division of Rare and Manuscript Collections, Cornell University Library

embellishment animate their rectilinear case pieces and seating furniture. With assertive and energetic designs, the firm appealed to equally daring, forward-looking customers. An article entitled "Gothic Revival," published in the April 24, 1875 issue of the *Cabinet Maker*, approvingly traces the evolution of the progressive style from its early manifestations at the beginning of the century, when furniture designs incorporated literal architectural elements, through to Reform or Modern Gothic, in which furniture construction embraced medieval practices. Lamenting that American craftspeople are ill-equipped to produce original art furniture because they lack formal art and design training, the author has solicited a "letter from one of the most celebrated of New York furniture designers, whose work is held in the highest esteem by the virtuoso and manufacturer" in support of developing national industrial design schools. The celebrated designer was Anton Kimbel, and his letter, which is printed in the article in full, gives voice to his thoughts and progressive vision:

> Dear Sir – I never was called upon to give any opinion in regard to furniture or furniture decoration, etc. except in private and hardly think I am able to do justice to your demand by giving you my own opinion on the subject. Much has been said and written about household taste, particularly in England, and the books published have exercised a great influence on this continent. Eastlake, Collins, Dresser, and others have published works to that effect and the first named gentleman is looked to as authority on such matter. Whatever their virtue may be, they have at least an impulse for the better, and it may be hoped that others will follow. What machinery could accomplish has been done to the fullest extent in this country, but all such furniture manufactured through these means has a cheap and vulgar look, which no damask or satin covering can take off. We may try to be original but the taste which is only acquired by long study and experience, is wasting. The opportunities offered to the people in Europe through institutions like the Polytechnic schools are wanting here and as long as we are not in possession of such disseminators of art knowledge, so long will we be dependent on European artists and manufacturers. Professor Andrew D. White, President of Cornell University in an address delivered before the New York State Agricultural Society has explained the advantage that would be derived through such institutions and I advise you to read the same address, published by D. Appleton & Co. and to give it a wider circulation.
>
> I remain, Sir, Yours Respectfully, A. K.[97]

FIG. 19 "Reception Room" from the "interiors" envelope in the A. D. White house building folder 2. Division of Rare and Manuscript Collections, Cornell University Library

A renowned professor, diplomat, co-founder of Cornell University, and its president for nearly twenty years, Andrew D. White eloquently advocated for higher education in all subjects, but was especially passionate about advancing studies in science, engineering, and industrial design. His address on "Scientific and Industrial Education in the United States," delivered before the New York State Agricultural Society, was published by D. Appleton and Company in *Popular Science Monthly* in 1874.[98] White's words clearly resonated with Kimbel, who wrote to him on May 10, 1875 respectfully requesting assistance with an introduction to Appleton's, "to speak to them of our style of work, as I would be willing to furnish some designs for the Art Journal published by them (fig. 18)."[99] Begun in England in 1849 and published in the United States from 1875, *Art Journal* was a significant publication of the era for affluent and cultured readers. Kimbel's pursuit of White's endorsement reveals an ambition to promote his firm's work. A photograph of White's reception room in his home in Ithaca, New York offers additional evidence of a connection with Kimbel and Cabus (fig. 19). Five Kimbel and Cabus chairs and a table (see pp. 107, 113) are featured prominently in the center of the richly decorated room.

That same year, articles published in prominent periodicals acknowledged Kimbel and Cabus in conjunction with other renowned New York City cabinetmakers and decorators as being in the vanguard of progressive design.[100] An evocative *Harper's Bazar* feature on "New York Fashions" states that "A fancy for medieval furniture is the caprice of the day with people of wealth, and to gratify this taste there are collections of artistic furniture gathered in the ware-rooms that make a visit there seem like going through some interesting museums of art."[101] The article elucidates furniture dealers' diverse interpretations of the Modern Gothic style. Descriptions of a walnut revolving bookstand "illuminated with color traceries" and topped by a carved owl that "looks as wise as Minerva herself" and "quaint" desks and cabinets with "large rings, keys, and ornaments of nickel or of gilt, or oxidized silver" correspond to Kimbel and Cabus's work (fig. 20 and see p. 177). The article concludes by thanking "Messrs. KIMBEL & CABUS" as well as Herter Brothers and L. Marcotte and Company for information received. Interestingly, although credit reports for the year indicate that Kimbel and Cabus continued to be viewed as "respectable, responsible, and prompt in meeting engagements," they were "not tho[ugh]t to have made much if any money in the past year" and were worth between $75,000 to $100,000, slightly less than two years prior.[102] By late November, embracing a common practice to raise capital and invest in new merchandise, they auctioned off their old stock.[103] The *American Cabinet Maker* describes "a handsome company" of "over 100 ladies and gentlemen" bidding on a four-piece "rich parlor suit, black gilt frame

FIG. 20 Revolving bookstand, from Album 1 [Furniture designed and sold by the New York firm of Kimbel and Cabus], ca. 1875

covered with *Maroon Satin*," which sold for $215, and an eight piece "rich black and gilt parlor suit . . . covered with tan colored silk coteline," which sold for $90.[104] Reports of a "rich black and gilt five-foot cabinet, very rich, brass ornaments; bronze center" that was sold for $235 and a "black and gilt venetian pedestal, Egyptian head" that was sold for $40 suggest a date of 1870–74 for an extant Kimbel and Cabus cabinet and pedestal (see pp. 101, 103).[105] The preponderance of "rich black and gilt" furniture being auctioned off—this description suggests Neo-Grec, a late-phase French classical revival style characterized by bold renditions of classical ornament such as acanthus and anthemion—indicates that Kimbel and Cabus were clearing house to make way for a new style. As the firm diversified their offerings, they established themselves as an influential force in the world of New York City cabinetmakers and decorators.

FIG. 21 Cabinet, from Album 1 [Furniture designed and sold by the New York firm of Kimbel and Cabus], ca. 1875

AN ALBUM OF PHOTOGRAPHS: EVIDENCE OF CREATIVITY AND VERSATILITY

A remarkable album of photographs in the collection of the Cooper-Hewitt, Smithsonian Design Museum Library in New York functions as the touchstone for identifying Kimbel and Cabus's work. In an era when businesses rarely retained records, the album offers valuable, even thrilling insights into Kimbel and Cabus's designs and forms.[106] One of two albums given to the museum in 1948 by Anton Kimbel's granddaughter Lillian Kimbel, it documents a broad range of Kimbel and Cabus's eclectic furniture from the period around 1875. Photographs of later work made by A. Kimbel and Sons after the partnership ended in 1882 comprise the second album. By the 1870s, photographic catalogues and salesman's portfolios were increasingly recognized as valuable marketing tools to share work with potential customers, and Kimbel and Cabus were not alone in their use of the medium. Kilian Brothers of New York City, Berkey and Gay of Grand Rapids, Michigan, and the Gorham Manufacturing Company of Providence, Rhode Island, for example, all used photography to represent their wares.[107] Reporting on the benefits of photographs for the traveling salesman, the *American Cabinet Maker* states that "nothing equals in satisfaction, to both buyer and seller, a photograph. There is no opportunity for artistic embellishment . . . there is certainty that things represented are what they seem."[108] The same article profiles R. G. Barcalow of 76 Bowery, "a photographer well known to the furniture trade of this city, and even country" who is described as "one of the oldest photographers in New York" and "the pioneer in furniture photography." According to the article, "The trucks of nearly all the prominent concerns of New York may be seen almost daily standing before the photographer's door laden with handsome sideboards, bedsteads, fancy chairs, parlor sets and the thousand and one different articles which represent the ingenuity of the modern furniture manufacturer."[109]

The album of Kimbel and Cabus's work consists of an assemblage of 109 prints mounted on 8 x 10-inch pages. The largest number of photographs depict case pieces such as bookcases, cabinets, desks, and sideboards, followed by seating furniture, hanging cabinets, easels and pedestals, tables, revolving bookcases and music stands, fire screens, and "quarrels," or large floor cushions (fig. 21).[110] Each object is identified with handwritten ink numerals, most likely production numbers, ranging from four to 468. Delicate graphite numerical notations in the margins next to and below the photographs indicate dimensions; occasionally they are encoded.[111] Additional graphite notations in the margins or on the photographs suggest prices that sometimes vary according to finish or treatment. For example, notations above a drop-front desk, object number 300, indicate that $65 and $75 versions are available (fig. 22, price notations not visible). Some photographs are stamped with the firm's name and address in blue ink, and one is signed "A Kimbel & J Cabus" in ink script, indicating the firm's proprietary interest in the images (figs. 21 and 22).

Organized in groups of related forms, such as cabinets, desks, seating furniture, tables, revolving bookstands, and other small forms, rather than the order in which they are numbered, the photographs display varied backgrounds and floor coverings that suggest they were taken at different times. When the photographs are examined in numerical order, however, a chronology can be discerned. Objects with numbers below 180 include "rich black and gilt" forms with Neo-Grec elements that correspond to the earlier pieces that Kimbel and Cabus auctioned off in 1875 as well as to a revolving bookstand with owl finial mentioned in the press that same year (see fig. 20; pp. 101,

FIG. 22 Desk and screen, from Album 1 [Furniture designed and sold by the New York firm of Kimbel and Cabus], ca. 1875

103). In contrast, objects numbered 207 to 468 encompass myriad eclectic Modern Gothic forms carved with stylized foliate and geometric ornament in low relief, or with owls or lion masks, often inset with turned spindles, ceramic tiles, or printed-paper panels and applied with bold metal strap hinges and hardware. Large and small-scale furniture forms display an infinite variety of interchangeable ornamental elements and demonstrate Kimbel and Cabus's striking creativity and adaptability in presenting customers with a range of aesthetic choices. Versions of pedestal number 330, cabinet number 363, and chair number 374 were featured in Kimbel and Cabus's display at the 1876 Centennial Exhibition in Philadelphia (fig. 23). A smaller percentage of objects in the album feature Asian and Islamic inspired forms—including rectilinear cabinets of Chinese derivation and furniture with decorative elements such as "Moorish" arches or inset tiles depicting pseudo-Kufic script—that were increasingly in vogue with proponents of the Aesthetic Movement and their patrons (figs. 24, 38, and 64).

In some photographs, studio props such as ewers, vases, a tazza, a sculpture, books, even long-stemmed smoking pipes and a hookah, indicate display options, scale, and utility for consumers so that they could imagine creating their own "Moorish" smoking room, for example. These sales tools evince a distinct informality. Kimbel and Cabus's trade card, on the other hand, also dated circa 1875, documents the firm's more formal and official public image (fig. 1). The card, for which an original design drawing survives (fig. 25), depicts an architectonic, richly carved Modern Gothic cabinet inspired by a design in Talbert's *Gothic Forms* (fig. 26).[112] Featuring pointed arches, columns and capitals, crockets and crenellations, carved bird finials, and a central compartment tantalizingly hidden behind textile hangings, Kimbel and Cabus's cabinet is an extroverted interpretation of Talbert's suggestion. Depicted in the trade card against a wainscoted wall, papered with a grid

FIG. 23 Kimbel and Cabus display at the Centennial Exhibition of 1876, Philadelphia. Photographic print, 3.9 × 6.3 in. (10 × 16 cm). Hagley Museum and Library, Centennial Exhibition Photograph and Ephemera Collection, Wilmington, Delaware

FIG. 24 Cabinet, ca. 1875. Ebonized cherry, gilding, earthenware, glass, metal, 79 ½ × 48 ½ × 14 ½ in. (201.9 × 123.2 × 36.8 cm). Collection of Michael and Marjorie Loeb

THE CENTENNIAL EXHIBITION: REALIZATION OF AN ARTISTIC VISION

The nineteenth-century world's fairs brought together an exhilarating range of artists and manufacturers from around the world to promote international trade, commerce, and the exchange of ideas. They provided Western audiences with their first introduction to non-Western arts and cultures, as well as to the latest styles from the UK and Continental Europe.[114] The Centennial Exhibition of 1876 was the first official world's fair in the United States. Conceived to mark the 100th anniversary of the signing of the Declaration of Independence and officially entitled the International Exhibition of Arts, Manufactures and Products of the Soil and Mine, the event was intended to promote a century of progress in the United States—a narrative benefitting the project of white settler colonialism. North American industries strove to present sophisticated wares on this international stage. During the exhibition's six-month duration, from May through November, more than 9 million Americans were introduced to and transfixed by arts, culture, and manufactures spanning the globe. For U.S. artists, designers, and manufacturers, as well as the general public, the first-hand exposure to new cultures and sources of inspiration, particularly the non-Western cultures of Japan, China, and North Africa, as well as British design reform ideology, had a profound impact on the nation's subsequent artistic developments.

Although the majority of the 177 U.S. furniture exhibitors in the main building were from New York and Philadelphia, over half of the states were represented, with a strong showing from the emerging Midwestern furniture-making centers of Michigan and Ohio.[115] Shortly before the Centennial Exhibition opened, U.S. critic Harriet Prescott

pattern of abstract botanical motifs, the cabinet is filled with *au courant* art objects that signify Kimbel and Cabus's alignment with the aesthetic sensibilities of the moment. For example, the inverted conical sugar bowl on the left side of the cabinet is recognizable as the work of British design reformer Christopher Dresser. Dresser's suggestions for progressive designs and motifs, along with those of Talbert and Eastlake, exerted significant influence on Kimbel and Cabus's interpretation of Modern Gothic.[113] Together, the photograph album and trade card offer insight into Kimbel and Cabus's ambitious business practices and a reputation well-established before their critically acclaimed display at the Centennial Exhibition.

Spofford wrote appreciatively about the "Gothic Style" in an article about household furniture for *Harper's Bazar*. Of the seven designs illustrated in her article, she thanked "Messrs. A. Kimbel & J. Cabus" for "the beautiful Gothic library, cabinet, window, and chair," and stated that they "make Gothic furniture a specialty."[116] Kimbel and Cabus's Centennial display, depicted in a newly identified photograph, received much attention from the press (fig. 23).[117] In June, the *American Cabinet Maker* stated that "the adaptation of Gothic to furniture has been

attained in an eminent degree by the American house of Kimbel & Cabus, and it is safe to state that in all the exhibition there is nothing of its kind which excels the exhibit of this concern."[118] Two weeks later, reporting on exhibitors, they published a description of the firm's display:

Kimbel & Cabus, New York, have an exhibit somewhat after the English style, and it receives very favorable criticism from members of the trade, who cannot be said to be poor judges. A heavy cornice, three feet

FIG. 25 Cabinet. Drawing, sheet: 11 × 14 in. (35.7 × 27.8 cm). Inv. Hdz 12968, Estate of Wilhelm Kimbel, Kunstbibliothek, Staatliche Museen, Berlin, Stiftung Preussischer Kulturbesitz

FIG. 26 Bruce James Talbert, *Gothic Forms Applied to Furniture, Metalwork, and Decoration for Domestic Purposes* (Boston: J. R. Osgood, 1873), plate 7 (detail)

FIG. 27 "Centennial Exhibition 1876 A. Kimbel & J. Cabus 7 & 9 East 20. Str. New York," *American Architect and Building News* (July 22, 1876)

wide, extends around two sides of their space: underneath this in the center is a large oil painting fresco, representing the arts and sciences, with rich frescoing in fine keeping on either side. Below the center is an unique door cornice, with heavy damask maroon curtains. The walls are draped with maroon hangings; between the hangings and the heavy panelled wainscoting completing the whole, is a space of about two feet which is frescoed in fancy designs. On the left is a mantle extending from the floor to the ceiling of ebonized cherry: the carving is exceedingly rich and the design

antique throughout; it also contains a tiled fireplace. A cabinet with heavy gilt hinges and hand painted panels, is a fine piece of workmanship. A writing desk, center table and pedestal of antique design to match the cabinet, and also two chairs and sofa in garnet satin, will bear comparison with any in the English section. The floor is maple, inlaid with cherry, rosewood and oak, of a showy pattern with star in the center and serpentine border. The exhibit as a whole takes a place in the front rank of American furniture and is a credit to the firm.[119]

Displaying a fully decorated and furnished interior was not a new idea. Anton was familiar with this concept from having worked with his uncle Anton Bembé. Furthermore, beginning with the 1873 Vienna world's fair, German cabinetmakers and upholsterers had increasingly been staging their work in complete room settings.[120] Several firms at the Centennial Exhibition, including London's Howard and Sons and New York's Pottier and Stymus and Herts and Company, also took this approach. Kimbel and Cabus were not alone in displaying Modern Gothic furniture. Mitchell and Rammelsburg of Cincinnati, Daniel Pabst of Philadelphia, and others exhibited furniture in this style.[121] Among their peers, however, Kimbel and Cabus particularly excelled in craftsmanship and presentation. Their display was prominently illustrated in the *American Architect and Building News* in July of the centennial year (fig. 27).[122] When compared with a photograph of their display, the illustration provides fascinating insight into the compelling vision Kimbel and Cabus sought to project. The photograph shows the furniture artfully arranged in an alcove which has been cordoned off, while the illustration depicts a less densely furnished drawing room. The papered walls are hung with

THE EXHIBIT OF MESSRS. KIMBEL & CABUS.

THE CENTENNIAL—ART FURNITURE.—Photographed by the Centennial Photographic Company.—[See Page 970.]

FIG. 28 "The Exhibit of Messrs. Kimbel & Cabus. The Centennial – Art Furniture – Photographed by the Centennial Photographic Company. – [See Page 970.]," *Harper's Weekly* (December 2, 1876)

portraits, artistic *objets* fill the cabinets, a figure of the Roman goddess Diana and her hound stands atop a pedestal, and a welcoming fire burns in the hearth.

Evocative newspaper articles illuminate visitor responses to the exhibition displays. A letter reprinted in the *Maine Farmer* asserts that many New York firms, including Kimbel and Cabus, "have set up glittering and tasteful booths, which are usually surrounded by eager crowds. To-day the ladies visited these establishments in thousands, then straightway went to make comparisons in the English, French and Italian departments."[123] A reporter praised Kimbel and Cabus for having excellent taste, then offered a criticism: they "need light

to take away the funereal look."[124] A British critic in the *Furniture Gazette* described their display "as an example of the work done by our cousins over the water," stating that "it does not differ very considerably from what is turned out at our own best factories. The furniture is in the prevailing American taste, extreme Gothic, a style which is not so prevalent [in the UK] as it is in the United States."[125] This description underscores the scale and exuberance of the American expression of the Modern Gothic style, characteristic of American excess. The firm's display earned awards in two categories: in Group VII for "originality of design and execution" for ceiling painting and "superior workmanship in cabinetmaking and upholstery,"

FIG. 29 Room with fireplace and writing desk. Drawing, sheet: 11 × 14 in. (35.7 × 27.8 cm). Inv. Hdz 12970, Estate of Wilhelm Kimbel, Kunstbibliothek, Staatliche Museen, Berlin, Stiftung Preussischer Kulturbesitz

FIG. 30 Writing desk. Drawing, sheet: 11 × 14 in. (35.7 × 27.8 cm). Inv. Hdz 12972, Estate of Wilhelm Kimbel, Kunstbibliothek, Staatliche Museen, Berlin, Stiftung Preussischer Kulturbesitz

and in Group XXVII for a chimney-piece displaying "symmetry and grace of design and admirable workmanship."[126] This led to the reprinting of versions of the *American Architect and Building News* drawing-room illustration in at least six different publications, ensuring they reached a broad range of trade and retail clients.[127] Although Kimbel and Cabus were a thriving, prominent firm prior to the Centennial Exhibition, their success at the fair generated national and international publicity that marked the apogee of their twenty-year partnership. In the years following, they capitalized on the accolades and secured multiple commissions for private and public interiors, becoming the preeminent U.S. purveyor of Modern Gothic.

FIG. 31 Interior design of a room with fireplace. Drawing, sheet: 11 × 14 in. (35.7 × 27.8 cm). Inv. Hdz 12969, Estate of Wilhelm Kimbel, Kunstbibliothek, Staatliche Museen, Berlin, Stiftung Preussischer Kulturbesitz

A FLOURISHING CABINETMAKING FIRM AND ITS INVENTIVE PRODUCTION

As reflected in the press, interest in the Modern Gothic style continued to build momentum after the Centennial. For example, *Harper's New Monthly Magazine* published Spofford's lengthy article on "Medieval Furniture" in November 1876.[128] Billed as "rich in quaint and entertaining facts" with illustrations that are "dazzling, embracing Gothic furniture in all its forms, from the ancient to the modern," the article includes designs by Talbert, British furniture-maker Collinson and Lock, and Kimbel and Cabus. Of the four Kimbel and Cabus designs illustrated, the original drawings for three of them, depicting a cabinet and two room interiors, are extant (figs. 29, 30, and 31). The fourth illustration depicts the firm's iconic Centennial Exhibition display. In December *Harper's Weekly* printed another illustration of that display based on the aforementioned photograph (fig. 23), with the addition of exhibition visitors (fig. 28). As reiterated the same month in the *American Cabinet Maker*, Kimbel and Cabus were synonymous with Modern Gothic: "The artistic, the durable and the commercial cabinet-maker have recognized the general demand for a species of Gothic ornament in the decoration of furniture and, under many names such as the Modern Gothic, Medieval, Early English, Eastlake and Kimbel, outlines are to be discerned of the Gothic style."[129]

The splendid interior of Kimbel and Cabus's shop at 7 and 9 East 20th Street, on the north side between 5th Avenue and Broadway, was featured in the *American Architect and Building News* the following February (see pp. 98–99).[130] The image shows a rectangular showroom featuring a staircase with figural newels and turned balusters illuminated by south-facing windows. Above plain walls, a frieze depicting a procession of musical putti

FIG. 32 "The Manufacture of Parlor Furniture.—
Factory of M. & H. Schrenkeisen, New York City,"
Scientific American 43, no. 15 (October 9, 1880):
223. Pennsylvania State University

This illustration, together with the photograph album, design drawings, trade card, and Centennial Exhibition images, provides invaluable documentation of the firm's sensibilities and production.

There are no extant images of Kimbel and Cabus's factory at 458 and 460 Tenth Avenue on the east side of the street between West 35th and 36th Streets. A city street map of 1879 locates them next-door to a silk factory, and the nearby presence of other factories, including a piano manufactory and a billiard-table factory, indicates a manufacturing district (fig. 12). The well-known profile of Messrs. M. and H. Schrenkeisen's New York City cabinetmaking firm, published in *Scientific American* in 1880, is a helpful resource for visualizing Kimbel and Cabus's furniture-making practices (fig. 32).[131] Although Schrenkeisen was a much larger business housed in two six-story buildings with machinery and a 100-horse power engine, Kimbel and Cabus utilized many of the same procedures, such as taking "the log as it comes from the woods, and do[ing] every part of the work necessary to make therefrom the completed furniture as it appears in the parlor." The article describes and illustrates the numerous steam-powered saws, planes, carving, turning, and joining machines that facilitated the production of multiple furniture forms. Like Cox and Son and other peers in Britain, Kimbel and Cabus employed modern mechanized production techniques to create their Modern Gothic furniture. Despite these faster production methods, handcraft still played a central role; Schrenkeisen employed thirty to forty expert woodcarvers to execute the firm's original artistic designs and adapt them to everchanging tastes. The upholstery and finishing work, which was finalized just before shipment, also required handwork and great care. Schrenkeisen also had an in-house photograph studio for documenting newly completed furniture sets, providing agents and

supports a cavetto cornice and ceiling decorated with Dresser-inspired geometric and attenuated botanical motifs. The Modern Gothic pier mirror and panoply of furniture forms, ranging from large and small case pieces to desks, chairs, hanging wall cabinets, and a humidor, demonstrate the firm's characteristic flat carved botanical and geometric motifs, turned spindles, and metal hardware. By filling the furniture shelves and surfaces with decorative objects, sculptures, and a globe, Kimbel and Cabus evoked a domestic setting meant to appeal directly to their style-conscious consumers.

FIG. 33 Sideboard, ca. 1875. Walnut, metal, 80 × 69 ¾ × 25 in. (203.2 × 177.2 × 63.5 cm). Collection of Lori Zabar

dealers with a reference when placing orders. All surviving evidence suggests Kimbel and Cabus employed similar marketing and documenting practices. The Products of Industry census for 1880 provides the only documentation of Kimbel and Cabus's workforce at this time. The firm had a capitalization of $150,000, one boiler, and one 40-horse-power steam engine. During the course of a year, the greatest number of employees was 104 people, with a regular work force of twenty-six male employees over the age of sixteen, four female employees over the age of fifteen, and eight youths or children. Employees worked ten hours a day, twelve months a year, with skilled mechanics earning $2.50 per day and ordinary laborers earning $1.00 per day. The firm owned materials valued at $30,000 and products valued at $170,000. Kimbel and Cabus were a much smaller operation than competitor Pottier and Stymus. For example, Pottier and Stymus had $300,000 capitalization, three boilers, and one 100-horse-power steam engine.

During the course of a year, the greatest number of employees was four hundred people, with a regular work force of three hundred male employees over the age of sixteen, thirty female employees over the age of fifteen, and twenty youths or children. Employees worked ten hours a day, twelve months a year, with skilled mechanics earning $3.00 per day and ordinary laborers $2.00. The firm owed materials valued at $143,000 and products valued at $432,000.[132] Kimbel and Cabus's capital exceeded those of furniture-makers George A. Schastey ($50,000)

FIG. 34 Desk, ca. 1875. Oak, nickel-plated brass, iron, lead-glazed earthenware, 59 × 48 × 15 in. (149.9 × 121.9 × 38.1 cm). Philadelphia Museum of Art, Gift of Frederick M. LaValley and John N. Whitenight in honor of James H. and Mayumi LaValley, 2016, 2016-203-1

FIG. 35 Bruce James Talbert, *Gothic Forms Applied to Furniture, Metalwork, and Decoration for Domestic Purposes* (Boston: J. R. Osgood, 1873), plate 15

FIG. 36 Parlor cabinet, ca. 1875. Ebonized cherry, paint, paper, gilding, brass, velvet, mirrored and transparent glass, 78 × 52 ¹⁵⁄₁₆ × 16 ⅛ in. (198.1 × 134.5 × 41 cm). Yale University Art Gallery. Gift of Thomas D. Cabot, Jr., and Charles Seymour, B.A. 1908, and bequest of Olive Louise Dann, by exchange

and Herts Brothers ($75,000) who reported slightly higher values for materials and products and offered comparable wages to their similarly sized workforce.[133] The fact that Schastey and Herts each maintained a steady headcount of one hundred to 125 people while Kimbel and Cabus's headcount fluctuated between thirty-eight to 104 people suggests that the latter operated conservatively and scaled up their workforce as needed when completing larger commissions.

A close study of extant objects and visual evidence drawn from primary sources elucidates the defining characteristics of Kimbel and Cabus's work at the peak of their success. Kimbel and Cabus's furniture designs are idiosyncratic and unmistakable among firms working in the Modern Gothic style. They produced a wide array of strikingly assertive forms charged with energy and decorated with rich assemblages of ornament in a range of media. They typically used ash, ebonized cherry, maple, oak, tulip poplar, and walnut—as well as rosewood in some early work—for furniture-making.[134] Case pieces predominate. They manufactured sideboards, cabinets, bookcases, desks, étagères, and smaller decorative pieces, among many other forms. These architectonic objects have the presence of small buildings, complete with gables, balustrades, capitals, columns, and doors. They are meant to be seen from the front, but decoration on the outer and inner sides and even at the base or feet ensured visual interest from multiple vantage points, which rewards the viewer either from afar or during more intimate use. Some pieces, such as a sideboard, one of the largest extant Kimbel and Cabus objects, combine a restrained rectilinear form with carved floral, vegetal, and geometric ornament (fig. 33).[135] These richly carved contrasting surfaces would have glimmered in gas or candlelight of the day. More often, objects display bold graphic qualities that conjure arresting abstractions, frequently combined with figural elements that fluidly bridge traditional Continental European vernacular with design reform ideals in entirely distinctive compositions (see pp. 8, 133–34, 183).[136] Alternately projecting and recessed components, such as carved lion's masks, owl finials, columns, galleries of turned baluster spindles, and arches, as well as cabinet doors, drawers, shelves, cubby and kneeholes, create a visually engaging interplay of light and shadow on these objects (fig. 34).

Crisply carved and incised surface decoration typically serves to complement the overall structure of each piece. Bands of geometric ornament—including zigzags, diaper patterns, projecting pyramidal forms, or series of alternating individual motifs such as diamonds and "x"s or stylized sprigs—emphasize the forms' horizontal and vertical lines. On the sides, straight lines frequently terminate in conventionalized flowerheads or tightly coiled foliage with projecting spear-form leaf tips, likely inspired by the designs of Talbert and Dresser (fig. 35). Cabinet doors display such Gothic motifs as carved quatrefoils (see p. 177), shields and armorial trophies, or stylized scrolling foliate sprays with the same spear-shaped leaves (see p. 119), among other motifs. Carved concentric geometric shapes, such as four squares within a square within a diamond, or stylized flower heads within roundels, punctuate forms at intervals. Although carved elements are usually unpainted, traces of polychromy on several objects offer evidence of color-enriched carved surfaces as well (see pp. 161, 165). The firm's ebonized examples predominantly feature bright gilded incised decoration, which creates a bold contrast with the glossy black surfaces.

Ceramic tiles, printed-paper panels, and, less frequently, hand-painted or marquetry panels and inset metalwork, further enrich many of the case pieces. A magnificent ebonized

FIG. 38 Cabinet, ca. 1875. Ebonized cherry, metal, 50 ¾ × 27 ¾ × 13 ¾ in. (128.9 × 70.5 × 34.9 cm). Collection of Ann Pyne

FIG. 37 Revolving bookstands, from Album 1 [Furniture designed and sold by the New York firm of Kimbel and Cabus], ca. 1875

cabinet, for example, features two hand-painted panels, one depicting Venus and the other the Virgin Mary as shepherdess in grisaille on a gold ground (fig. 36).[137] Identifiable tiles found on extant Kimbel and Cabus objects include examples made by the French firm of Creil et Montereau and the English firms of Maw and Company; Minton, Hollins, and Company; and W. B. Simpson and Sons.[138] Kimbel and Cabus would have been able to purchase such tiles from any number of suppliers within New York City. The *American Cabinet Maker* identified Thomas Aspinwall at 39 Murray Street, New York as a purveyor of Minton's 6 x 6 inch picture tiles for furniture, stating, "The reader of Shakespeare will delight in those new turquoise glaze tiles in Persian style, recalling as they do, familiar scenes from King Lear, Twelfth Night, Romeo and Juliet, etc.; besides from fables, fairy stories, scriptural, industrial and historical subjects which may be found in all colors adapted to any style of furniture."[139] Scottish designer John Moyr Smith, colleague of Talbert and Dresser, designed picture tiles for Minton, Hollins, and Company, and examples of his work can be seen on English furniture forms as well as on a Kimbel and Cabus desk (see pp. 172–75).[140]

Marquetry panels, integral to Kimbel and Cabus's earlier work in the Neo-Grec style (see p. 101), feature less prominently on their Modern Gothic forms. A diamond-shaped example is the crowning element in the peaked gable of an exceptional Kimbel and Cabus drop-front desk (see p. 183). Printed-paper panels that simulate marquetry or ceramic tiles bearing a multitude of motifs—ranging from stylized grotesques based on Dresser's designs to Moyr Smith's medieval-style allegorical figures, musicians, dancing and reclining figures, rampant lions, and abstract geometric and botanical motifs—are more frequent, being impactful, less expensive alternatives to marquetry (see pp. 145, 166). Although the maker of the printed-paper panels is not identified, one candidate would be Charles W. Spurr of Boston, Massachusetts, who won an award at the Centennial Exhibition for papered wood hangings or veneers. Spurr advertised wood and paper veneers suitable for hangings and marquetries for furniture, pianoforte, and organs, and promoted himself as the sole manufacturer of this technique, suggesting that he may have been a source for the panels.[141] Photographs in the Kimbel and Cabus album reveal that Japanese prints were also applied to furniture, although no extant examples are currently known (fig. 37). An étagère of Chinese inspiration and four related forms are most unusual in that they incorporate a reticulated cast metal panel of stylized botanical motifs into the central cabinet door (fig. 38). A small number of photographs depict accent pieces for the display of art, including an easel, pedestal, wall cabinets, and a cabinet inset with relief-molded metal panels depicting classical figures or motifs.

FIG. 39 Armchair and sofa, from Album 1 [Furniture designed and sold by the New York firm of Kimbel and Cabus], ca. 1875

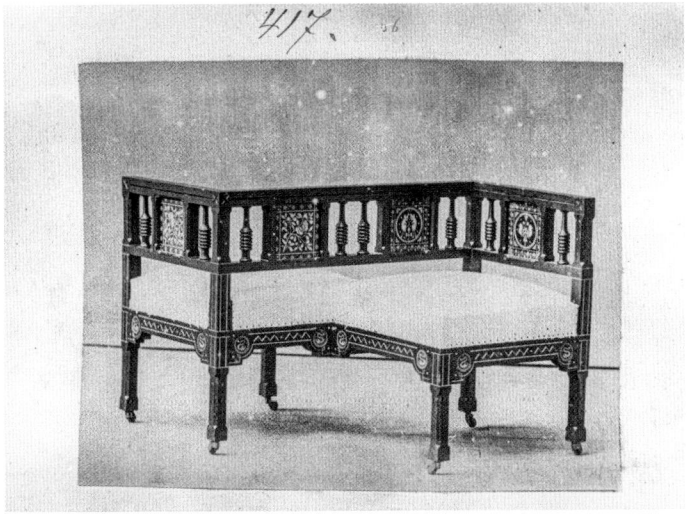

FIG. 40 *Vis-a-vis* sofa, from Album 1 [Furniture designed and sold by the New York firm of Kimbel and Cabus], ca. 1875

Bold brass and nickel-plated brass hardware also served as prominent decorative features of Kimbel and Cabus's furniture. The elongated strapwork hinges, large escutcheons,

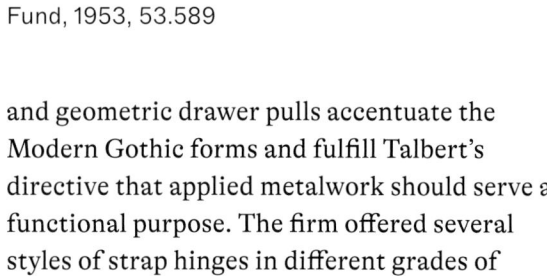

FIG. 41 Plate 26 [advertisement for Yandell], from *Kimball's Book of Designs: Furniture and Drapery*, 1876, The Metropolitan Museum of Art, The Elisha Whittelsey Collection, The Elisha Whittelsey Fund, 1953, 53.589

FIG. 42 Cabinet, from Album 1 [Furniture designed and sold by the New York firm of Kimbel and Cabus], ca. 1875

and geometric drawer pulls accentuate the Modern Gothic forms and fulfill Talbert's directive that applied metalwork should serve a functional purpose. The firm offered several styles of strap hinges in different grades of metal. Spear-shaped or rectangular hinges that included detailed cast ornamentation were likely most expensive (see p. 189); the more frequently used stamped scrolling or spiky strap hinges display a range of detail that also suggests varied

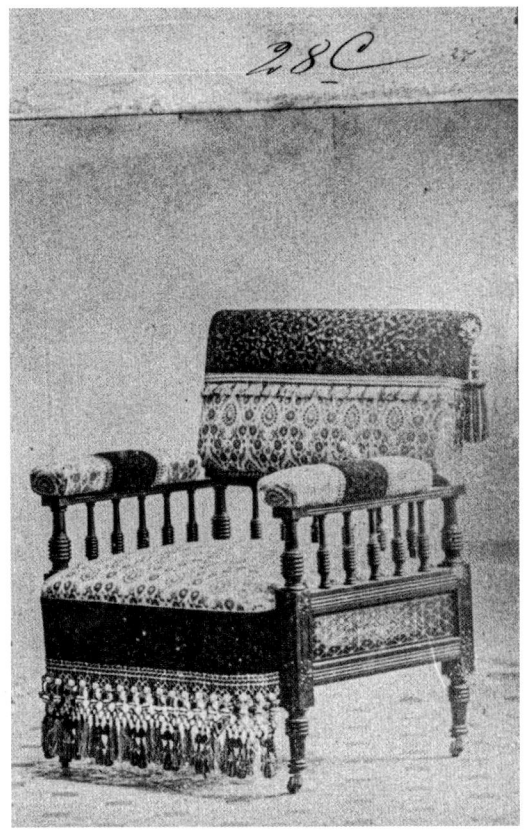

FIG. 43 Armchair, from Album 1 [Furniture designed and sold by the New York firm of Kimbel and Cabus], ca. 1875

price points (see p. 173). Because numerous, typically English, firms manufactured hardware, it is unlikely Kimbel and Cabus acquired all their hardware from the same maker.[142] Several pieces of their furniture bear locks with marks for Shannon of Philadelphia and C. A. Stock of New York.[143] There is evidence to suggest that Stock might have provided them with hardware, as surviving images of Stock's offerings illustrate hinges, drawer pulls, and escutcheons found on Kimbel and Cabus's casework (see p. 156).[144]

Album photographs and other surviving records suggest that seating furniture was Kimbel and Cabus's second largest category of production. Illustrations feature sets of sumptu-

ously upholstered sofas, armchairs, and side chairs, richly decorated with passementerie, as well as individual armchairs (fig. 39). Predominately rectilinear in form, many had characteristic incised and gilded decoration on the straight members and incorporated rows of turned spindles between the backrest and seat or between the arms and seat rail. Furniture forms intended to accommodate confidential conversation, such as the two-seated *vis-a-vis*, or face to face, depicted here with muslin covers, and the three-person *indiscret*, include Dresser-inspired printed-paper panels (fig. 40). Restrained wooden dining and side chairs, at times caned or upholstered in leather, also feature in their offerings. Many of the chairs, such as a side chair with original leather upholstery stamped with a gilded diaper pattern of stylized flowerheads, illustrate the firm's distinctive use of angled rear legs, likely an adaptation from the German designer Oppler (see p. 121).[145]

New evidence suggests that Kimbel and Cabus may have acquired leather and fabrics from Charles R. Yandell and Company, located nearby at 744 Broadway. At the Centennial Exhibition Yandell's firm received an award for leather lambrequins characterized by "excellence of work and elegance of design" and praise for exhibiting "some of the most exquisite patterns of stamped, gilded, and colored leather, that have ever been produced."[146] Yandell advertised their art leather manufactures, embossed velvets, satin, and plush in J. Wayland Kimball's illustrated furniture catalogue, *Kimball's Book of Designs: Furniture and Drapery*, published in 1876 (fig. 41).[147] Among their offerings depicted in plate 26, two patterns correspond to fabrics used on Kimbel and Cabus's furniture. Fabric in Yandell's pattern number nine lines the coved hood of a cabinet (fig. 42).[148] The upholstery pattern depicted on the Yandell side chair on the left (fig. 41) corresponds to velvet used on the top of a Kimbel and Cabus armchair (fig. 43).

FIG. 45 Hanging Cabinet, ca. 1875. Tulip poplar, paint, paper, 22 × 24 ⅜ × 6 ¾ in. (55.9 × 61.9 × 17.1 cm). Collection of Ann Pyne

FIG. 44 Hanging Cabinet, ca. 1875. Tulip poplar, paint, paper, 39 × 27 ¼ × 9 ⁹⁄₁₆ in. (99.1 × 69.2 × 24.3 cm). Collection of Ann Pyne

Substantial library tables informed by Oppler's medieval-inspired designs (see p. 139), as well as tiered side tables, represent a smaller proportion of Kimbel and Cabus's production. Fanciful hanging wall cabinets for the display of art objects (figs. 44 and 45), and quirky revolving bookstands (see pp. 143–45) and music stands (see p. 147) with eclectic silhouettes, printed-paper panels, and turned spindles are distinct standouts among their repertoire of smaller furniture. Easels and pedestals in a range of styles from Neo-Grec and Egyptian revival to Modern Gothic and Asian and Islamic-inspired were offered for displaying art in the home (figs. 46 and 47). Advertisements document that Kimbel and Cabus offered "rich, decorated and plain" furniture "within reach of

all," but there are few known examples of their "plain" work because high-end objects were more likely to be kept, and thus survive over time. A labeled bedroom set (see p. 163) and library table (fig. 48), both characterized by plain wood and a limited used of restrained incised decoration, do provide some insight into this aspect of the firm's production. Leveraging artistic flair, efficient manufacturing techniques, and strategic partnerships to their economic advantage, Kimbel and Cabus appealed to a broad range of customers with a limitless variety of stylish goods at diverse price points.

In the words of English cleric and author Charles Caleb Colton (1780–1832), "Imitation is the sincerest form of flattery." As much as Kimbel and Cabus drew inspiration from

Talbert, Eastlake, Dresser, Oppler, and others, they too spawned imitators. For example, an advertisement for the New York City firm of Killian Brothers in the *American Cabinet Maker* in March 1878 illustrates a staid version of the Kimbel and Cabus desk featured prominently in their Centennial Exhibition display (fig. 49 and see p. 119). Where the Kimbel and Cabus desk has oblique-angled front legs that imbue the form with energetic tension, the Killian version is frontal and static. Brooklyn furniture-makers Lang and Nau of 292 and 294 Fulton Street, Brooklyn, were even more flagrant in their imitation. They appropriated the renowned Kimbel and Cabus Centennial image, added a vase of sunflowers at the side, and used it as

FIG. 48 Library Table, ca. 1875. Ebonized cherry, metal, 30 ¾ × 34 × 22 in. (78.1 × 86.36 × 55.88 cm). Collection of the Hudson River Museum, INV.306

FIG. 47 Pedestal, ca. 1875. Ebonized, gilt and poly-chromed wood, 42 × 14 × 14 in. (106.7 × 35.5 × 35.5 cm). Detroit Institute of Arts, Gift of the Post Road Gallery, T2020.550.1

FIG. 46 Easel, ca. 1875. Walnut, metal, 88 ½ × 26 × 28 in. (224.8 × 66 × 71.1 cm). Collection of Federico Santi and John Gacher, Newport, Rhode Island

their own trade card (fig. 50). Clearly, associating their name with this image signaled quality.

COMMISSIONS AND CLIENTELE

Kimbel and Cabus's prominent public commissions for the Fifth Avenue Presbyterian Church and the Seventh Regiment Armory have defined our thinking about the firm's work as decorators. Although few of their private commissions are known to survive, recent research has uncovered several domestic projects that offer further insight into their approach to conceiving and furnishing interiors. In 1867, just four years into their partnership, they advertised as "Cabinet Makers and Decorators" who routinely provided room designs on request. Nearly a decade later, their drawing-room display at the Centennial Exhibition attested to their aspirations and achievement in domestic interior decoration. As a result of that success, they received

FIG. 49 Advertisement for Killian Brothers, *American Cabinet Maker* (March 30, 1878): 40

FIG. 50 Lang and Nau (Brooklyn, NY) trade card, ca. 1882. Paper, 4 ⅞ × 6 ⅝ in. (12.4 × 16.8 cm). Lent by Kevin L. Stayton

unprecedented attention in the press between 1876 and 1877. For example, *Harper's Bazar, Harper's New Monthly Magazine,* and *Harper's Weekly* illustrated seven of the firm's designs for furniture and interiors alongside images of the Centennial Exhibition display in multiple articles.[149] The *American Architect and Building News* published the firm's showroom and two designs for interiors in addition to the Centennial display.[150] These illustrations, along with a group of thirteen newly discovered design drawings given by Anton's great-nephew Martin (1905–1993) to the Kunstbibliothek, Berlin, provide rare insight into the firm's proposals for domestic interiors. Five of the thirteen drawings appear to be preparatory drawings for illustrations in two of the *Harper's* articles.[151] The majority of these illustrations and design drawings depict elevations for mantels, often flanked by contiguous bookcases or cabinets,

indicating designs for libraries or drawing rooms (figs. 51 and 52). There are also elevations for a window, a pier mirror, and two corner views of furnished drawing rooms that provide greater context for the viewer. Four of the drawings depict sideboards. All of the designs contain the eclectic combinations of columns, crockets, crenellations and dentillations, trefoils, incised carving, inset tiles, and bold metal hardware characteristic of Kimbel and Cabus's distinctive take on the Modern Gothic style.

Customers who patronized Kimbel and Cabus during the 1870s were aesthetically adventurous and aligned themselves with the progressive design ideals espoused by Talbert, Eastlake, Dresser, and others. This clientele consisted of doctors, merchants, and stockbrokers who shared the same energy and drive as the British industrialist patrons of Reformed

Gothic furnishings.[152] As we will see, William A. Hammond (1828–1900), a prominent New York City doctor, and John Bond Trevor (1822–1890), a successful stockbroker of New York City and Yonkers, exemplify the firm's forward-looking clientele. Period illustrations, a painting, and photographs of domestic interiors containing Kimbel and Cabus furniture help us to identify the firm's customers and better understand the scope of its business. Newspaper reports offer additional insight. For example, in March 1877 the *New York Herald* announced an auction of the contents of a private residence at 60 West 17th Street as containing "very elegant household furniture made to order by Kimbel and

Cabus, and almost new."[153] Between March 28 and April 5, 1878, the *New York Daily Tribune*, the *Evening Post*, and the *Evening Telegram* announced that Kimbel and Cabus were exhibiting "several pieces of Italian furniture, intended for San Francisco, showing carved work of the highest artistic order," revealing an intriguing European business connection that is in need of further scholarly exploration.[154] A June 1877 *Harper's Bazar* article entitled "The Art of Furnishing" describes another type of customer:

But if one has neither taste nor aptitude in this direction, yet desires fit furnishing, and has the

FIG. 51 Design for a wall with fireplace. Drawing, sheet: 11 ¼ × 14 in. (28.4 × 35.5 cm). Inv. Hdz 12971, Estate of Wilhelm Kimbel, Kunstbibliothek, Staatliche Museen, Berlin, Stiftung Preussischer Kulturbesitz

FIG. 52 Dining room: fireplace and chair. Drawing, sheet: 14 × 11 in. (35.5 × 27.8 cm). Inv. Hdz 12966, Estate of Wilhelm Kimbel, Kunstbibliothek, Staatliche Museen, Berlin, Stiftung Preussischer Kulturbesitz

wealth which that demands, the best course is to put the whole house into the hands of accomplished upholsterers. They will enter at the moment the masons leave, and they will not only attend to every detail, but will render those details into a homogeneous whole. The frescoes of the ceilings, the colors of the carpet and curtains and furniture covers, the wood-work of the furniture and of the walls, will be designed exactly to correspond with each other; doors and fire-places, windows and mirrors, will be a part of the picture; and if the result does not express any individuality of the owner, it is yet necessarily full of harmony and grace and beauty, for it is the work of skill and art, and that skill and art which command a price, as one may believe who knows that the great furniture houses pay [cost] from thirty to fifty thousand dollars a year for the drawing of their designs alone.[155]

In thanking Kimbel and Cabus, Pottier and Stymus, Herter Brothers, and William Morris and Company of London, among others, for information received, the author of this article offers further evidence that Kimbel and Cabus

FIG. 53 Drawing room, William Hammond House, in *Artistic Houses: Being a Series of Interior Views of a Number of the Most Beautiful and Celebrated Homes in the United States*, vol. 1 (New York: D. Appleton, 1883)

catered to a broad spectrum of customers. They created *Gesamtkunstwerk*—completely coordinated artistic interiors—for the affluent, as well as furniture that was "within reach of all" (see fig. 11). Despite Kimbel and Cabus's success, enthusiasm for the Modern Gothic and other progressive styles was by no means universal. The author of a June 1877 *New York Times* article asked, "Is it not almost time to rebel against the professors of household art? They are so numerous, persistent and dogmatic that they make life a burden."[156] A December 1877 article in the *American Cabinet Maker* also provides a different perspective. It reports on the Bowery, the "people's boulevard," as being lined with furniture stores that are "not much on the Eastlake, Queen Anne" and know "very little about Bruce J. Talbert."[157] The "honest" men and women shopping there "are not interested in furniture of the high art style" and "buy furniture that does not pay [cost] monstrous prices for the design."

From William Hammond, the esteemed military physician, we can glean insight into the firm's ambitious clientele. Surgeon general of the U.S. Army for much of the Civil War, Hammond was the first U.S. physician to specialize in neurology, a founding member of the American Neurological Association, a professor, and a prolific author. In 1873 he corresponded with Andrew D. White of Cornell University to propose the formation of Cornell Medical College in New York City.[158] Hammond's relationship with White may explain how he knew or became interested in Kimbel and Cabus. That same year Hammond was overseeing the construction of his house at 43 West 54th Street, New York City, which was modelled on a house he had admired in Nuremberg. Years later, reporting on the Hammond house for the *Art Amateur*, an author stated that "the doctor uses his own ideas and selects his designs, and himself gives instructions to the artisans he employs."[159] Hammond's eclectic, richly

FIG. 54 Edward Bierstadt (German, 1824–1906), Glenview, ca. 1885. Photogravure, 12 ¾ × 10 ⅛ in. (32.38 × 26.1 cm). Collection of the Hudson River Museum, INV.0023

decorated rooms, considered some of the earliest "artistic interiors" in New York City, were illustrated in *Artistic Houses* (1883–84), the lavish four-volume publication compiling descriptions and photographs of elite, fashionable domestic interiors. From ceiling to floor, Hammond's drawing room dazzled visitors with ornament and objects incorporating global references: a Celtic-inspired pattern on the ceiling, a frieze depicting scenes from the Bayeux Tapestry, walls lined with cabinets of ceramics from Asia and the Islamic world, and ebonized furniture in a range of styles including at least three examples by Kimbel and Cabus: an armchair, a side chair, and a two-person sofa or love seat (fig. 53).

FIG. 55 Edward Bierstadt (German, 1824–1906), Glenview Parlor, ca. 1886. Photogravure, 10 ¼ × 12 ¾ in. (32.38 × 26 cm). Collection of the Hudson River Museum, Gift of Mr. and Mrs. John Bond Trevor, Jr., 1973, 73.6.2

Kimbel and Cabus furniture also appears in interior photographs of Glenview, John Bond Trevor's country house in Yonkers, an early pastoral suburb of New York City favored by professionals as a refuge from the increasingly dense and disease-ridden city (fig. 54). Beginning in 1861, Trevor, his first wife Louisa, and their son resided at Seven Pines, also in

Yonkers. After Louisa's death, Trevor married Emily Norwood (1842–1922) and purchased twenty-three acres of adjoining land on which to build Glenview. Architect Charles W. Clinton (1838–1910) designed this majestic, thirty-seven-room house in the Gothic and French Second Empire style, and it was constructed of locally quarried greystone between 1876 and 1877. From

FIG. 56 Edward Bierstadt (German, 1824–1906). Glenview Sitting Room, Looking toward the Ebony Library, ca. 1886. Photogravure, 10 × 13 in. (25.4 × 7.62 cm). Collection of the Hudson River Museum, Gift of Mr. and Mrs. John Bond Trevor, Jr., 1973, 73.6.1

indoor plumbing to gas lighting, the new residence was equipped with all the modern conveniences for Trevor's family of six, who resided there from April through December and spent the winter months in their Manhattan townhouse. The Trevors were equally modern in their interior design choices, employing prominent Philadelphia cabinetmaker Daniel

Pabst (1826–1910), another proponent of Modern Gothic, to create the interior woodwork.[160] Given his preference for the Modern Gothic style, Trevor was naturally familiar with Kimbel and Cabus as well. He was a Philadelphia native, and most certainly attended the Centennial Exhibition with his wife; this may have been what led them to

FIG. 57 Exterior, Duncraggan,
residence of Anna Smith Cochran,
ca. 1875

acquire examples of the firm's work. Edward Bierstadt's photographs of the Glenview interiors published in *Homes on the Hudson* (ca. 1887), an illustrated volume tracing the architectural history of the region, document the Kimbel and Cabus furniture in the Trevor house. Among the parlor furnishings, a rectilinear Kimbel and Cabus armchair with inset paper panels can be seen in the foreground and a side chair at the window in the background (fig. 55). The view showing both the sitting room and part of the ebonized library provides tantalizing partial views of the firm's forms—a corner chair at the left of the library entrance, cropped so the arm is

FIG. 58 Walter Thomas, Duncraggan Parlor, ca. 1880s. Black-and-white photograph, 6 × 8 in.
(15.24 × 20.32 cm). Collection of the Hudson River Museum, INV. 5024 B

visible, an armchair to the right facing the splendid fireplace, and a side chair in the background near the portrait on the easel (fig. 56).[161] The location of these objects is not currently known—the contents of Glenview were dispersed after Emily Trevor's death in 1922. The Trevors were an example of a successful professional and his wife looking to appoint their new home in the latest style.

Duncraggan, another Gothic-style country home in Yonkers that is no longer standing, was also illustrated in the 1887 *Homes on the Hudson*. It belonged to William F. Cochran (1833–1901), secretary and treasurer of the Smith Carpet Mills in Yonkers and a notable philanthropist, and his wife Eva (1845–1909), daughter of Smith Carpet Mills founder Alexander Smith (fig. 57).[162] Interior photographs of the Cochrans' parlor and library depict several examples of Kimbel and Cabus furniture in situ among other

furnishings. In the parlor, a Modern Gothic cabinet, one of the firm's most elaborate forms, can be seen to the right of the window in the background, underneath a painting (fig. 58 and see p. 195). A monumental Kimbel and Cabus desk features prominently in the photograph of the library, suggesting that the library table to the left, which resembles an extant example attributed to Kimbel and Cabus, is also probably by the firm (figs. 59 and 60 and see p. 177).

In 1879, the author of the *Art Journal* column "New York Interiors" profiled the residence of William H. DeForest (1837–1896), built by architects Lamb and Wheeler at 12 West 57th Street. DeForest was a leading silk wholesaler, served as the U.S. agent of the well-known French firm of Guanet Brothers, and invested and speculated in real estate in Upper Manhattan and New Jersey.[163] Although Kimbel and Cabus are not mentioned in the column, the

FIG. 59 Unknown photographer. The Library Looking East, 1904. In an album of Duncraggan, 11 ¼ × 14 ¾ × 31 ¼ in. (28.5 × 37.5 × 79.3 cm). Collection of the Hudson River Museum, Gift of Jo Magram, 2001, 2001.02 u

FIG. 60 Table, ca. 1875. Oak, pine, leather. 29 ½ × 40 × 30 in. (74.9 × 101.6 × 76.2 cm) Collection of David Petrovsky

accompanying illustration of DeForest's library depicts versions of the firm's distinctive library table and armchair (fig. 61 and see pp. 133, 139). The arrangement of the fireplace mantel and clock with flanking bookcases corresponds to Kimbel and Cabus's design drawing for a Gothic library, a version of which was published in *Harper's Bazar* in 1876 (fig. 51), suggesting that the design may have been from the commission for DeForest. An evocative description of the room, beginning with the peacock-green tiled mantel, provides rare insight into the color scheme:

> The roof, so to speak, of the fireplace is one mass of tiles overlapping each other . . . The curtains and hangings are of a very dark blue; the carpet a Persian rug of dark blue and green; the chairs covered with the thick blue velvet of the curtains. Around the room tiles set thick in wood-work carry out the idea suggested in the fireplace. The wood is solid, of a light colour. It is a beautiful room, very original, very perfect, a triumph of colour in its sobriety and neatness. The little clock which puts forth from the mantel is worthy of Nuremberg; in fact, the whole thing suggests that lingering home of the Middle Ages. What do we want better than Nuremberg? . . . The square, solidly-cut-out table, how well it supplements this solid room! . . . Bronzes, a few quiet pictures, a medallion or two, a student-lamp, low book-shelves, convenient to the hand, and we have a *conscientious* library.[164]

A second illustration of the boudoir includes two side chairs that relate closely in design to Kimbel's chair patent of 1871. DeForest's home is also described and illustrated in *Artistic Houses*, coincidentally following Dr. Hammond's entry. A photograph depicting DeForest's library does not match the earlier *Art Journal* illustration, nor does it resemble a conventional library, as there are no bookshelves. It is likely

Library.—Residence of W. H. DeForest, Esq.

FIG. 61 "New York Interiors. Residence of W. H. DeForest, Esq.," *Art Journal* 5 (1879): 141–42

that the photograph depicts a second library located upstairs, described as connecting two suites of rooms.[165]

During the same year, 1879, the *Art Journal's* columnist reported on another "New York Interior," the residence of James P. Kernochan, Esq. (1831–1897) at 824 Fifth Avenue.[166] Kernochan, the New York-born son of a wealthy Louisiana sugar planter, and his wife Catherine Lorillard, an heiress of the Lorillard Tobacco Company, were affluent members of New York society.[167] In addition to managing his and his wife's combined fortunes, Kernochan was socially well-connected and involved with many clubs and organizations. He was governor of the exclusive Metropolitan Club, for example. Kimbel and Cabus are not cited in the article, but an illustration of the dining room displays chairs as well as a mantel and cabinetry of recognizable Kimbel and Cabus design (see pp. 121–22). Again, the descriptive text is evocative:

Should and [*sic*] unexpected comet visit us and wipe off our atmosphere, or a shower of ashes descend to keep us in *intaglio* for the next two thousand years, the New-Zealander who should explore our deserted streets would scarcely find a more typical dining room that that of Mr. James P. Kernochan. . . . Spacious and lofty, it tells a story of the prosperity of New York, its solid fortunes, its steady and its ephemeral growths. . . . This beautiful room has few superiors in New York, and yet there are in that street of palaces—the Fifth Avenue—enough to bear it company, so that, instead of presenting a picture of isolated beauty, it is a typical room. . . . The color, then, of this charming dining-room is peacock-green, and the eye appears in the ceiling and borders. Not to be too monotonous, another royalty is introduced, and the three feathers of the Prince of Wales, in gold, light up the blue and green. The solid wood work, of a light tint

FIG. 62 Vincent Stiepevich (American, born Italy, 1841–after 1910). *Victorian Interior*, 1880. Oil on paper, 10 × 14 in. (25.4 × 35.6 cm). Collection of Ann Pyne

shows out gracefully and well against this mass of colour, and steel fixtures to the fireplaces give a diamond glitter to that most comforting of winter landscapes, a wood-fire. Heavy draperies of woollen stuffs, of the same colour as the wall or screen, which breaks the distance and rests the eye; a long, solid table and Eastlake chairs complete the silent picture.[168]

An 1880 rendering entitled *Victorian Interior*, by the Italian-born painter Vincent G. Stiepevich (1841–1910), depicts the Kernochan dining room from a different angle (fig. 62).[169] Seated at the dining table quietly reviewing papers,

the Kernochans are the focal point of the composition. Stiepevich evidently relished capturing the play of light and shadow on the pleats and folds of Catherine Kernochan's blue silk dress. More importantly, and with meticulous attention to detail, the artist masterfully recorded the colors, textures, and reflective qualities of the objects and materials—from fabric to wood, metal, and fur—present within the room. Close examination of the cabinet on the left between the mantel and door reveals carved panels, enriched with white, blue, and red, on the doors—a glimpse of Kimbel and Cabus's

FIG. 63 Company K Room. "The Seventh Regiment Armory," *Decorator and Furnisher* 6, no. 2 (May 1885): 42–46

polychromatic woodwork. *Victorian Interior* offers rare and colorful insight into a Kimbel and Cabus interior.

Between 1879 and 1880, Kimbel and Cabus received an important commission that placed them at the forefront of New York furniture-manufacturing and interior-decorating companies: to furnish the 10th Company K Room at the Seventh Regiment of the New York Militia Armory on Park Avenue in New York City. The Seventh Regiment, which traced its origins to 1806 and counted men from elite New York families such as the Van Rensselaers and the Roosevelts among its members, was the first militia to defend Washington, D.C. at the outbreak of the Civil War.[170] After the war, the regiment moved its headquarters from Tompkins Market on the Lower East Side to an uptown Park Avenue location, commissioning architect and regiment member Charles W. Clinton to design and construct the new, privately-funded armory. Evocative of a fortified Italian palazzo with a central tower and turrets at the four corners, the massive three-story building, red-brick with granite trim, occupies the entire city block between East 66th and 67th streets. It houses meeting rooms for the regiment's ten companies and a drill hall that stretches the width of the block to Lexington Avenue. Members held a grand fair in November 1879 to raise funds for decorating the interior. The companies competed in a "tournament of taste," creating display booths of Byzantine, Chinese, Egyptian, Moorish, Persian, Queen Anne, and Venetian inspiration, among other themes, and raffled and sold goods with the goal of achieving the highest earnings and thus winning a prize silver punch bowl donated by Brooks Brothers, designer of the regiment's regalia.[171] Visitors to the fair enjoyed a variety of entertainments including painting and model yacht exhibitions, a shooting range, and magic and Punch and Judy shows. They could purchase confections, curiosities, groceries, and toys. The

fair was an astounding success, raising $140,550—the equivalent of about $2.2 million in 2021—over a two-week run. Each company received a $6,000 allotment from the proceeds and then strove to outdo one another in the decoration of their private rooms. Firms hired to complete the other company rooms included Kimbel and Cabus's illustrious competitors Herter Brothers, Pottier and Stymus, and Louis C. Tiffany's Associated Artists. The Company K Room, designed by company member Sidney Stratton of New York's premier architectural firm of McKim, Mead and White, was awarded to Kimbel and Cabus (fig. 63). In contrast to the Renaissance revival style predominant elsewhere in the building, Stratton's design was in the Queen Anne style, another fashionable mode of the 1870s characterized by an eclectic combination of classical architectural elements, including triangular pediments, paterae, volutes, dentilated borders, rounded arches, and balustrades of turned spindles. Company members' wood-paneled lockers lined the walls, and the frieze above depicted wreath-enclosed K motifs and paterae that echoed the carved woodwork below.[172] The May 1885 *Decorator and Furnisher* illustrated the Company K Room in an article on the Armory, with accompanying text:

Our last view is that of one of the company rooms, the 10th Company K, supposed to be the most elaborately arranged of the entire number. It is finished in maple and mahogany, has a handsomely decorated wall, hung with trophies and portraits of former officers of the company. The work in the room was done by Messrs. Kimball & Cabus after designs by S. V. Stratton, a member of the company, and of the firm McKim, Mead & White. There are traces of at least the influence in style from Messrs. Tiffany & Co. in the room and there are very many choice and beautiful items of decorative fancy about worthy of notice and preservation.[173]

FIG. 64 Cabinet, ca. 1875. Ebonized wood, leather, paper. 57 × 27 × 12 in. (144.8 × 68.6 × 30.5 cm). Courtesy Dr. John S. Wadlington family collection

Although opinions about whether the Company K Room was the most elaborately appointed vary, it underlines Kimbel and Cabus's adaptability to working in a range of styles. This limitless creative versatility sustained their long-term success.

By the late 1870s the Modern Gothic style was on the wane, as noted by Cook in *The House Beautiful*:

> There was a little while ago quite a rage for a certain style of furniture that made a great display of seeming steel hinges, key-plates, and handles, with inlaid tiles, carving of an ultra-Gothic type, and an appearance of the most ingenuous truth-telling in the construction. The chairs, tables and bedsteads looked

as if they had been on the dissecting-table and flayed alive,—their joints and tendons displayed to an archaeologic and unfeeling world. One particular firm introduced this style of furniture, and for a time, had almost the monopoly of it. It had a great run, for the purchaser was made to feel that in buying it he got an immense deal more for his money than he could get in any other style of furniture.[174]

Interest in the Aesthetic Movement, which embraced art for art's sake, was on the rise throughout Europe and the United States. World's fairs, especially the Centennial in the United States, had introduced exciting new sources of artistic inspiration. Artists and designers enthusiastically appropriated forms and motifs from China, Japan, North Africa, the Middle East, and other parts of the globe, which they synthesized to create the striking, hybrid designs characteristic of the Aesthetic Movement. Kimbel and Cabus objects, such as an ebonized display cabinet featuring Moorish-style arches, Chinese-style fretwork, and canted front legs with cloven-hoof feet (fig. 64), as well as the multiple forms documented in their photographs (figs. 24 and 38), demonstrate a fluency in this idiom. The firm's positive credit reports throughout 1880 reflect these changes, stating that the business, worth $75,000 and held in high esteem by the trade, was "Like many others in this line" in that "they carried for several years a considerable stock of fine goods, there being no demand—this has been sold without serious loss."[175]

THE END OF A PARTNERSHIP AND THE BEGINNING OF A NEW CHAPTER

In May of 1882 Kimbel and Cabus dissolved their partnership; the decision "was caused by a difference of opinion regarding the class of work they should make."[176] That February the firm had

FIG. 65 A. Kimbel and Sons. Étagère, ca. 1887. Cherry, metal, glass, 69 ¾ × 41 ¾ × 16 in. (177.2 × 106 × 40.6 cm). The Metropolitan Museum of Art, Sansbury-Mills Fund, 1991, 1991.230

informed their patrons and the public via newspaper announcements that they were liquidating their stock of "high class Parlor, Library, Dining-room, Chamber, and Fancy Furniture" at "greatly reduced prices" in preparation for the dissolution of their business on May 1.[177] Auctioneer R. Somerville started selling off remaining stock on April 19.[178] Although a remarkable partnership of nearly twenty years had come to an end, Kimbel, aged fifty-nine, and Cabus, aged fifty-seven, laid the foundations upon which their sons each built prosperous businesses, having assumed control of their now independent firms.

Retaining the Kimbel and Cabus show-room and factory addresses, Kimbel established A. Kimbel and Sons. The new firm continued making furniture in the fashionable Aesthetic Movement style, as illustrated by an étagère enriched with Chinese-inspired fretwork (fig. 65). Eventually, however, A. Kimbel and Sons focused on producing furniture and decorating interiors in the more conservative European revival styles that returned to favor during the last decade of the nineteenth century. After Anton Kimbel's death in 1895, his sons and grandsons continued the business into the 1940s, moving to new locations several times.[179]

Cabus built a cabinetmaking factory at 506 West 41st Street in which he employed between thirty-five and forty men, collaborating with McKim, Mead and White, and Louis Comfort Tiffany, as well as other esteemed firms, to carve and finish woodwork interiors. For example, working with Stanford White and Louis Comfort Tiffany, he executed interiors for the Villard Houses in New York City, and the Baltimore home of John Work Garrett.[180] Until his death in 1898, Cabus and his son Alex carved picture frames for White according to his designs.[181]

After working so closely together for nearly a third of their lives, it is fitting that Kimbel and Cabus are both interred in family plots in Brooklyn's historic Green-Wood Cemetery. Theirs is an inspiring New York City story of immigrant success. They took artistic talent and technical skill rooted in Old World training and combined them with an assertive New World entrepreneurial spirit to achieve national recognition, making inventive furniture and interiors that defined the Modern Gothic ethos in the United States and became their legacy. By garnering clients and commissions through business acumen and stylistic versatility, they sustained long-term success over two decades, and thus provided economic security for their children and future generations.

1   "Gothic" is derived from "Goths," the name given to Germanic people who invaded the Roman Empire. "*Gothic*," in *Oxford English Dictionary*, 11th ed., eds. Catherine Soanes and Angus Stevenson (Oxford: Oxford University Press, 2008).

2   See also the essay by Max Donnelly in this volume.

3   For confirmation of Anton Kimbel's birthdate see "Stadtarchiv Mainz; Mainz, Deutschland; *Zivilstandsregister, 1798–1875*; Signatur: *50 / 25*, entry 726," under "Mainz, Germany, Births, Marriages and Deaths, 1798–1875," *Ancestry.com*. For confirmation of Kimbel family birthdates see Heidrun Zinnkann, *Mainzer Möbelschreiner der ersten Hälfte des 19. Jahrhunderts* (Frankfurt am Main: Historischen Museums, 1985), pp. 152–53 nn. 649, 673–74. Anton's siblings were: Marie (b. 1824), Barbara (b. 1828), Elisabeth and Eva (twins b. 1829), Katarina (b. 1832), Wilhelm (b. 1833), Martin (b. 1835), Johann (Jean) (b. 1837), Helene (b. 1840), and Franziska (b. 1842).

4   For information regarding Wilhelm Kimbel see Zinnkann 1985 (as in note 3), pp. 152–66.

5   For information regarding Philipp Anton Bembé, referred to as Anton, see ibid., pp. 166–83; see also Tim Möst, *Anton Bembé. Möbel für Adel und Bürgertum*, on the website of Instituts für Geschichtliche Landeskunde an der Universität Mainz e.V., http://www.wirtschaftsgeschichte-rlp.de/a-z/a/anton-bembe.html (last accessed February 10, 2014).

6   Zinnkann 1985 (as in note 3), p. 177.

7   Ibid., p. 157 n. 714. Pallenberg was a leading firm in Cologne and supplier to the Prussian royal families. The French Emperor Napoleon III and Empress Eugénie patronized the prominent Parisian cabinet-making firm of Alexandre-Georges Fourdinois. See also the essay by Melitta Jonas in this volume.

8   September 15: Anton Kimbel, aged twenty-six, arrives in New York, NY, on the *Zurich* from Le Havre. "Year: 1848; Arrival: New York, New York; Microfilm Serial: M237, 1820–1897; Microfilm Roll: Roll 075; Line: 35; List Number: 1062; Page Number: 2" s.v. "New York, Passenger and Crew Lists (including Castle Garden and Ellis Island), 1820–1957," *Ancestry.com*.

9   Stanley Nadel, *Little Germany, Ethnicity, Religion, and Class in New York City, 1845–80* (Chicago: University of Illinois Press, 1990), pp. 1, 17–18.

10   Ibid., p. 16.

11   Ibid., p. 63.

12   For a discussion of cabinet and furniture making in New York City at this time see Catherine Hoover Voorsanger, "From the Bowery to Broadway: The Herter Brothers and the New York Furniture Trade," in Katherine S. Howe, Alice Cooney Frelinghuysen, Catherine Hoover Voorsanger et al., *Herter Brothers: Furniture and Interiors for a Gilded Age* (New York: Harry N. Abrams in association with the Museum of Fine Arts, Houston, 1994), pp. 56–77; Catherine Hoover Voorsanger, "'Gorgeous Articles of Furniture': Cabinetmaking in the Empire City," in *Art and the Empire City: New York, 1825–1861*, eds. Catherine Hoover Voorsanger and John K. Howat (New York: Metropolitan Museum of Art, 2000), pp. 287–325.

13   Nadel 1990 (as in note 9), p. 64.

14   Elizabeth A. Ingerman, "Personal experiences of an old New York cabinet-maker," *ANTIQUES* 84 (November 1963): 577.

15   "A. KIMBEL, having been for six years designer in Mr. Badouine's manufactory, brings ample experience to the task." See "BEMBE & KIMBEL, FURNITURE AND UPHOLSTERY," *New York Daily Times* (September 1, 1854): 7.

16   According to Zinnkann 1985 (as in note 3), p. 157, during these early years Kimbel returned to Mainz with three hundred of his current design drawings to present to his father and uncle. No further documentation is known at the time of publication.

17   Ingerman 1963 (as in note 14), p. 578.

18   Voorsanger 2000 (as in note 12), p. 313; Anna Tobin D'Ambrosio, ed., *Masterpieces of American Furniture from the Munson-Williams-Proctor Institute* (Utica: Munson-Williams-Proctor Institute, 1999), pp. 82–87.

19   "Designing and Designers," *American Cabinet Maker* 13, whole no. 337 (November 4, 1876): 4. This is also the reference for the preceding sentence. Begun on May 14, 1870, the *A Cabinet Maker* was a trade journal published by J. Henry Symonds, Boston, that reported on the major furniture-making centers in the United States and published articles on furniture forms, patents, woods, decorative techniques, machinery, exhibitions, interior decoration and design, and other media as well as advertisements. Its name changed to the *American Cabinet Maker, Upholsterer and Furniture Reporter* in 1875.

20   For confirmation of Pauline Blank's birthdate of February 8, 1822 see "Family Number 5604" s.v. "Mainz, Germany, Family Registers 1760–1900," *Ancestry.com*. This record also confirms her departure for the United States in May 1849. Interestingly, passenger records for the ship *Queen Victoria*, arriving in New York, NY, from Le Havre, France, on June 5, 1849, list a twenty-seven-year-old male Paulie Blank traveling with a nineteen-year-old Elisa Kimbel and a group of seven others. It is likely that this is Pauline, recorded as male by accident or perhaps on purpose, accompanying one of Anton's sisters. "Year: 1849; Arrival: New York, New York; Microfilm Serial: M237, 1820–1897; Microfilm Roll: Roll 080; Line: 15; List Number: 659" s.v. "New York, Passenger and Crew Lists (including Castle Garden and Ellis Island), 1820–1957," *Ancestry.com*. For confirmation of Anton and Pauline's children's names and ages see "United States Federal Census, 1860, New York, New York, Ward 20, District 1, p. 11, lines 18–27" and "United States Federal Census, 1870, New York, New York, 10th Election District, Ward 20, District 10, p. 19, lines 26–31," *Ancestry.com* and Brooklyn Museum curatorial files.

21   *New York City Directory* (New York: Charles R. Rode, 1854/55), p. 394.

22   Voorsanger 2000 (as in note 12), p. 320.

23   Zinnkann 1985 (as in note 3), pp. 157–58 n. 715 and "A. BEMBE & A. KIMBEL, No. 56 Walker st.," *New York Daily Times* (September 1, 1854): 7.

24   Ibid.

25   "A Parlor View in a New York Dwelling House," *Gleason's Pictorial Drawing-Room Companion* 7, no. 19 (November 11, 1854): 300. This is the reference for the following two sentences as well. The article incorrectly describes Bembé and Kimbel as a French house. The statement that the firm has a manufactory at "Mayence," France, is likely a misunderstood reference to Mainz. The confusion may have resulted from the fact that during the first sixteen years of Bembé's life Mainz was under French occupation. During the occupation, 1793–1815, the Bembé name was given its French form, and (Philipp) Anton Bembé became fluent in French. Reminiscences of

the Kimbel sons show that Bembé and his sisters frequently spoke French. Thus it is unsurprising that Americans thought that Bembé and Kimbel was a French firm. See Zinnkann 1985 (as in note 3), p. 167 n. 783.

26   *New York City Directory* (New York: John F. Trow, 1855/56), p. 67.

27   "New York, State Census, 1855, New York City, New York County, 5th Ward, 3rd Election District (unpaginated), lines 22–27," *Ancestry.com*.

28   *New York City Directory* (John F. Trow, 1857/58), p. 67.

29   See "April 16, 1857 New York," vol. 191, p. 401 Z, R. G. Dun & Co. credit report volumes, Baker Library, Harvard Business School, Boston, MA.

30   August 12: "I received today from Bembe and Kimbel of New York a letter with a bill for two chairs and two desks which they say have been sent for inspection. They ask a less price than that I have agreed to pay to [Doe], Hazleton, and Co. of Boston for the desks of which they brought me specimens. I am surprised at the price they charge being so low. But I have not seen the chairs." August 14: "The desk and chairs by Bembe and Kimbel have arrived. The chairs are better than the Boston chairs, the desks not so good. All are cheaper." August 19: "At the office. Mr. Kimbel of Bembe and Kimbel is here to make a bargain for the chairs for the House of Representatives. He will, I fear, not be able to make them in time. I shall probably give to him a small portion only of the number required." August 27: "I made a bargain with Mr. [John T.] Hammitt [of the Hammitt Desk Manufacturing Company] of Philadelphia for one-half of the chairs for the House of Representatives at $75 each, delivered. I have telegraphed to Bembe and Kimbel of New York that they might make the other half at $70 each, not including the packing. This makes 262 chairs and the same number of desks in all for the House of Representatives which are now engaged." Wendy Wolff, ed., *Capitol Builder: The Shorthand Journals of Montgomery C. Meigs, 1853–1859, 1861, A Project to Commemorate the United States Capitol Bicentennial 1800–2000* (Washington, D.C.: Prepared under the direction of the Secretary of the Senate. U.S. Government Printing Office, 2001), pp. 520–24. See also Donald C. Pierce, *Art, and Enterprise: American Decorative Art, 1825–1917: The*

Virginia Carroll Crawford Collection (Atlanta: High Museum of Art, 1999), pp. 366–67.

31   See "June 1, 1858; July 18, 1859 New York," vol. 191, R. G. Dun & Co. credit report volumes (as in note 29).

32   See "June 1, 1858; December 16, 1858 New York," vol. 191, R. G. Dun & Co. credit report volumes (as in note 29).

33   *New York City Directory* (New York: John F. Trow, 1858/59), p. 438.

34   "United States Federal Census, 1860, New York, New York, Ward 20, District 1, p. 11, lines 18–27," *Ancestry.com*.

35   *New York City Directory* (New York: John F. Trow, 1861/62), pp. 68, 463.

36   Letter from Anton Kimbel's daughter Elizabeth Kimbel Mehlbach to her son William K. Mehlbach, July 23, 1925, p. 2. A photocopy of the original letter is in the curatorial files in the American Wing of the Metropolitan Museum of Art, New York.

37   Ibid., pp. 1–2, and Zinnkann 1985 (as in note 3), pp. 157–58 n. 716. See also "May 19, 1862, New York," vol. 191, R. G. Dun & Co. credit report volumes (as in note 29). These are also the sources for the following four sentences.

38   *New York City Directory* (New York: John F. Trow, 1863/64), p. 69; (New York: John F. Trow, 1864/65), p. 71; (New York: John F. Trow, 1865/66), p. 75; (New York: John F. Trow, 1866/67), p. 79.

39   For confirmation of Pauline Kimbel's June 29, 1861, birthdate see "1934; Arrival: New York, New York, USA; Microfilm Serial: T715, 1897–1957; Microfilm roll 5534; Line: 2; Page Number: 52 s.v. "New York, s.v. Passenger and Crew Lists (including Castle Garden and Ellis Island), 1820–1957," *Ancestry.com*.

40   Letter from E. K. Mehlbach to W. K. Mehlbach, July 23, 1925 (as in note 36), pp. 1–2. Family letters referenced in the following discussion are those of E. K. Mehlbach. Death date for Pauline Blank Kimbel confirmed by headstone in lot 26651, section 143, Green-Wood Cemetery, Brooklyn.

41   Ibid. These letters are the source for the following sentence as well. The identity of the competing firm is not known. A Simon Gerber is listed: "Gerber, Simon, mer. 6 Liberty, h 75 Amity," in *New York City Directory* (New York: John F. Trow, 1862/63, p. 323); "Gerber, Simon cheese, 144

Chambers Street, h. Belvedere, as are Gerber F. & J. Cheese 207 Duane," in *New York City Directory* (New York: John F. Trow, 1877/78), p. 505. A. Kimbel as well as S. Gerber departed on the ship *Donau* bound for Bremen in June 1878, offering further evidence that Simon Gerber was likely the friend and benefactor of Anton mentioned in E. K. Mehlbach's letters. "Departures for Europe," *New York Times* (June 15, 1878): 3.

42   Calmoutier is in the Haute-Saône department in the Franche-Comté region of France. For confirmation of Joseph's birthdate see "Passport application No. 13846, June 29, 1894, National Archives and Records Administration (NARA); Washington, D.C.; Roll #: 426; Volume #: Roll 426 - 23 Jun 1894–09 Jul 1894" s.v. "U.S. Passport Applications, 1795–1925," *Ancestry.com*. For confirmation of arrival in New York of Claude, age thirty-four, his wife Anne, thirty-four, and their sons Joseph, nine, Victoire, six, and George, four, see "New York, Passenger and Crew Lists (including Castle Garden and Ellis Island), 1820–1957, 1833, New York, New York, USA; Year: 1833; Arrival: New York, New York; Microfilm Serial: M237, 1820–1897; Line 21; List number 136; Page number 3," *Ancestry. com*. Although Joseph is listed as age nine, recent confirmation of his birthdate indicates that he was in fact still eight. For documentation of Claude and his sons' identification as farmers see "New York, New York, Index to Passenger Lists, 1820–1846," *FamilySearch.org*; "Butt - Cam > image 1310-14 of 5491; citing NARA microfilm publication M261," National Archives and Records Administration, Washington, D.C.

43   For further discussion see Leonard Dinnerstein and David Reimers, *Ethnic Americas: A History of Immigration* (New York: Columbia University Press, 2009), pp. 23–55.

44   *New York City Directory* (New York: Thomas Longworth, 1838/39), p. 136; *New York City Directory* (New York: Thomas Longworth, 1839/40), p. 141.

45   "United States Federal Census, 1840, New York, New York, Fourteenth Ward, roll 307, page 320, Family History Library film 0017197," *Ancestry.com*.

46   *New York City Directory* (New York: John Doggett, Jr., 1850/51), p. 87.

47   "United States Federal Census, 1850, New York, New York, Ward 8, District 1,

page 23b, lines 11–13," *Ancestry.com*. Joseph Cabus was naturalized on June 11, 1851 at the Common Pleas Court, New York County, see "Soundex code C120" s.v. "Soundex Index to Petitions for Naturalizations Filed in Federal, State, and Local Courts in New York City, 1792–1906," *fold 3*, *Ancestry.com*.

48   *New York City Directory* (New York: John F. Trow, 1852/53), p. 101; *New York City Directory* (New York: John F. Trow, 1853/54), p. 110.

49   "New York, State Census, 1855 NYC, Ward 8, District 1, sheet 36, lines 21–33," *Ancestry.com*. This is the reference for the following sentence as well.

50   Voorsanger 2000 (as in note 12), pp. 317–18.

51   Ingerman 1963 (as in note 14), p. 579.

52   From at least 1849, Roux's business address is at 479 Broadway. See *New York City Directory* (New York: John Doggett, Jr., 1849/50), p. 364. Voorsanger 2000 (as in note 12), p. 317 n. 203. This is the reference for the following sentence as well.

53   *New York City Directory* (New York: Doggett and Rode, 1851/52), p. 462.

54   *New York City Directory* (John F. Trow, 1857/58), p. 129; *New York City Directory* (John F. Trow, 1858/59), p. 127; *New York City Directory* (John F. Trow, 1859/60, p. 133). Cabus's work address, 479 Broadway, was the same as Roux's. Cabus's home address was on Grand Street at that time.

55   For confirmation of Cabus's role as Roux's foreman and partner see "December 14, 1858 New York," vol. 190, p. 397, R. G. Dun & Co. credit report volumes, Baker Library, Harvard Business School, Boston, MA. This is also the reference for the following sentence. Offering further documentation of their partnership, Joseph Cabus's name is seen on the lower right corner of Roux's paper label affixed to a serving table. See Eileen Dubrow and Richard Dubrow, *American Furniture of the 19th Century, 1840–1880* (Exton, PA: Schiffer Publishing, 1983), p. 167. For confirmation of the woods used at Roux's firm see Ingerman 1963 (as in note 14), p. 579.

56   For Alexander's and Theresa's birth years see "United States Federal Census, 1860, New York, New York, 8th Ward, 2nd District, p. 279, line 40 and p. 280 lines 1–7," s.v. "Family History Library Film 803794," *Ancestry.com*. The Cabuses also resided

with a female Irish servant. Between 1855 and 1860 Joseph's third child, William, died; he is no longer listed in the 1860 census. For Frank's birth year see "New York, State Census, 1865, Kings County, New York, Brooklyn, Ward 8, p. 50, line 25," *Ancestry.com*. Theresa died between 1860 and 1865; she is no longer listed in the New York State Census of 1865. *New York City Directory* (New York: John F. Trow, 1861/62), p. 132.

57   See "January 10 and 16, 1860, New York," vol. 190, p. 397, R. G. Dun & Co. credit report volumes (as in note 55).

58   June 1863: Joseph Cabus, aged thirty-nine, cabinetmaker, living between 3rd and 4th Avenues. Former military service is listed as "55th regiment NY V" (the abbreviation possibly standing for "New York Veteran"). See "Consolidated list of all persons of Class II subject to do military duty in the 8th ward, 2nd Congressional District, in the City of Brooklyn, NY" in the U.S. Civil War draft records at the National Archives and Records Administration (NARA), Washington, D.C. (*Consolidated Lists of Civil War Draft Registration Records (Provost Marshal General's Bureau; Consolidated Enrollment Lists, 1863–1865)*; Record Group: *110, Records of the Provost Marshal General's Bureau (Civil War)*; Collection Name: *Consolidated Enrollment Lists, 1863–1865 (Civil War Union Draft Records)*; NAI: *4213514*; Archive Volume Number: *4 of 5*.

59   *New York City Directory* (New York: John F. Trow, 1862/63), p. 134.

60   See passport applications: "Anton Kimbel No. 18197, issued May 26, 1888," s.v. "U.S., Passport Applications, 1795–1925, National Archives and Records Administration (NARA); Washington, D.C.; Roll #: 306; Volume #: Roll 306–22 May 1888–31 May 1888," *Ancestry.com*; "Joseph Cabus No. 13846, issued June 29, 1894," s.v. "U.S., Passport Applications, 1795–1925, National Archives and Records Administration (NARA); Washington, D.C.; Roll #: 426; Volume #: Roll 426–23 June 1894–09 Jul 1894," *Ancestry.com*.

61   See letter from E. K. Mehlbach to W. K. Mehlbach, July 23, 1925 (as in note 36), p. 3.

62   *New York City Directory* (New York: John F. Trow, 1863/64), p. 470.

63   See "February 26, 1863, New York," vol. 191, R. G. Dun & Co. credit report volumes (as in note 29).

64   "HOUSES, ROOMS & C., TO LET," *New York Herald* (April 14, 1863): 5.

65   See "April 11, 1866, New York," vol. 191, R. G. Dun & Co. credit report volumes (as in note 29).

66   Mary Ann Saunders' life dates are confirmed by a headstone in lot 26651, section 143, Green-Wood Cemetery, Brooklyn. See also "United States Federal Census, 1870, New York, New York, Ward 20, District 10, Roll: M593_1007; Page: 274A," s.v. "Family History Library Film: 552506," *Ancestry.com*. For Richard Kimbel's birth year, 1866, see "Passport application 83816, stamped October 29, 1912," s.v. "U.S., Passport Applications, 1795–1925, National Archives and Records Administration (NARA); Washington, D.C.; Roll #: 172; Volume #: Roll 0172 – Certificates: 83529-84480, 22 Oct 1912–15 Nov 1912," *Ancestry.com*. For Laura Kimbel's birth year, 1872, see the passport bureau notice attached to Anton Kimbel's application of May 25, 1888 (see note 60).

67   *New York City Directory* (New York: John F. Trow, 1865/66), p. 527; (New York: John F. Trow, 1866/67), p. 549; (New York: John F. Trow, 1867/68), p. 561.

68   *New York City Directory* (New York: John F. Trow, 1864/65), p. 137; (New York: John F. Trow, 1865/66), p. 148; (New York: John F. Trow, 1866/67), p. 155; (New York: John F. Trow, 1867/68), p. 157.

69   According to family history, Carl had "a riotous life of a few years" and neglected the business. Kimbel rescued Carl from "the gutter" and had him looked after. See letter from E. K. Mehlbach to W. K. Mehlbach, July 23, 1925 (as in note 36), p. 3; *New York City Directory* (New York: John F. Trow, 1867/68), p. 561.

70   Ibid., p. 561.

71   "Business Cards," *Chicago Tribune* (September 6, 1867): 1; "General Notices," *Chicago Tribune* (November 6, 1867): 1. These are the references for the following sentence as well.

72   "Furniture," *New York Observer and Chronicle* (May 14, 1868): 160. The firm published the same advertisement in the *Observer* in 1868 on July 9: 224; July 16: 232; July 23: 240; August 13: 264; September 10: 296; October 15: 336; October 22: 344; November 5: 360; November 12: 368;

December 3: 392; December 24: 416; December 31: 424; and on January 7, 1869: 8; January 14: 16; January 28: 32; February 4: 40; February 18: 56; March 4: 72; March 11: 80; March 18: 88. "Furniture, & c." *The Jewish Messenger* (July 1868). Recent digitization of primary sources has made clear that a plethora of publications existed in which firms advertised in order to reach a broad range of customers.

73   See "August 7, 1868 and April 3, 1869, New York," vol. 191, R. G. Dun & Co. credit report volumes (as in note 29).

74   *New York City Directory* (New York: John F. Trow, 1868/69), p. 589; (New York: John F. Trow, 1869/70), p. 599.

75   "United States Federal Census, 1870, New York, New York, Ward 20, 10th Election District, p. 19, lines 26–33," *Ancestry.com*. Kimbel had moved to 356 West 35th Street in 1868 and then to 337 West 32nd Street in 1869. *New York City Directory* (New York: John F. Trow, 1868/69), p. 589; (New York: John F. Trow, 1869/70), p. 599. These are the sources for the following three sentences as well.

76   "United States Federal Census, 1870, New York, King's County, Brooklyn, Ward 8, p. 28, lines 13–19," *Ancestry.com*; *New York City Directory* (New York: John F. Trow, 1870), p. 177. These are the sources for the following two sentences as well.

77   Cabus's Brooklyn address changed to 156 17th Street between 1871 and 1874. In 1874 he and his family moved to West 30th Street in Manhattan, near Kimbel. See *New York City Directory* (New York: John F. Trow, 1874/75), p. 186.

78   See "March 24, 1870 and April 15, 1871, New York," vol. 193, p. 700EE, R. G. Dun & Co. credit report volumes, Baker Library, Harvard Business School, Boston, MA.

79   Anton Kimbel, Design for a Chair, United States Patent 4634, issued February 7, 1871; Anton Kimbel, Design for a Chair, United States Patent 4635, issued February 7, 1871.

80   See "labor," in Kenneth T. Jackson, ed., *The Encyclopedia of New York City* (New Haven: Yale University Press; New York: New York Historical Society, 1995), pp. 646–49; M. R. Werner, "That Was New York, The Great Strike," *New Yorker* (September 28, 1946): 70–81; Howard Zinn, *A People's History of the United States* (New York: Harper Collins, 2015), pp. 240–41.

81   "The New York Strikes," *Cabinet Maker* 3, no. 6 (June 15, 1872): 44. This is the source for the following two sentences as well (see also note 19).

82   "The New York Strikes," *Cabinet Maker* 3, no. 7 (June 22, 1872): 52. This is the source for the following four sentences as well.

83   *Cabinet Maker* 5, whole no. 229 (October 10, 1874): 8.

84   See "March 12 and October 14, 1873, New York," vol. 193, R. G. Dun & Co. credit report volumes (as in note 78).

85   "Furniture," *New York Daily Tribune* (July 22–24, 1873): 3; (August 9, 26, 1873): 7; (September 2, 5, 1873): 7; (September 17, 20, 24, 1873): 11; see "Furniture," *New York Tribune* (July 31, 1873): 3; see "Furniture," *New York Herald* (July 27, 1873): 9; (July 29, 1873): 11; (August 4, 1873): 7; (August 13, 1873): 2; (August 14, 1873): 3; (August 30, 1873): 11; (September 14, 1873): 4; (September 22, 1873): 8; see "Furniture," *New York Times* (August 19, 1873): 7.

86   "Church Celebrates Centennial Today," *New York Times* (December 20, 1908): 8.

87   For a brief history of the church, see the website of the Fifth Avenue Presbyterian Church, https://www.fapc.org/history.

88   *Brooklyn Daily Eagle* (June 10, 1873): 2.

89   *Brooklyn Union* (May 10, 1875): 2.

90   Select church minutes pertaining to the Kimbel and Cabus bids and contract are excerpted in a letter by church archivist Effrieda A. Kraege, New York, to David A. Hanks, New York, October 3, 1989, Archives, Fifth Avenue Presbyterian Church, New York, NY. This letter is the reference for the following four sentences.

91   According to Fifth Avenue Presbyterian Church archivist Dale W. Hansen, records indicate that Joseph Cabus "bought" ground-floor pew number 105 on May 19, 1876 and became a member of the church on May 31, 1877. He bequeathed the pew to his daughter, Sarah P. Cabus, who had joined the church on February 10, 1876. It was transferred to her on September 30, 1898 shortly before his death on October 3, 1898.

92   Records describe an improvement without indicating if it was made by architect Carl Pfeiffer or Kimbel and Cabus.

93   For more on Edwin Oppler see the essay by Melitta Jonas in this volume.

94   "The Illustrations," *American Architect and Building News* (March 24, 1883): 139–40. According to the article, "sculptured work was done by Ellin & Kitson and some by Edward Plassman. The exterior of the building is faced with Belleville, N.J. stone. The mason's and stone-cutter's work was contracted for by James Stewart; the carpenter's work by Jennings & Brown. The painting and interior decoration was done by John. H. Mohr. The organ is furnished by Jardine & Son."

95   Bruce James Talbert, *Gothic Forms Applied to Furniture, Metal Work and Decoration for Domestic Purposes* (Birmingham: S. Birbeck; London: the author, 1867–68). See also Charles Locke Eastlake, *Hints on Household Taste* (Boston: J. R. Osgood, 1872) and the essay by Max Donnelly in this volume.

96   A colleague of Oppler, the German architect and professor Johann Heinrich Wilhelm Luer (1834–1870) also participated in the Hanoverian School of Architecture under the leadership of Conrad Wilhelm Hase. Luer's designs evidently influenced Kimbel and Cabus, for two chairs depicted in the Cooper Hewitt period inventory photos are variations of Luer's designs. See chairs number 285 and 342. We thank Wayne Mason for this insight.

97   "Gothic Revival" in "New York Trade News," *Cabinet Maker* 6, whole no. 257 (April 24, 1875): 9, 12.

98   *"Scientific and Industrial Education in the United States, An Address," Delivered before the New-York State Agricultural Society by Andrew D. White, LL.D., President of Cornell University [Revised by the Author for The Popular Science Monthly]* (New York: D. Appleton, 1874), pp. 3–23.

99   Letter from Anton Kimbel, New York, NY, to Andrew Dickson White, Ithaca, NY. May 10, 1875. Andrew Dickson White (American, 1832-1918) papers. Volume/Box: 19, Folder 4, Division of Rare and Manuscript Collections, Cornell University Library.

100   "New York Trade News," *Cabinet Maker* 6, whole no. 262 (May 29, 1875): 28.

101   "New York Fashions—House Furnishings," *Harper's Bazar* 8 (July 3, 1875): 427. This is the source for the following three sentences as well.

102   See "August 4, 1875, New York," vol. 193, R. G. Dun & Co. credit report

volumes (as in note 78). Given the Panic of 1873 and subsequent depression, it is not surprising that they did not make money that year.

103   See "Sales at Auction," *New York Herald* (November 24, 1875): 1; "Fine Arts," *Daily Graphic* (November 26, 1875): 203; "New York Trade News," *American Cabinet Maker* 6, whole no. 289 (December 4, 1875): 6.

104   *American Cabinet Maker* 6, whole no. 289 (December 4, 1875): 6.

105   The cabinet that sold for $235 was worth the equivalent of about $5,700 in 2021 and approximately two times what furniture maker C. and F. Vogel charged for a seven-piece parlor suit in 1876. See "C. & F. Vogel advertisement," in *Kimball's Book of Designs: Furniture and Drapery* (Boston: J. Wayland Kimball, 1876), p. 17.

106   See "Album 1 [Furniture designed and sold by the New York firm of Kimbel & Cabus] call number NK2435.N7K56 ca. 1875 folio," Cooper-Hewitt Rare Books Collection, Smithsonian Libraries. The album is accessible on the Smithsonian Libraries website, https://library.si.edu/ image-gallery/collection/kimbel-and-cabus. See also Steven Van Dyk, "Focus On . . . A Unique Kimbel & Cabus Furniture Album," *19th Century* 28 (Spring 2008): 30–33.

107   For discussion of Berkey and Gay's factory photo studio see Kenneth L. Ames, "Grand Rapids Furniture at the Time of the Centennial," *Winterthur Portfolio* 10 (1975): 28; and then see also "Kilian Brothers, 1875–ca. 1900" in Winterthur Library, Decorative Arts Photographic Collection; Gerald Carbone and Holy Snyder, "Gorham Silver and American Industrialism," in *Gorham Silver, Designing Brilliance, 1850–1970* (New York: Rizzoli Electa, 2019), pp. 25–26.

108   *American Cabinet Maker* 7, whole no. 286 (November 13, 1875): 8.

109   Ibid.

110   For description of the quarrel "a little seat coming again into vogue" see "Household Furniture – Minor Articles," *Harper's Bazar* (December 9, 1876): 786. According to the article, "It is frequently made of what seems like two cushions piled upon another. The use of it may be a remnant of that fashion . . . of sitting on carpets, and cushions, borrowed from the Oriental fashion." We thank Wayne Mason for this reference.

111   Some photographs are inscribed with numerical dimensions, some with dimensions preceded by a letter, and some with letters only. The photograph of sideboard number 69, for example, is inscribed at the bottom with a width of O 4' 7" and with a presumed height of T.

112   See also the essay by Max Donnelly in this volume.

113   For more on the influence of Talbert and Eastlake see the essay by Max Donnelly in this volume. Dresser's sketch for the sugar bowl is one of many daring new designs documented in his Ipswich sketchbooks of 1862–67. See Widar Halén, *Christopher Dresser* (Oxford: Phaidon, Christie's, 1990), pp. 24–25.

114   For a discussion of world's fairs see Jason T. Busch and Catherine Futter, eds., *Inventing the Modern World: Decorative Arts at the World's Fairs, 1851–1939* (New York: Skira Rizzoli, 2012).

115   Robert C. Post, ed., *1876 A Centennial Exhibition* (Washington, D.C.: National Museum of History and Technology, Smithsonian Institution, 1976), p. 103.

116   "Household Furniture – The Gothic Style," *Harper's Bazar* (April 29, 1876): 277–78. The Gothic cabinet illustrated in the article corresponds to the cabinet on the Kimbel and Cabus trade card and in the associated design drawing (see pp. 36 fig. 1, and 61 fig. 25). The Gothic chair illustrated matches chair 286 in the Kimbel and Cabus period inventory photographs.

117   Of the eight Kimbel and Cabus furniture forms exhibited at the Centennial, versions of five can be identified in the period inventory photographs. See number 73 for a related table; 317 and 359, as well as 374 and 390 for related armchairs; 330 for a related pedestal; 363 for a related cabinet; for a related desk see showroom image (pp. 98–99). For positive press see "The Centennial Exhibition. III," *Art Journal* 2 (1876): 232; George Bell et al., *The Illustrated Catalogue of the Centennial Exhibition, Philadelphia, 1876* (John Filmer, 1876), p. 75; "Furniture at the Centennial," *American Cabinet Maker* 6, whole no. 312 (May 13, 1876): 9; "Furniture Exhibitors," *American Cabinet Maker* 13, whole no. 313 (May 20, 1876): 10; "The Centennial," *American Cabinet Maker* 13, whole no. 316 (June 10, 1876): 7; "The Centennial," *Maine Farmer* (June 10, 1876): 2; "American Exhibitors," *American Cabinet Maker* 13,

whole no. 318 (June 24, 1876): 8; "Directory," Centennial supplement presented with the issue of *American Cabinet Maker* 13, whole no. 319 (July 1, 1876): 3; "Interior Perspective of a Room. Messrs. Kimbel and Cabus, Decorators," *American Architect and Building News* 1 (July 22, 1876): 237; "The Centennial Awards," as reported in a supplement published with the *American Cabinet Maker* 13, whole no. 332 (September 30, 1876): after p. xvi; "The Centennial," *American Cabinet Maker* 13, whole no. 332 (September 30, 1876): 7; Charles Wyllys Elliott, "Art Applied to Life, Seen at the Centennial," *The Galaxy. A Magazine of Entertaining Reading* 22, no. 4 (October 1876): 494; "Our Separate Plate, American Art Furniture and Decoration," *Furniture Gazette* (October 7, 1876): 216; "Design at the Centennial," *American Cabinet Maker* 13, whole no. 336 (October 28, 1876): 11; Harriet Prescott Spofford, "Medieval Furniture," *Harper's New Monthly Magazine* (November 1876): 826; "Sayings and Doings," *Harper's Bazar* 9 (November 4, 1876): 711; "After the Centennial," *American Cabinet Maker* 14, whole no. 340 (November 25, 1876): 2; "Note," *Harper's New Monthly Magazine* 54, no. 31 (December 1876): 143; "The Centennial," *Harper's Weekly* (December 2, 1876): 969–70; "Decorative Fine-Art Work at Philadelphia, American Furniture," *American Architect and Building News* 1 (December 23, 1876): 412.

118   "The Centennial," *American Cabinet Maker* 13, whole no. 316 (June 10, 1876): 7. Kimbel and Cabus are also mentioned within the context of the American Bible Society, for whom they designed and executed an ash bookcase "in Eastlake fashion" for the society's Centennial book display. See "Individual Book Exhibits," in *Centennial Exhibition Number of the Publisher's Weekly* X, 1 (July 1, 1876): 13–18. We thank Ian Ehling for this reference.

119   "American Exhibitors," *American Cabinet Maker* 13, whole no. 318 (June 24, 1876): 8. According to the article, Mr. F. B. Carrington, the proprietor of a Philadelphia cabinetmaking and decorating business and also an exhibitor, represented Kimbel and Cabus at the Centennial. The fact that Kimbel and Cabus called on a colleague for assistance illustrates the interconnected nature of the cabinetmaking industry. In August Anthony Kimbel, Jr. registered with the Centennial Bureau as representing the

firm, "The Centennial," *American Cabinet Maker* 13, whole no. 326 (August 19, 1876): 10.

120 Stefan Muthesius, "Communications between Traders, Users and Artists, The Growth of German Language Serial Publications on Domestic Interior Decoration in the Later Nineteenth Century," *Journal of Design History* 18, no. 1, *Publishing the Modern Home: Magazines and the Domestic Interior 1870–1965* (Spring 2005): 7–20. We thank Wayne Mason for this reference.

121 "Decorative Fine-Art Work at Philadelphia, American Furniture," *American Architect and Building News* 1 (December 23, 1876): 412.

122 "Interior Perspective of a Room. Messrs. Kimbel and Cabus, Decorators," *American Architect and Building News* 1 (July 22, 1876): 237. *American Architect and Building News* published two more Kimbel and Cabus designs later that year. See "Interior Designed by Messrs. Kimbel and Cabus, New York," *American Architect and Building News* 1 (September 23, 1876): 308; "Decorative Interior. Messrs. Kimbel and Cabus," *American Architect and Building News* 1 (November 25, 1876): 381. The interior illustrated in the September issue, which Kimbel and Cabus said they executed, closely relates to a design by Edwin Oppler and architect Schorbach for Prince Solms's dining room in his villa in Baden-Baden and offers evidence of Oppler's influence on their designs. See Edwin Oppler, ed., *Die Kunst im Gewerbe* (*Industrial Art*) 4, issue 1 (1875): 4.

123 "The Centennial," *Maine Farmer* (June 10, 1876): 2.

124 Charles Wyllys Elliott, "Art Applied to Life, Seen at the Centennial," *The Galaxy. A Magazine of Entertaining Reading* 22, no. 4 (October 1876): 494.

125 "Our Separate Plate, American Art Furniture and Decoration," *Furniture Gazette* (October 7, 1876): 216.

126 Their "interior of a room, and ceiling painting" was recognized for "originality of designs and execution" and "for superior workmanship in cabinet work and upholstery" in Group VII. Their "chimney-piece in wood" was "commended for symmetry and grace of design and admirable workmanship" in Group XXVII. See United States Centennial Commission, *International Exhibition, 1876*, vol. 3, *Reports and Awards:*

Group VII, ed. Francis A. Walker (Philadelphia: J. B. Lippincott, 1877–78), p. 11; United States Centennial Commission, *International Exhibition, 1876*, vol. 5, *Reports on Awards: Group XXVII*, ed. Francis A. Walker (Philadelphia: J. B. Lippincott, 1877–78), p. 47.

127 "The Centennial Exhibition. III," *Art Journal* 2 (1876): 232; George Bell et al., *The Illustrated Catalogue of the Centennial Exhibition, Philadelphia, 1876* (John Filmer, 1876), p. 75; "Our Separate Plate, American Art Furniture and Decoration," *Furniture Gazette* (October 7, 1876): 216; "Medieval Furniture," *Harper's New Monthly Magazine* (November 1876): 826; [George Titus Ferris], *Gems of the Centennial Exhibition: Consisting of Illustrated Descriptions of Objects of an Artistic Character, In the Exhibits of the United States, Great Britain, France,* [. . .] *at the Philadelphia International Exhibition of 1876* (New York: D. Appleton, 1877), p. 138; Harriet Prescott Spofford, *Art Decoration Applied to Furniture* (New York: Harper and Brothers, 1878), p. 86.

128 Harriet Prescott Spofford, "Medieval Furniture," *Harper's New Monthly Magazine* (November 1876): 809–29. Three of the four illustrations depicting Kimbel and Cabus's designs are incorrectly attributed to Pottier and Stymus in this article: "Modern Gothic Drawing-Room," p. 825; "Sideboard," p. 827; "Drawing Room," p. 828. A correction was run in the December 1876 *Harper's*: "Note.—In the paper on 'Medieval Furniture' in our November number, the modern drawing-rooms illustrated on pages 825 and 828, and the modern Gothic sideboard, on page 827, which were inadvertently credited to Messrs. Pottier and Stymus, were designed and executed by Messrs. A. Kimbel and J. Cabus, Nos. 7 and 9 East Twentieth Street, New York.—ED. HARPER'S MAGAZINE." *Harper's New Monthly Magazine* 319, vol. 54 (December 1876): 143. The correction also appears in "The Centennial," *Harper's Weekly* (December 2, 1876): 970. We thank Wayne Mason and Walter Ritchie for bringing these references to our attention.

129 "Modern Gothic Ornaments," *American Cabinet Maker* 14, whole no. 341 (December 2, 1876): 2.

130 "Interior. Messrs. Kimbel and Cabus (7 & 9 East Twentieth Street, New York, NY)," *American Architect and Building News* 2, no. 61 (February 24, 1877): 60.

131 "American Industries," *Scientific American* 43, no. 15 (October 9, 1880): cover, 223, 229.

132 For "Kimball [sic] and Cabus and Pottier & Stymus Mfg. & Upholstery" see United States Census, City of New York. Products of Industry. Tenth Census. 1880. New York. Schedule 3. Manufactures. New York State Library, Albany, pp. 126, 133.

133 For Herts Brothers and George A. Schastey, Furniture see ibid., p. 90.

134 Wood analysis undertaken in conjunction with Harry Alden of Alden Identification Service, Chesapeake Beach, Maryland, has enabled us to document many of the woods used by Kimbel and Cabus. Of the twenty-three objects sampled, most were made from cherry or American black walnut. Maple, tulip poplar, white oak, and less frequently ash and rosewood were also used.

135 A version of this sideboard can be seen in the 1877 showroom illustration in *American Architect and Building News* (see note 130 and pp. 98-99).

136 See also the essay by Melitta Jonas in this volume.

137 An ebonized music cabinet in William Turner's collection features two hand-painted panels on the lower doors, one depicting Chaucer and the other Dante. The figures are mirror images of designs emanating from the London studio of Cottier and Co., which appear on at least one ceramic plaque depicting Dante, also in William Turner's collection, as well as other commissions for stained glass and interior decoration. We do not know how Kimbel and Cabus secured the original Cottier designs, although it may have been through the New York branch of Cottier and Co., which opened in 1873. We thank William Turner and Max Donnelly for these insights. For further information see Petra Ten-Doesschate Chu, Max Donnelly, Andrew Montana, and Suzanne Veldink, eds., *Daniel Cottier: Designer, Decorator, Dealer* (London and New Haven: Paul Mellon Centre for Studies in British Art and Yale University Press, 2021), pp. 169, 195, 218 n. 123.

138 For further information on these tile manufactories see J. Austwick and B. Austwick, *The Decorated Tile* (London: Pitman House, 1980); Hans van Lemmen, *Minton Hollins Picture Tiles* (Stoke-on-Trent: Gladstone Pottery Museum, 1985);

Tiled Furniture (Princes Risborough: Shire, 1989); *Victorian Tiles* (Princes Risborough: Shire, 2000); Terrence Lockett, *Collecting Victorian Tiles* (Antique Collector's Club, 1979); Lezli Richer, "Training for Industrial Design and the Decline of Maw & Co," *Glazed Expressions* 33 (1996): 3–5; D. S. Skinner and Hans van Lemmen, eds., *Minton Tiles 1835–1935* (Stoke-on-Trent: City Museum and Art Gallery, 1984); Annamarie Stapleton, *John Moyr Smith 1839–1912: A Victorian Designer* (Shepton Beauchamp: Richard Dennis, 2002).

139   "Tiles," *Cabinet Maker* 6, whole no. 270 (July 24, 1875): 156.

140   The British firms of Collinson and Lock and Cox and Sons also used tiles and painted panels in their "art furniture." See the essay by Max Donnelly in this volume.

141   See United States Centennial Commission, *International Exhibition, 1876*, vol. 3, *Reports and Awards: Group VI*, ed. Francis A. Walker (Philadelphia: J. B. Lippincott, 1877–78), p. 50; [Charles W. Spurr advertisement], *Boston Daily Globe* (August 17, 1876): 1; "Imitation of Marquetry," *Canadian Mechanics Magazine and Patent Office Record* (September 1876): 262. For a discussion of imitation inlay and marquetry that includes Charles Spurr see Clive Edwards, "'Improving' the Decoration of Furniture: Imitation and Mechanization in the Marquetry Process in Britain and America, 1850–1900," *Technology and Culture* 53 (April 2012): 411–16. We thank Wayne Mason and Laura Vookles of the Hudson River Museum for these references.

142   We thank Joan Parcher for her insights on this subject.

143   For example, a desk in the collection of the Museum of Fine Arts, Boston (1992.6) bears a lock marked "SHANNON/PHILA." and a desk in Ann Pyne's collection (see p. 119) bears a lock marked "C. A. STOCK / NEW YORK."

144   Photocopies of three photographic plates depicting hardware seen on Kimbel and Cabus furniture are inscribed on the reverse "C. A. Stock, 118 Wooster Street" and are in curatorial files in the American Wing, Metropolitan Museum of Art, New York. The original photographs are in the collection of Childs Gallery, Boston. The *New York City Directories*, published by John F. Trow between 1870 and 1877, list Casper A. Stock, hardware at 116 and 118 Wooster Street (see p. 156).

145   For more on Oppler see the essay by Melitta Jonas in this volume. See also the entry on p. 121 for the side chair.

146   United States Centennial Commission, *International Exhibition, 1876*, vol. 3, *Reports and Awards: Group VII*, ed. Francis A. Walker (Philadelphia: J. B. Lippincott, 1877–78), p. 28; "Decorative Fine-Art Work at Philadelphia," *American Architect and Building News* 2 (January 13, 1877): 12. We thank Wayne Mason for his insights and observations about Charles R. Yandell.

147   Both a furniture maker and a distributor for smaller manufacturers, J. Wayland Kimball published an illustrated catalogue of various firms' work from which retailers could place orders on behalf of customers without having samples in stock. For Charles R. Yandall and Co. see J. Wayland Kimball, *Kimball's Book of Designs: Furniture and Drapery* (Boston: J. Wayland Kimball, 1876): pp. 3, 26–28; plates 9, 20, 26.

148   In addition, the fabric lines the coved hood of cabinet 464 and hanging wall cabinet 451.

149   See *Harper's Bazar* (April 29, 1876): 277–78; in addition to the designs for a Gothic chair and cabinet discussed in note 116, a Gothic library and window are illustrated. See note 128 for *Harper's New Monthly Magazine* (November 1876): 809–29; the fourth illustration depicts the firm's Centennial display. For another illustration of the firm's display see "The Centennial," *Harper's Weekly* (December 2, 1876): 969–70 (p. 63 fig. 28).

150   See notes 122 and 130.

151   For design drawings for the Gothic cabinet and library illustrated in *Harper's Bazar* (April 29, 1876): 277–78, see p. 61 fig. 25, and p. 77 fig. 51. For design drawings for Modern Gothic drawing rooms and sideboard illustrated in *Harper's New Monthly Magazine* (November 1876): 809–29, see pp. 64–65 figs. 29, 30, 31.

152   For more on British patrons see the essay by Max Donnelly in this volume.

153   "SALES AT AUCTION," *New York Herald* (March 25 and 26, 1877): 3 and 2 respectively.

154   "Amusements," *Evening Telegram* (March 28–9, 1878): 4; "Amusements," *New York Daily Tribune* (April 1 and 5, 1878): 3; "Amusements," *Evening Telegram* (April 4 and 5, 1878): 4 and 1 respectively. Other cabinetmakers, such as Herter Brothers

(Mark Hopkins House), offered Italian furniture to their clients as well.

155   "Household Art, The Art of Furnishing," *Harper's Bazar* 10 (June 16, 1877): 370–71.

156   As reprinted in "The Furniture Craze," *American Cabinet Maker* 15, whole no. 370 (June 23, 1877): 21.

157   "Items," *American Cabinet Maker* 16, whole no. 393 (December 1, 1877): 23. This is the reference for the following sentence as well.

158   Letter from William A. Hammond, New York, NY, to Andrew Dickson White, Ithaca, NY, September 14, 1873. Box 17, microfilm reel 14, Division of Rare and Manuscript Collections, Cornell University Library.

159   Curio, "Private Collections: Dr. Hammond's Bric-A-Brac," *Art Amateur* 1 (June 1879): 13. Kimbel and Cabus forms seen in the *Artistic Houses* photograph of Hammond's drawing room correspond to the Kimbel and Cabus period inventory photographs as follows: side chair, 304; love seat, 431; armchair, 389.

160   See Mary Jean Smith Madigan, *Eastlake-Influenced American Furniture, 1870–1890* (Yonkers, NY: Hudson River Museum, 1973); see also the Hudson River Museum website https://www.hrm.org/.

161   In the Glenview parlor view, the armchair in the foreground is a variation of forms 421 and 421a in the Kimbel and Cabus period inventory photographs and corresponds to a sofa and two armchairs with fragments of original upholstery in Wayne Mason's collection. One of the armchairs was tested by Harry Alden (see pp. 99, 207) and the frame is ebonized hard maple. Wayne Mason's suite displays printed-paper panels depicting a diaper pattern, stylized foliage, and an ibex and a stag. Both the ibex and stage derive from murals by the German painter Gisbert Munster (active 1868–70) for the Neo-Gothic Villa Cahn, built by German architect Edwin Oppler in 1868–70 in Bonn for banker Albert Cahn (see p. 146). In 1873 Oppler published images of Munster's murals in his design periodical *Die Kunst im Gewerbe* (*Industrial Art*) 2, issue 3: pl. 16–17, figs. 6, 7—the likely source of inspiration for the creator of these paper panels (see the essay by Melitta Jonas in this volume). We thank Wayne Mason for this insight. The side chair depicted at the window corresponds to number 304 or 307 in the Kimbel and Cabus period inventory photographs. In

the Glenview sitting room and library view, the side chair corresponds to numbers 28C, 421, and 421a; the corner chair to 399; the side chair to the left of the fireplace to 304 or 307; and the side chair to the right of the fireplace to 308.

162 See "W. F. Cochran's Will," *New York Tribune* (January 10, 1902): 9; see also Michael P. Rebic, *Landmarks Lost and Found: An Introduction to the Architecture and History of Yonkers* (Yonkers: Yonkers Planning Bureau, 1986).

163 William H. DeForest was born in New York, NY, in 1837 and died in Summit, NJ, on July 16, 1896. See "William H. DeForest," *Findagrave.com*. The United States Federal Censuses for 1870 and 1880 confirm his profession and that he, his wife Frances Rundel DeForest, and three children lived at Madison Avenue around 45th Street.

164 "New York Interiors. Residence of W. H. DeForest, Esq," *Art Journal* 5 (1879): 141–42. We thank Wayne Mason for this reference.

165 See "Mr. W. H. DeForest's House," in George William Sheldon, *Artistic Houses: Being a Series of Interior Views of a Number of the Most Beautiful and Celebrated Homes in the United States*, vol. 1 (New York: D. Appleton, 1883), p. 99.

166 "New York Interiors. Residence of James P. Kernochan, Esq," *Art Journal* 5 (1879): 46–47.

167 The Lorillards were prominent members of New York society and also patrons of Herter Brothers, Kimbel and Cabus's competitors. For confirmation of life dates (October 22, 1831–March 5, 1897) and profession as "retired merchant, Capitalist" and "Trus. Lorillard, Marshall and Spencer Estates" see "James P. Kernochan, Dead," *New York Times* (March 6, 1897); "James P. Kernochan," *Findagrave.com*.

168 "New York Interiors. Residence of James P. Kernochan, Esq" (as in note 166). The term Eastlake refers to a style not a maker.

169 Known for fresco painting, Stiepevich was born in Venice and trained in London at the Royal Academy. He arrived in the United States in 1872. By 1877 he had established himself in New York, NY, and worked primarily on private commissions for decorative wall paintings and frescoes. He painted exotic scenes as well as genre scenes such as this work, and exhibited paintings at the National Academy of

Design, among other prominent venues. See Catherine Hoover Voorsanger, "Dictionary of Architects, Artisans, Artists and Manufacturers," in Doreen Bolger et. al, *In Pursuit of Beauty: Americans and the Aesthetic Movement* (New York: Metropolitan Museum of Art, 1986), pp. 468–69.

170 See Colonel Emmons Clark, *History of the Seventh Regiment of New York, 1806–1889*, vol. 2 (New York: Seventh Regiment, 1890).

171 "The Seventh Regiment Armory," *New York Times* (November 14, 1879): 8, quoted in Mary A Hunting, "The Seventh Regiment Armory in New York City—Restoration of the Historic Site," *New York Magazine Antiques* (January 1999): 17–21.

172 Jay Shockley, *Landmarks Preservation Commission* (July 19, 1994), Designation List 259, pp. 2, 3, 8, 9. Shockley cites Clark 1890 (as in note 170); *New York Times* (April 10, 1880); Minutes of the Board of Officers (June 7, 1879); *Seventh Regiment Gazette* (1891–1933); Tenth Company Minutes (1895–1913); Holbrook, *A Handbook of Company K, Seventh Regiment* (New York, 1940). The room survives with relatively few alterations. The few notable changes are the covering of the original stenciled frieze, the replacement of the fireplace surround and mirror with an elaborate bronze World War I memorial tablet in 1922, and the replacement of the original gas chandelier.

173 "The Seventh Regiment Armory," *Decorator and Furnisher* 6, no. 2 (May 1885): 42–46. In contrast, Clark 1890 (see note 170), p. 1880 states that the "Tenth Company room is of oak and mahogany, quaint in design and delicate in detail."

174 Clarence Cook, *The House Beautiful: Essays on Beds and Tables, Stools and Candlesticks* (New York: Scribner, Armstrong, 1878), p. 325. Although Cook does not name the firm cited, we can deduce that it was Kimbel and Cabus.

175 See "May 4, 1880, New York" and "November 24, 1880, New York," vol. 193, pp. 700 A69, 700 A132 R. G. Dun & Co. credit report volumes (as in note 78).

176 See "May 15, 1882, New York," in vol. 193, p. 700 a/155 R. G. Dun & Co. credit report volumes (as in note 78). According to a November 1881 credit report, "the copartnership of Kimbel and Cabus will expire in May and will not be renewed." "November 21, 1881, New York," in ibid., p. 700 A132.

177 "SPECIAL NOTICES," *New York Daily Tribune* (February 15, 1882): 5. This ad ran on March 2: 5, and 12: 7; March 19 and 28: 5 and "SPECIAL NOTICES," *New York Times* (February 19, 1882): 9.

178 "Sales at Auction," *New York Herald* (April 20, 1882): 3. It was also announced in the *Evening Post* on the same date under "Special Notices."

179 For Anton Kimbel's death certificate see State of New York Certificate and Record of Death for the County and City of New York, No. 33339, September 23, 1895. For his obituary, which records the value of his estate as $200,000, see *New York Times* (October 10, 1895): 20, col. 5. He was buried at Green-Wood Cemetery, Brooklyn, lot 26651, grave 8, section 143. City directory listings indicate that in 1895 A. Kimbel and Sons move their shop to 395 Fifth Avenue, and their workshop continues to be located at 458 10th Avenue. The business is described as "house furnishers," "decorators," and "furniture makers." (*New York City Directory*, John F. Trow, 1895/96). Research into A. Kimbel and Sons is housed in the Metropolitan Museum of Art's American Wing curatorial files and the Brooklyn Museum's curatorial files.

180 See "May 15, 1882, New York," vol. 193, p. 700a/155, R. G. Dun & Co. credit report volumes (as in note 78). Regarding collaborations on interiors see Wayne Craven, *Gilded Mansions: Grand Architecture and High Society* (New York: W. W. Norton, 2009), p. 247. See also Lance Humphries and Roberta A. Mayer, "Gilding an Antebellum Baltimore Townhouse: The Lost Mansion of John Work Garrett and Mary Elizabeth Garrett," *Nineteenth Century: The Magazine of The Victorian Society in America* 39, no. 1 (Spring 2019): 19, citing McKim, Mead, and White Papers and Garrett Papers MS 797, Box 16, Maryland Historical Society, Baltimore.

181 Nina Gray and Suzanne Smeaton, "Within Gilded Borders: The Frames of Stanford White," *American Art* 7, no. 2 (1993): 34. For Joseph Cabus's death certificate see State of New York Certificate and Record of Death, New York City, No. 28437, October 4, 1898. He was buried at Green-Wood Cemetery, Brooklyn, lot 9321, grave 7-8-13-12, section 121. Research into the Cabus cabinetmaking firm is housed in the Metropolitan Museum of Art's American Wing curatorial files and the Brooklyn Museum's curatorial files.

A. Kimbel & J. Cabus, 729 East. 20th Str. New-York.

EXHIBITION OBJECTS

Author's note: In the entries, some objects with black surfaces are described in the media line as painted, while most are described as ebonized. This distinction does not reflect different techniques or materials but, instead, different approaches to acknowledging that there were many techniques used and we do not know precisely what they were. All objects examined by the Brooklyn Museum use "painted" in the medium line, and all others use "ebonized." In the entry texts, the term "ebonized" is employed according to the definition of "to ebonize," which means "to make something look black."

Harry Alden of Alden Identification Service performed wood analysis on certain objects as noted on the following pages, thus those media lines reflect the results of his study.

"Showroom illustration for A. Kimbel & J. Cabus, 7 & 9 East 20th Str. New York," *American Architect and Building News* (February 24, 1877). Collection of Andrew VanStyn

CABINET, circa 1870

This masterfully decorated monumental cabinet is emblematic of late-nineteenth-century American excess and evocative of grand exhibition pieces. Kimbel and Cabus's aspirational customers would have featured the cabinet as a dramatic focal point in their parlor or drawing room to signal their wealth and sophistication. Sumptuous woods in shades of gold, brown, red, and black combined with luminous gilded ornament created a striking effect that would have been further enriched by the display of sculptures or a garniture. The rectilinear cabinet's curving sides flank a raised pedestal and marquetry medallion above an inverted breakfront. In spite of its broad form, the storage space the cabinet affords is modest. Behind the medallion there is empty space, suggesting that visual impact was prioritized over function. The cabinet is a rare example of Kimbel and Cabus's work in the Neo-Grec style, a late-phase French classical revival style fashionable during the 1860s and 1870s, characterized by bold renditions of classical ornament, seen here in the carved acanthus leaves, fluted columns, egg-and-dart border, and incised, gilt-enriched classical vase. The central marquetry medallion, depicting a centaur and youth inspired by *The Education of Achilles by the Centaur Chiron*, a 1783 painting by Jean-Baptiste Regnault (1754–1829), as well as the marquetry side panels depicting vases amplify the classical aesthetic. Applying marquetry panels consisting of small pieces of costly woods arranged as a picture or pattern to a less costly wood surface as a decorative veneer was common in fashionable nineteenth-century furniture worldwide, an aesthetic that contrasts markedly with that of the British design reform movement and the Modern Gothic style (see the essay by Max Donnelly in this volume).[1]

When the Brooklyn Museum received the cabinet as a gift in 1945, it was accessioned as being from France. During the 1970s, curatorial exploration of the Kimbel and Cabus period inventory photographs in the Cooper-Hewitt, Smithsonian Design Museum Library led to the identification of Kimbel and Cabus as the cabinet's makers. There are six known versions of the form, which is an indication both of its popularity and of Kimbel and Cabus's success at providing customers with a wealth of options.[2] In December 1875, the *American Cabinet Maker* reported that Kimbel and Cabus had auctioned off their old stock to make way for the new. They described what may very well have been a seventh version of this cabinet, a "rich black and gilt five-foot cabinet, very rich, brass ornaments; bronze center" that was sold for $235.[3]

In the period inventory photograph the cabinet is identified as number 4, and a graphite notation of 200 may indicate the price.[*]

Rosewood, cherry, other woods, brass, gilding.
62 ½ × 19 ¼ × 68 in. (158.8 × 48.9 × 172.7 cm)

Brooklyn Museum, Anonymous gift, 45.96

1   There were many skilled craftspeople in New York City by 1870, and thus it is unclear whether the marquetry panels were made locally or imported from Europe. See Donald C. Pierce, *Art and Enterprise: American Decorative Art, 1825–1917: The Virginia Carroll Crawford Collection* (Atlanta: High Museum of Art, 1999), pp. 136–37.

2   In addition to this example, there are at least five other known versions of the form. Two, one in the High Museum of Art collection (1985.317) and the other in a private collection, share the same central marquetry panel but have different marquetry side panels. Another privately owned version has a central painted ceramic medallion and the same marquetry side panels as those on the Brooklyn Museum's cabinet. Two further examples in private collections display painted central medallions, one depicting a classical maiden, the other a cockatoo among flowers.

3   *American Cabinet Maker* 6, whole no. 289 (December 4, 1875): 6.

*   Wood analysis of this cabinet was performed by Harry Alden of Alden Identification Service.

Cabinet, from Album 1 [Furniture designed and sold by the New York firm of Kimbel and Cabus], ca. 1875

PEDESTAL, circa 1870

In late 1875, Kimbel and Cabus auctioned off their stock of "rich black and gilt" Neo-Grec furniture to raise capital as they shifted their focus from historical revivalism to the new Modern Gothic style (see p. 56).[1] Among the objects listed was a "black and gilt venetian pedestal, Egyptian head," likely a version of this form, that sold for $40. Bold renditions of classical ornament, in this case a fluted column with volutes and medallions depicting classical profiles and Egyptian-inspired elements such as the pharaonic mounts, characterize the Neo-Grec and Egyptian-revival styles. The opening of the Suez Canal in 1869 and subsequent celebrated debut of Verdi's opera *Aida* in New York City in 1873 sparked a renewed interest in Egypt and its culture. Competing furniture firm Pottier and Stymus incorporated Egyptian masks, busts, and animal heads into some of their furniture designs, perhaps inspiring Kimbel and Cabus's herme-form pedestal, with opposing busts and whimsical projecting bare feet. Prominently situated in a drawing room or parlor, the pedestal could function for the display of art, as well as signaling the owner's erudition and artistic sensibilities. Period ephemera suggests that this pedestal design was a success for Kimbel and Cabus, as a version can be seen among the furniture forms on the cover of the 1881 catalogue for Robert Mitchell Furniture Company of Cincinnati, Ohio, indicating that it had inspired imitation. A photograph of the famous actor Edwin Booth (1833–1893) portraying Cardinal Richelieu in Edward Bulwer-Lytton's play *Richelieu* incorporates a version of the pedestal, which is further evidence of the prominence and popularity of the design.

In the period inventory photograph the pedestal is identified as number 125, and a graphite notation of 46 may indicate a price.[*]

Painted hard maple, zinc, copper alloy, gilding
42 ½ × 17 ½ × 17 ½ in. (108 × 44.5 × 44.5 cm)

Brooklyn Museum, Gift of the American Art Council, 86.81

1   See "Sales at Auction," *New York Herald* (November 24, 1875): 1; "Fine Arts," *Daily Graphic* (November 26, 1875): 203; "New York Trade News," *American Cabinet Maker* 6, whole no. 289 (December 4, 1875): 6.

*   Wood analysis was performed by Harry Alden of Alden Identification Service.

PHOTO. BY SARONY.   ARTOTYPE, E. BIERSTADT, N. Y.

BOOTH AS RICHELIEU

Edward Bierstadt (German 1824–1906),
Edwin Booth as Richelieu in "Richelieu"
Photomechanical print, 3 ½ × 5 ¼ in.
(8.89 × 13.33 cm). University of Illinois
Theatrical Print Collection, B725te-45

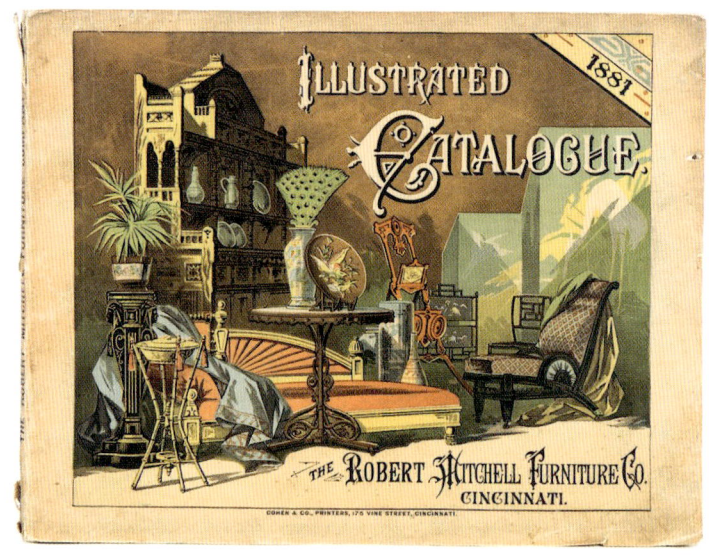

Catalogue of the Robert Mitchell
Furniture Co., Cincinnati (1881)

Pedestals, from
Album 1 [Furniture
designed and sold by
the New York firm of
Kimbel and Cabus],
ca. 1875

TABLE, circa 1874

Given prominence in the foreground of Kimbel and Cabus's 1876 Philadelphia Centennial display, a version of this rectangular table was one of eight forms selected by the firm to represent its finest work (see p. 59, fig. 23). In revealing its own construction, evident in the bold mortice and tenon joints connecting the aprons and stretchers, the table exemplifies Kimbel and Cabus's embrace of Modern Gothic tenets as espoused by British architects and designers A. W. N. Pugin and Bruce James Talbert. Pugin and Talbert praised medieval furniture, of which the latter said "the wood is solid, the construction honestly shewn, and fastened by tenons, pegs, iron clamps, nails, &c."[1] Yet the canted, spiral-carved legs and the scrolling foliage, carved in low relief on the apron panels and in higher relief at the leg joins, enliven the table's rectilinear form. It has antecedents in German vernacular furniture from the Bavarian town of Tolz. Illustrations of a Tolz table, with which Anton Kimbel may have been familiar, were published in European and U.S. design journals targeting cabinetmakers and upholsterers during the 1860s and 1870s, including by North American critic Clarence Cook in his column for *Scribner's Monthly* in April 1877 (see p. 108).[2] Cook stated, "A few years ago, Messrs. Kimbel & Cabus made several tables after a design similar to this, but they were decorated with carving rather than painting, and this made them more costly. I remember, however, that they were very pretty, and seemed all the prettier for breaking up the monotony of New York furniture shops with something altogether new on this side of the water." Perhaps it was the allure of the new that enticed Andrew Dickson White, Cornell University cofounder and its first president, to acquire a version of Kimbel and Cabus's table, along with four side chairs and an armchair, for the house he commissioned in 1871 in Ithaca, New York (see p. 55, fig. 19). The quarter-sawn tabletop, constructed to match the wood's grain pattern, is accented by an incised scrolling foliate border that incorporates symbols representing carpentry and woodworking tools in each of the four corners.[3]

In the period inventory photograph, the table is identified as number 73 and a graphite notation of 70 may indicate the price.[*]

American black walnut, cherry, metal.
30 × 43 ½ × 31 in.
(76.2 × 110.5 × 78.7 cm)

Collection of Ann Pyne

1 Bruce James Talbert, *Gothic Forms Applied to Furniture, Metal Work and Decoration for Domestic Purposes* (Birmingham: S. Birbeck; London: the author, 1867–68), p. 1.

2 "Nr. 27 n. 28 Sogenannte Tölzer Möbel," *Gewerbehalle, Organ für d. Fortschritt in allen Zweigen d. Kunst-industrie* 2 (1864): 31; "Meubles de la fabrique de Toelz, Tyrol Bavarois," in Rodolphe Pfnor, *Ornementation Usuelle de Toutes Les Époques dans les Arts Industriels et en Architecture* 37 (Paris: A La Librairie Artistique De E. Devienne Et Cie. Éditeurs, 1866): 37; "Table and Chair with painted Ornament for a garden Pavilion," *Cabinet Maker's Album* 2 (New York, 1871): 27; "Cut No. 7 is a copy . . ." in "Beds and Tables, Stools and Candlesticks," *Scribner's Monthly* 12, no. 6 (April 1877): 820. Special thanks to Wayne Mason for these references.

3 The symbols depict carpentry squares, a compass and square, and a mallet and chisel, all of which were associated with architecture, carpentry, and woodworking, but also with masonic symbolism. There is a second version of this table in private hands with a leather top, matching carpentry symbols in the corners, and a different scrolling foliate pattern on the apron.

* Wood analysis was performed by Harry Alden of Alden Identification Service.

Table and Chair from Tyrol, Bavaria.
No. 78.

Clarence Cook, *The House Beautiful: Essays on Beds and Tables, Stools and Candlesticks* (New York: Charles Scribner's Sons, 1881), p. 255

Table (detail), ca. 1874

Table, key cabinet, side chair, from Album 1
[Furniture designed and sold by the New
York firm of Kimbel and Cabus], ca. 1875

HANGING KEY CABINET, circa 1874

With elements derived from Gothic architecture such as a peaked gable, foliate trefoil finial, columns, crockets, and lacey tracery, this elaborate hanging cabinet, intended for the storage of keys, is a transitional object in Kimbel and Cabus's production. It is from the period in which they shifted from historical revivalism to the clean-lined, rectilinear Modern Gothic aesthetic advocated by British architect and designers Bruce James Talbert and Charles Locke Eastlake. Displayed in a foyer or entrance hall, the cabinet would have signaled a homeowner's embrace of the fashionable Gothic revival style. Fluidly carved interlacing foliate tendrils at the peaked top and pendant base demonstrate the virtuosity of the firm's craftspeople, who were highly accomplished carvers and spared no effort in the creation of this object. A calligraphic metal hinge and escutcheon amplify its overall richness. Another example of the key cabinet in oak resembles a version displayed in the Kimbel and Cabus showroom (see pp. 98-99) and illustrates variations on the foliate carving, columns, pendants, finals, and hardware.

The key cabinet is identified as number 74 in the period inventory photograph, and a graphite notation of 25 may indicate the price.

Rosewood, oak, and pine secondary woods, metal
38 ¼ × 12 ³⁄₁₆ × 3 ½ in.
(96.5 × 31.1 × 8.9 cm)

Collection of Associated Artists, LLC

Hanging key cabinet, ca. 1875. Oak, metal
41 ¾ × 12 ⅞ × 5 ½ in.
(106 × 32.7 × 14 cm).
The Metropolitan Museum of Art, Sansbury-Mills Fund, 1981. 1981.211

SIDE CHAIR, circa 1875

In her April 1876 article for *Harper's Bazar* on "The Gothic Style," critic Harriet Prescott Spofford prominently illustrated a version of this side chair.[1] With straight, chamfered members secured by prominent mortice-and-tenon joints, the chair epitomizes the "honest" or revealed construction promoted by British architects and designers Bruce James Talbert and Charles Locke Eastlake. In fact, some of the mortice and tenon joints are simulated, and thus reveal Kimbel and Cabus's interpretation of Modern Gothic ideals in style, if not entirely in practice. The chair displays angled legs, an openwork back with a splat pierced by quatrefoils, and stiles carved with geometric motifs at the top rail joints. The distinctive use of angled stiles and rear legs is characteristic of many of the firm's chairs (see pp. 121, 125) and was inspired by German architect Edwin Oppler's chair designs for Marienburg Castle, Schulendburg (see p. 31, fig. 6). In 1872, Oppler published images of his chair designs in his periodical *Die Kunst im Gewerbe* (*Industrial Art*) and credited the architect Georg Gottlob Ungewitter (1820–1864) with the design.[2] Ungewitter aimed to create a chair that was sturdy, comfortable, and aesthetically pleasing, which he achieved by setting the back of the chair and rear leg at angles. The arrangement makes a strong yet light and graceful support. Kimbel and Cabus were not the only firm to appreciate Oppler's designs. Working for the Chicago furniture maker Frederic W. Krause, German cabinetmaker Henry Rumpke (active 1870s, died 1876) created a version that closely matched Oppler's design, with the addition of a decorative apron under the front seat rail. Rumpke appears to have brazenly claimed credit for the design by applying for a patent.[3]

Evidently Andrew Dickson White, a cofounder and first president of Cornell University, appreciated this design, for three of the chairs can be seen in a photograph of his reception room (see p. 55, fig. 19).

In the period inventory photograph the chair is identified as number 286, and a graphite notation of 8–10 may indicate the price.

Walnut, needlepointed textile
36 ⅜ × 16 ⅝ × 21 ½ in. (92.4 × 42.2 × 54.6 cm)

The Metropolitan Museum of Art, Gift of Marco Polo Stufano, in honor of Deedee and Barrie A. Wigmore, 2001, 2001.67

1   "Household Furniture – The Gothic Style," *Harper's Bazar* (April 29, 1876): 277–78.

2   "Gothische Stühle, entworfen vom Baurath Oppler in Hannover," *Die Kunst im Gewerbe* (*Industrial Art*) 1, issue 1 (1872): pl. 5, fig. 2.

3   Henry Reupke's patent number 166,555 for an improvement in chairs, to which he was assignor for himself and Frederick W. Krause, was granted on August 10, 1875. The Brooklyn Museum's version of Krause's chair, 87.19, is impressed on the back of the crest rail: PAT'D AUG. 10 1875 / MANUF'D BY / F.W. KRAUSE / 47 W. WASHINGTON ST. / CHICAGO.

Side chair, from Album 1
[Furniture designed and
sold by the New York firm
of Kimbel and Cabus],
ca. 1875

Frederick W. Krause
(American, born Germany,
1829–?). "Star" Side Chair,
patented August 10, 1875.
Walnut, paint, modern
caning, 38 × 17 ¼ × 17 ½ in.
(96.5 × 43.8 × 44.5 cm).
Brooklyn Museum, H.
Randolph Lever Fund, 87.19

PEDESTAL, circa 1875

A version of this ebonized pedestal was one of the eight forms chosen by Kimbel and Cabus to represent their best work at the 1876 Philadelphia Centennial Exhibition (see p. 59, fig. 23). Although it seems to have been exhibited without supporting an object, an illustration published in the *American Architect and Building News* of July 1876 depicts the pedestal with a sculpture of Diana of the Hunt as the focal point of the firm's celebrated display (see p. 62, fig. 27). To the aspirational customer, the message was clear: the display of artworks was integral to the artistic home and, furthermore, revealed what you knew of the world and your place in it. For their customers, Kimbel and Cabus created myriad forms that were both functional and fashionable in themselves and in their decoration, such as: revolving bookcases and music stands, and easels and pedestals for the display of art.

One of eleven pedestals documented in the Kimbel and Cabus period inventory photographs, this example is evocative of a Gothic baptismal font as well as an hourglass.[1] Supported by four bracket feet separated by carved trefoils, a central rectangular shaft—surrounded by four slender columns with foliate capitals—rises from a pyramidal base. The shaft supports a tapered form echoing the springer of a Gothic arch, surmounted by a square top with canted sides and corners. The ebonized surface is incised with signature Kimbel and Cabus ornament—sharp-edged, stylized foliate motifs including spiraling tendrils, spear-tipped leaf forms, and zigzags enriched with gilding. With gilt accents, its dark tone would have created a dramatic contrast with a white marble or Parian sculpture, or a work in bronze. A variation of this pedestal is also illustrated in the Kimbel and Cabus period inventory photographs. Although the variation retains the same overall arrangement of central shaft and surrounding columns, it is a pared-down version of the design that is more aligned with the Anglo-Japonesque taste characteristic of the Aesthetic Movement.[2] Turned elements replace the foliate capitals, and bands of geometric printed-paper decoration replace the incised, gilded decoration. This is evidence of the firm's ceaseless adaptability to consumer demand.

In the period inventory photograph the pedestal is identified as number 330, and a graphite notation of 35 may indicate the price. The second pedestal is identified as number 444.

Ebonized wood, gilding
Height: 41 ¹⁵⁄₁₆ in. (106.6 cm)

The Toledo Museum of Art, Purchased with funds from the Florence Scott Libbey Bequest in Memory of her Father, Maurice A. Scott, 1987.220

1   Joel Rosenkranz, R. Ruthie Dibble, and Avis Berman, *The Art of Display: The American Pedestal, 1830–1910* (New York: Conner-Rosenkranz, 2018), p. 30.

2   Ibid., p. 33.

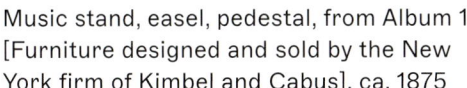

Music stand, easel, pedestal, from Album 1
[Furniture designed and sold by the New
York firm of Kimbel and Cabus], ca. 1875

DESK, circa 1875

A version of this desk featured prominently in Kimbel and Cabus's display at the 1876 Philadelphia Centennial (see p. 59, fig. 23) and was also positioned in the foreground of their showroom illustration in the *American Architect and Building News* of 1877 (see pp. 98–99). In comparison to the firm's monumental drop-front desks, this form is petite, and the relatively large number of extant examples suggests its success.[1] Sprightly canted front legs recall Kimbel's 1871 design patent (see p. 50, fig. 13) and energize an otherwise rectilinear form with mortice and tenon-joined stretcher and rails. Two lower cabinets, with carved linenfold side panels, flank the kneehole below the fold-out desktop that lifts to reveal a storage compartment. The upper section consists of three alcoves, topped by small drawers and a central architectonic, upright square cabinet with a sloping roof. Possibly inspired by tastemaker Charles Locke Eastlake's illustration in *Hints on Household Taste* (1867), the roof lifts to reveal a storage compartment.[2] Chamfered edges, carved quatrefoils, and incised geometric and scrolling foliate borders enliven the surface of the desk. An incised open book on the desktop and elaborate, scrolling hinges on the cabinet doors add visual interest. Surviving examples include walnut, oak, and ebonized versions, as well as one with an unusual white finish.[3] The white desk displays an openwork arcade between the lower and upper sections that is also seen on the version exhibited by Kimbel and Cabus at the Centennial, evidence of the myriad modifications the firm made to designs in order to produce varied offerings.

This desk descended in the family of New York financier and railroad director Charles Handy Russell (1796–1884) whose initials "CHR," in addition to "33778 Store," are inscribed on the back. A member of the social elite, Russell divided his time between a Fifth Avenue residence in New York City and a villa, "Oaklawn," in Newport, Rhode Island.[4] Although nothing further is presently known about the provenance of the desk, Russell's social spheres included individuals such as New York money manager James P. Kernochan (1831–1897), owner of the "Seaview" residence in Newport and newly identified as a Kimbel and Cabus client.[5] Affluent, style-conscious consumers, undoubtedly attracted by Kimbel and Cabus's Centennial success, were also attuned to one another's decorating and furnishing choices.[6]

Walnut, metal
57 × 36 ½ × 30 in.
(144.8 × 92.7 × 76.2 cm)

Collection of the Mint Museum, Charlotte, NC, Museum Purchase: Exchange Funds from the Gift of Harry and Mary Dalton, 2000.116.1

1   In addition to these two examples, there are versions of the desk in the following collections: Baltimore Museum of Art, 1998.1358; Los Angeles County Museum of Art, 88.4a-b; Metropolitan Museum of Art, 2000.58; Museum of Fine Arts, Boston, 1992.6; Newark Museum, 2005.41A-F; Saint Louis Art Museum, 206:2017; Smithsonian, National Museum of American History, 1980.689.1; Sweetbriar College; and two and a half examples in private collections.

2   Charles Locke Eastlake, *Hints on Household Taste* (Boston: J. R. Osgood, 1872), p. 131. The British edition was first published in 1867, followed by further editions.

3   Wood analysis was performed by Harry Alden of Alden Identification Service.

4   Charles Howland Russell, *Memoir of Charles H. Russell, 1796–1884* (New York 1903), pp. 50–2, https://archive.org/details/memoirofcharlesh00russ.

5   "Cottage Life at Newport," *New York Herald* (July 19, 1873): 8. See also the essay by Barbara Veith and Medill Higgins Harvey in this volume.

6   The Sweetbriar version was acquired at auction from the estate of Samuel J. Tilden, former governor of New York.

Desk, circa 1875. American black walnut, metal, 59 × 36 ½ × 20 ¼ in. (149.9 × 92.7 × 51.4 cm). Collection of Ann Pyne

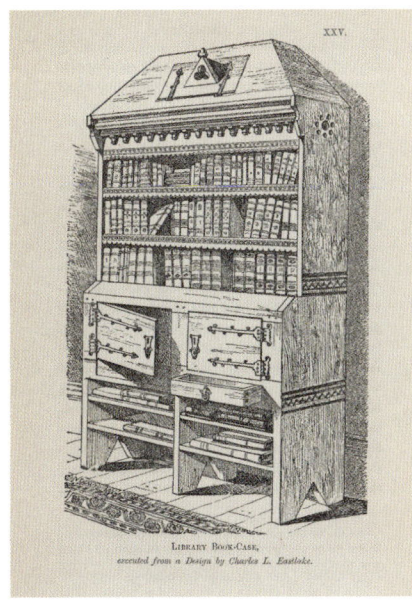

Charles Locke Eastlake, *Hints on Household Taste* (Boston: J. R. Osgood, 1872), p. 131

SIDE CHAIR, circa 1875

The number of known examples of this chair suggest it was popular with clients. Versions of it can be seen in period images documenting the fashionable domestic interiors of James P. Kernochan, a New York City money manager; Andrew Dickson White, cofounder and first president of Cornell University; and John Bond Trevor, a New York City stockbroker (see pp. 55, 80–81, 122). The Fifth Avenue Presbyterian Church in New York City retains an armchair version of this chair in its chancel (see p. 53, fig. 17). With rectilinear lines, a row of turned baluster spindles between the chair back and seat, and inventive angled rear legs derived from German architect Edwin Oppler's designs, the chair signaled the owner's preference for progressive taste. It was versatile, serving as part of a dining or parlor suite.

Unlike the tufted and fabric upholstered versions of the chair depicted in the Kimbel and Cabus period photographs, this example retains its exceedingly rare original red leather upholstery, now faded. It is stamped with abstract gilded rosettes within a diamond-shaped trellis, while a horizontal band, enclosing three short vertical bands of rosettes, bisects the design at the chair's back.[1] The fact that the upholstery is leather, a material considered appropriate for the dining room during this period, suggests that this chair was part of a dining suite. Kimbel and Cabus may have acquired the leather from Charles R. Yandell and Company, located nearby at 744 Broadway (see the essay by Barbara Veith and Medill Higgins Harvey in this volume). Yandell's firm "received the highest award" at the 1876 Philadelphia Centennial Exhibition for figured leatherwork and claimed to be "the only [firm] . . . having facilities for doing this artistic work in the country."[2] Their advertisement in J. Wayland Kimball's illustrated furniture catalogue, *Kimball's Book of Designs: Furniture and Drapery*, published in 1876, describes leather tapestries in "fifty different Diamond and Square Line Patterns, Highly Embossed and Picked Out in Gold" that could be "enlarged or contracted to suit all sizes of Chairs, Sofas, etc.," offering further evidence that Yandell was the likely source.

In the period inventory photographs, the side chair is identified as 212 with a graphite notation of 11 which may indicate the price and 304 with a graphite notation of 12.

Ash, original stained patent and gilt leather
35 ½ × 18 ½ × 21 in. (90.2 × 47 × 53.3 cm)

Brooklyn Museum, Purchased with funds given by the Wigmore Foundation, 1998.46

1   A different chair form—an armchair—that is numbered 361 in the period inventory photographs displays part-leather upholstery impressed with a similar rosette.

2   Advertisement for Charles R. Yandell and Co. in J. Wayland Kimball, *Kimball's Book of Designs: Furniture and Drapery* (J. Wayland Kimball: Boston, 1876), p. (3). This is the reference for the following sentence as well.

Dining-room.—Residence of James P. Kernochan, Esq.

"New York Interiors. Residence of James P. Kernochan, Esq." *Art Journal* 5 n.s. (1879): 46-47

Armchair and side chair, from Album 1 [Furniture designed and sold by the New York firm of Kimbel and Cabus], ca. 1875

ARMCHAIRS, circa 1875

These two innovative armchairs, from different sets, exemplify Kimbel and Cabus's vigorous chair designs. The example on page 127 displays the overall design and the dynamic diagonal front legs patented by Kimbel on February 7, 1871 (see the essay by Barbara Veith and Medill Higgins Harvey in this volume and p. 50, fig. 13). The down-turned diagonal legs, attached to the back stiles under the seat and secured by additional stretchers to each other and the front underside of the seat, are a defining characteristic of the firm's seating furniture and energize an otherwise restrained rectilinear form incised with stylized foliate motifs. The chair opposite exhibits distinctive angled rear legs, an adaptation of German architect Edwin Oppler's chair designs (see p. 31, fig. 6). Mortice and tenon joints between the H-stretcher reveal the construction, and segmented, turned legs and striking free-standing armrests connect to the sides of the seat.[1] Pointed aprons incised with geometric motifs add visual interest to the sides of the chair. According to a July 1875 article on "New York Fashions" published in *Harper's Bazar*, in which Kimbel and Cabus were acknowledged along with Herter Brothers and L. Marcotte and Company for providing insights, chairs for dining rooms, halls, and libraries were "upholstered with leather, plain or stamped, in bright colors or sombre, either brown, dark green, or crimson" while the wood was "most usually black-walnut, though there is a fancy for oak suites."[2] Aesthetic preferences as well as cost considerations may have dictated the selection of wood. Dining chair sets or suites typically included two armchairs and up to a dozen side chairs.

In the period inventory photograph, armchair number 284 has a graphite notation of 8, which may indicate a price, and the matching side chair is illustrated but not identified by number. Armchair number 282 has a graphite notation of 14, and the matching side chair is number 283½ with a graphite notation of 8. Below the chairs, ink notations indicate that 282 is "45 plain leather" and 283½ is "23 plain leather," likely indicating the cost of the upholstery.

American black walnut, leather
35 ⅝ × 23 × 23 ¾ in.
(90.5 × 58.4 × 60.3 cm)

Collection of Andrew VanStyn

Ash, leather, brass
39 × 20 ⅞ × 20 ¼ in.
(90.5 × 58.4 × 60.3 cm)

Museum gift in loving memory of Robert Kaufmann, by his sister Catherine Tatum. Cooper-Hewitt, Smithsonian Design Museum, Smithsonian Institution, 2009-45-2

1   Wood analysis of the chair on p. 125 was performed by Harry Alden of Alden Identification Service.

2   "New York Fashions: House Furnishing," *Harper's Bazar* 8 (July 3, 1875): 427.

Armchair, from Album 1
[Furniture designed and
sold by the New York firm
of Kimbel and Cabus],
ca. 1875

Armchair and side chair,
from Album 1 [Furniture
designed and sold by the
New York firm of Kimbel
and Cabus], ca. 1875

SOFA, circa 1875

An example of Kimbel and Cabus's creativity and inventiveness, this visually arresting sofa is a paradox. The everted arms and canted legs suggest adjustability or flexibility, but the bold mortice and tenon joints securing the legs and rails render motion impossible. A row of turned spindles separates the sofa back from the seat. Incised zigzags on the rails and sharply cut stylized flowerheads at the joints punctuate the form while emphasizing its structure. As documented in the period inventory photographs, the sofa was part of a suite that included an armchair and a side chair. By ingeniously inverting German architect Edwin Oppler's angled rear chair leg, seen in its original form on the side chair, the firm created sofa and armchair designs that are related but different, and surprisingly forward-looking (see p. 31, fig. 6). In the Kimbel and Cabus reinterpretation, the shape of the angled rear chair legs from Oppler's design are adapted to become the everted arms on the sofa, and his back stiles become the canted sofa legs. Even with the design turned upside down, Oppler's observation that an angled rear leg makes a chair (or, in this case, a sofa) sturdy and aesthetically pleasing remains relevant.

A series entitled "The Homes of America," published in the *Art Journal* in 1878, features an illustrated profile of "Old Morrisania," the ancestral home of U.S. politician and diplomat Gouverneur Morris (1752–1816), then owned by his son, in what was at the time Westchester County, New York. An illustration of the reception room depicts the striking armchair version of this form, seen from the back, prominently placed in the center of the room on a fur rug, facing a blazing hearth. The room was described as having had "modern Eastlake judicious restorations" that "have added the freshness, and safety, and comfort of today."[1]

In the period inventory photographs the sofa is number 213, and a graphite notation of 25 may indicate a price. The armchair is number 211 with a graphite notation of 18, and the side chair is number 212 with a graphite notation of 11.*

American black walnut, modern textile
32 × 70 × 27 in. (81.3 × 177.8 × 68.6 cm)

Collection of Ann Pyne

1   M.E.W.S., "The Homes of America. 'Old Morrisania'," *Art Journal* 4 (1878): 81–85.

*   Wood analysis was performed by Harry Alden of Alden Identification Service.

Sofa, from Album 1
[Furniture designed and
sold by the New York firm
of Kimbel and Cabus],
ca. 1875

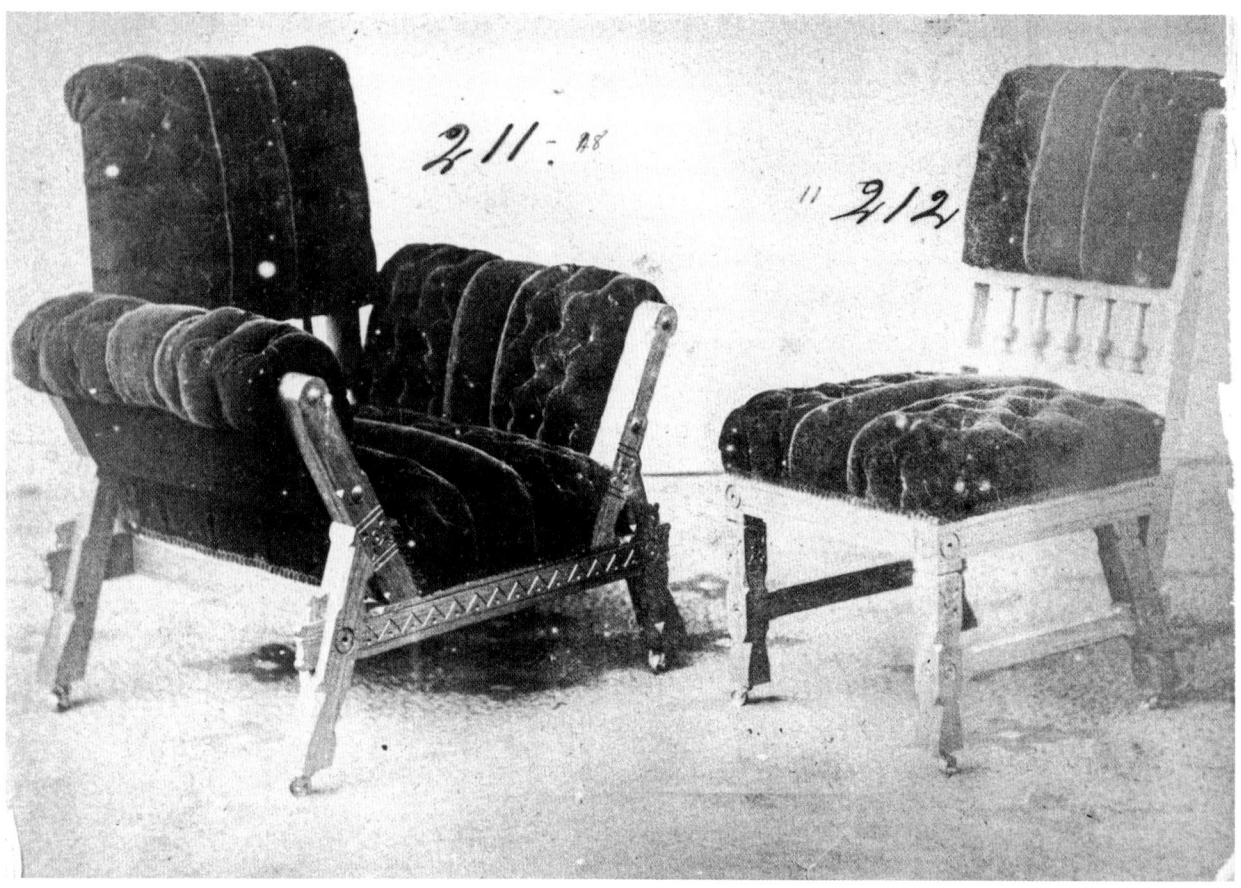

Armchair and side chair, from Album 1
[Furniture designed and
sold by the New York firm
of Kimbel and Cabus],
ca. 1875

Reception Room, " Old Morrisania."

M. E. W. S., "The Homes of
America. 'Old Morrisania',"
Art Journal 4 (1878): 81–85

ARMCHAIR, circa 1875

This robust armchair, with its rectilinear, ebonized frame, was part of a suite of furniture, consisting of a sofa, armchairs, and side chairs, that would have made a dramatic impression when displayed as a whole in a drawing room or parlor.[1] According to a July 1875 article on "New York Fashions" in *Harper's Bazar*, for which Kimbel and Cabus, along with Herter Brothers and L. Marcotte and Company, were consulted, "Ebony is the wood selected for great drawing rooms, especially when they are fitted up somewhat in medieval fashion. It is used in the whole suite of furniture; appears in the straight backs, arms, and clawed feet of long sofas and deep square chairs."[2] Because ebony was costly, less expensive wood was ebonized—stained or painted black—to emulate it. Of the seven suites documented in the Kimbel and Cabus period photographs, this example displays the most vigorous carved Gothic ornamentation in the form of bold, blind quatrefoils between the side rails, bands of pyramidal forms, and roaring lion masks on the front arm posts. Rows of turned baluster spindles studded with pyramidal bosses create a lively interplay of light and shadow, or solid and void, by separating the chair back and arms from the seat and sides. The effect is continued with the turned upper chair rail, from which the upholstered back appears to be suspended. As per the observations in *Harper's Bazar*, in some examples of the suite "the decorations for brightening this solemn wood are gilt traceries" that would have glimmered in daylight or gaslight for further animation. A version of the armchair may be seen in the fashionable Gothic style library designed by Kimbel and Cabus for leading New York City silk wholesaler William H. DeForest (see p. 84, fig. 61).

In the period inventory photograph, the armchair is identified as 306 and a graphite notation of 28 may indicate the price.

Ebonized wood
34 ¼ × 26 ½ × 25 ¼ in.
(87 × 67.3 × 64.1 cm)

Collection of Andrew VanStyn

1   The sofa is identified as 305 with a graphite notation of 30 and the side chair as 307 with a graphite notation of 15.
2   "New York Fashions: House Furnishing," *Harper's Bazar* 8 (July 3, 1875): 427.

Armchair and side chair, from Album 1 [Furniture designed and sold by the New York firm of Kimbel and Cabus], ca. 1875

CORNER CHAIR, circa 1875

This corner chair, with its arresting angularity and dramatic ebonized surface, resembles Anglo-Japonesque furniture forms, as well as examples by the progressive English architect and designer Edward William Godwin (1833–1886), whose reductive forms presaged the taste for abstraction that characterized early-twentieth-century modern furniture design. Incised, gilt-enriched decoration on the stiles and rails creates a luminous contrast with the ebonized surface and highlights the structure. British designer and theorist Christopher Dresser's amusing grotesques (see p. 20, fig. 11) published in *Studies in Design* (1874–76) inspired the fanciful motifs of paired mice and birds on printed-paper panels on the chair's back. Dresser stated that "in ornament humor finds expression in the grotesque" and that "the grotesque must reveal, by its nature or formation, knowledge on the part of its producer."[1]

Less expensive than hand-painted panels or ceramic tiles, the printed-paper panels were a cost-effective means of amplifying the design reform vocabulary embodied by the chair. Customers could also purchase a related two-seated *vis-à-vis* (see p. 71, fig. 40). With their striking forms and imaginative iconography, these fashionable seating pieces attested to the owner's progressive tastes.

In the period inventory photograph, the corner chair is identified as number 399, and a graphite notation of 20 may indicate the price. The *vis-à-vis* is identified as number 417 with a graphite notation of 36.*

Painted soft maple, gilding, paper, copper alloy, rubber, modern textile
27 ½ × 18 ½ × 18 ½ in.
(69.9 × 47 × 47 cm)

Brooklyn Museum, Bequest of DeLancey Thorn Grant in memory of her mother, Louise Floyd-Jones Thorn, by exchange, 1992.9

1   Christopher Dresser, *Studies in Design* (London: Cassell, Petter and Galpin, 1874–76), pp. 33–34.
*   Wood analysis was performed by Harry Alden of Alden Identification Service.

Corner chair, from Album 1 [Furniture designed and sold by the New York firm of Kimbel and Cabus], ca. 1875

ARMCHAIR, circa 1875

The pared-down ebonized elements of this striking geometric armchair create a visually engaging interplay of positive and negative space. Gilt-enriched incised lines and stylized flowerheads emphasize the chair's horizontal and vertical lines. Rectangular diaper-printed paper-decorated panels form the sides between the rail and seat rail, and rows of turned baluster spindles create visual interest along the openwork arms. On the front and back, the rectangular back splat displays printed-paper panels depicting Medieval-inspired figures personifying "Wisdom" as a scholar and "Folly" as a jester, both derived from designs by British painter and designer Charles Rossiter (1827–1897) for Minton and Company tiles and found on ebonized British furniture (see the essay by Max Donnelly in this volume). Replicating Rossiter's patterns on printed-paper panels was a less expensive means of achieving a fashionable British aesthetic than marquetry, intricate carving, or even transferware tiles. In contrast to Kimbel and Cabus's sumptuous suites of upholstered sofas, armchairs, and side chairs, this armchair was a singular statement piece that would have captured attention through its progressive form and decoration.

In the period inventory photograph the armchair is identified as number 401, and a graphite notation of [?22] may indicate the price.

Ebonized cherry, gilding, paper, modern textile
35 × 20 ¼ × 24 ½ in.
(88.9 × 51.43 × 61.59 cm)

The Metropolitan Museum of Art, Promised Gift of Barrie A. and Deedee Wigmore, L.2019.66.30

Table and armchair, from Album 1 [Furniture designed and sold by the New York firm of Kimbel and Cabus], ca. 1875

TABLE, circa 1875

This ebonized rectangular table richly decorated with printed-paper panels of flowers and butterflies, bands of geometric motifs, and abstract medallions is another manifestation of German architect Edwin Oppler's influence on Kimbel and Cabus's designs (see Melitta's essay). As editor of *Die Kunst im Gewerbe* (*Industrial Art*), a German design periodical published between 1872 and 1878 under the direction of the Hanoverian Association of Architects and Engineers, Oppler promoted European Medieval and Renaissance works of art, "the rich treasures of our fatherland," and Gothic revival designs of his own and others as sources of artistic inspiration.[1] His table design for Marienburg Castle, published in *Die Kunst* in 1872, evidently inspired this Kimbel and Cabus form, of which the firm made large and small versions (see p. 141). Oppler had reinterpreted a fourteenth-century table and honored the original construction principals, but modified the appearance. In turn, Kimbel and Cabus retained Oppler's overall design, adding a second stretcher below the tabletop and shifting the visually engaging x-shaped stretcher down to the feet. The printed-paper panels of flowers and butterflies were a cost-effective means of emulating Oppler's richly carved and reticulated side panels. Everted scroll supports placed at intervals underneath the edge of the tabletop also echo Oppler's design.

Kimbel and Cabus created fewer tables than case pieces and seating furniture. Of the fifteen tables illustrated in the period photographs, six are large in scale and the remainder are smaller tiered forms and accent pieces.

In the period inventory photograph (see p. 136) this table is number 400, and a graphite notation of 35 may indicate the price.

Ebonized wood, gilding, paper, metal
30 ⅞ × 42 × 27 in.
(78.4 × 106.7 × 68.6 cm)

Collection of Barrie and Deedee Wigmore

1 *Die Kunst im Gewerbe* (*Industrial Art*) 1, issue 1 (1872): 1–2.

Edwin Oppler, *Die Kunst im Gewerbe* (*Industrial Art*) 1, issue 2 (1872): pl. 8, fig. 6 (detail)

3. Sophatisch,
entworfen vom Baurath Oppler in Hannover.

REVOLVING BOOKSTANDS, circa 1875

These striking ebonized revolving bookstands are two of the myriad smaller forms, including easels, pedestals, and music stands, that Kimbel and Cabus created as functional and fashionable accent pieces for the display of art, music, and literature in the home. As book publishing flourished during the last quarter of the nineteenth century, so too did private libraries. Although Kimbel and Cabus also made large bookcases, portable revolving bookstands allowed owners to have books at hand, perhaps even the latest home-decorating manuals, in the parlor or drawing room. In the "artistic" home, an appreciation of literature and music, along with the display of art objects, demonstrated cultural awareness and refinement.

The largest of the eight revolving bookstands illustrated in the Kimbel and Cabus period photographs was "illuminated with colored traceries" and displayed an elaborately carved owl finial (p. 56, fig. 20).[1] A three-tiered example (opposite) with an angular silhouette, balustrades of turned spindles, incised, gilt-enriched decoration, and six ornamental printed-paper medallions depicting pointed quatrefoils was created in two sizes, of which this example is the larger.[2] A squat, cylindrical bookstand (see p. 145) with six side openings for books is one of three variations of this form.[3] Zigzag borders and printed-paper panels depicting musicians based on Minton and Company's tile designs encircle the sides.

In the period inventory photographs, the three-tiered example is number 392, and a graphite notation of 35 may indicate the price. The cylindrical example is number 427 with a graphite notation of 35.

Ebonized wood, paper
37 ⅞ × 22 ¼ in.
(96.2 × 56.5 cm)

Collection of Barrie and Deedee Wigmore

Ebonized cherry, paper, metal
30 × 20 in.
(76.2 × 50.8 cm)

Museum of Fine Arts, Boston, Gift of Barrie A. and Deedee Wigmore, 2020.384

1   "New York Fashions – House Furnishings," *Harper's Bazar* 8 (July 3, 1875): 427.

2   There is another example of this form in a private collection with grotesque panels in the style of Christopher Dresser.

3   There are two further examples of this form in private collections with decoration on the circular top. One has printed-paper panels of classical figures centering a geometric roundel and the other displays the same decoration in metal relief. There is another version depicted in the parlor of Joseph B. Thresher's home in Dayton, Ohio, designed by Edward Colonna, circa 1885–88. See the essay by Martin Eidelberg in *E. Colonna*, exh. cat. (Ohio: Dayton Art Institute, 1983), p. 11, fig. 7. I thank Nonie Gadsden, Museum of Fine Arts, Boston, for this reference.

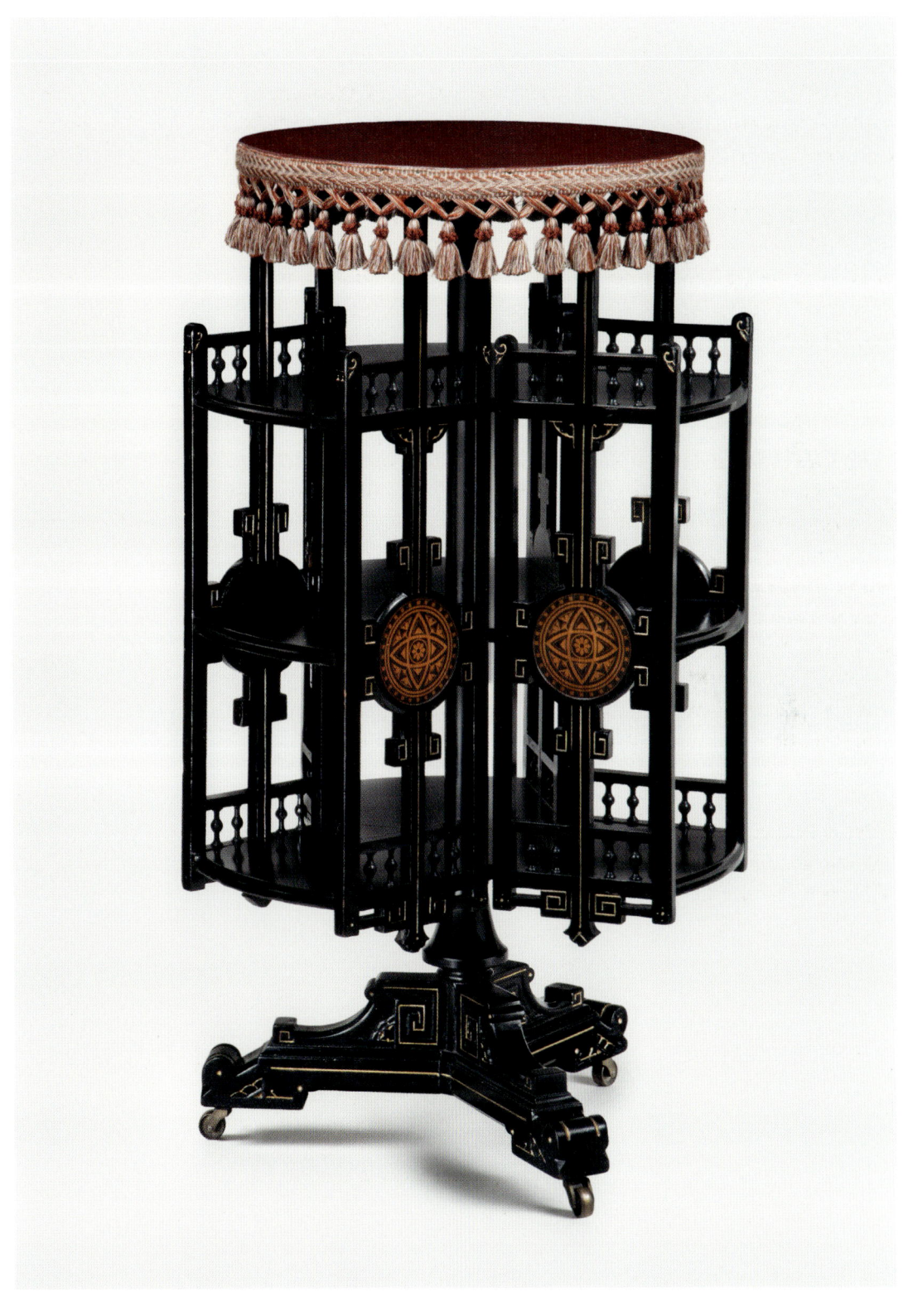

Pipe shelf and revolving
bookstands, from Album 1
[Furniture designed and sold
by the New York firm of
Kimbel and Cabus], ca. 1875

Hanging wall cabinet and
revolving bookstand, from Album 1
[Furniture designed and sold by
the New York firm of Kimbel and
Cabus], ca. 1875

MUSIC STAND and WALL POCKET, circa 1875

To provide artful storage and decorative accents for fashionable interior décor, Kimbel and Cabus created quirky, smaller accent pieces, as exemplified by this ebonized music stand and wall pocket. In a drawing room or parlor, music stands functioned as repositories for sheet music and folios. With its exaggerated vertical elements balanced by horizontal supports that create a harmonious grid, Kimbel and Cabus's upright version evokes Anglo-Japonesque furniture forms. It consists of a lower cabinet with interior storage and double doors on the front and back, and an upper shelf with H-form openwork sides and turned balustrades that terminate in stylized animal masks with drop rings. The doors, secured by squat, pointed metal hinges, and the sides of the cabinet display a total of six printed-paper panels depicting Medieval-style male musicians, each playing a different instrument, based on the British firm Minton and Company's popular tile designs.[1] The printed-paper panels were a cost-effective means of decorating a small form with eye-catching, not to mention appropriate, iconography. The music stand bears a Kimbel and Cabus label underneath the base, a rare instance of the firm labeling its furniture.

A printed-paper panel depicting a Medieval-style musician also features prominently on an ebonized baluster wall pocket utilized for the discreet storage of pencils, pens, notes, gloves, or other small personal items. The rectangular compartment displays a printed-paper panel depicting a scene of figures in an arbor drinking wine, reading books, playing a lute, and relaxing, placed within a geometric double border. The scene derives from murals of grape harvesting and winemaking by the German painter Gisbert Munster (active 1868–70). These murals decorated the neo-Gothic Villa Cahn, built by German architect Edwin Oppler between 1868 and 1870 in Bonn for banker Albert Cahn. In 1874, Oppler published images of Munster's murals in his design periodical, *Die Kunst im Gewerbe* (*Industrial Art*), the likely source of inspiration for the creator of this paper panel (see p. 149 and the essay by Melitta Jonas in this volume). The striking small wall pocket illustrates Kimbel and Cabus's inventive melding of British and Continental European design sources to create distinctive objects for a North American audience.

In the period inventory photograph, the music stand is number 328, and a graphite notation of 32 may indicate the price (see p. 117). The wall pocket is number 408 with a graphite notation of 10.*

Ebonized cherry, paper, gilding, brass
36 ½ × 23 × 13 ¼ in.
(92.7 × 58.4 × 33.7 cm)

The Metropolitan Museum of Art, Promised Gift of Barrie A. and Deedee Wigmore, L.2019.66.32

1   The musicians are playing a harp, a viol, drums, a portable organ-like instrument, a viol da Gamba, and double pipes.
*   Wood analysis of the wall pocket was performed by Harry Alden of Alden Identification Service.

Ebonized cherry, paper, metal
22 ⅝ × 16 ⅜ × 5 ⅛ in.
(57.5 × 41.6 × 13 cm)

Collection of Andrew VanStyn

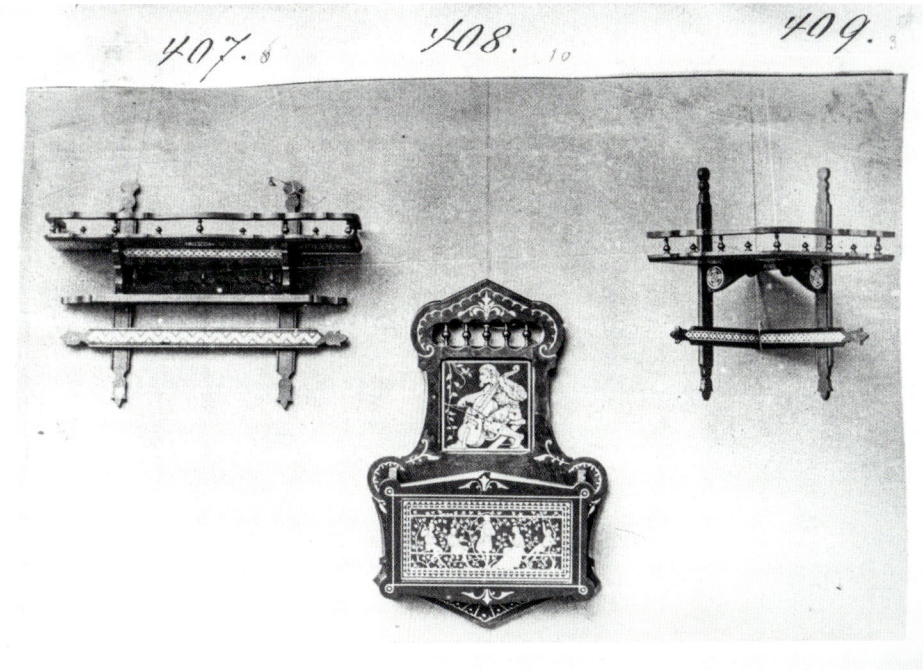

Hanging shelves and wall pocket, from Album 1 [Furniture designed and sold by the New York firm of Kimbel and Cabus], ca. 1875

Edwin Oppler, *Die Kunst im Gewerbe* (*Industrial Art*) 3, issue 3 (1874), pl. 9, fig. 9

HANGING CABINET, circa 1875

Although Kimbel and Cabus's hanging wall cabinets served many purposes, the majority, including this ebonized rectilinear example, were intended for the display of artistic objects in the drawing room or parlor. Ceramic, glass, and metal objects adorned cabinets, étagères, and side-boards. A hanging wall cabinet was ideal for displaying smaller works. This cabinet has four shelves: a shallow bottom shelf; a middle shelf with central alcove flanked by two painted panels depicting Medieval-style figures "Wisdom" and "Folly" in the guise of a scholar and jester; and two upper shelves with partial turned balustrades. Printed-paper geometric borders horizontally accent the front edges of the shelves. Tiles for Minton and Company by British painter and designer Charles Rossiter (1827–1897), as seen on an ebonized cabinet by the British firm of Cox and Son, were the source of inspiration for these fashionable but less expensive painted panels (see the essay by Max Donnelly in this volume).

In contrast to Kimbel and Cabus's richly carved, incised, and embellished case pieces, the twenty-seven hanging wall cabinets recorded in the firm's inventory photos are distinguished by eclectic silhouettes, turned elements, and ebonized surfaces enriched with visually engaging printed-paper panels depicting a range of motifs. This formula ensured that Kimbel and Cabus produced a wide range of options at lower cost to attract customers.

Two variations on this cabinet appear in the period inventory photo-graphs. One, numbered 426, has a graphite notation of 36 that may indicate price, and on the other, numbered 422, the graphite notation is obscured.*

Painted cherry, gilded and painted wood panels, paper, metal
34 × 30 7/8 × 7 3/16 in.
(86.4 × 78.4 × 18.3 cm)

Brooklyn Museum, Promised gift of Dr. Barry R. Harwood

*   Wood analysis was performed by Harry Alden of Alden Identification Service.

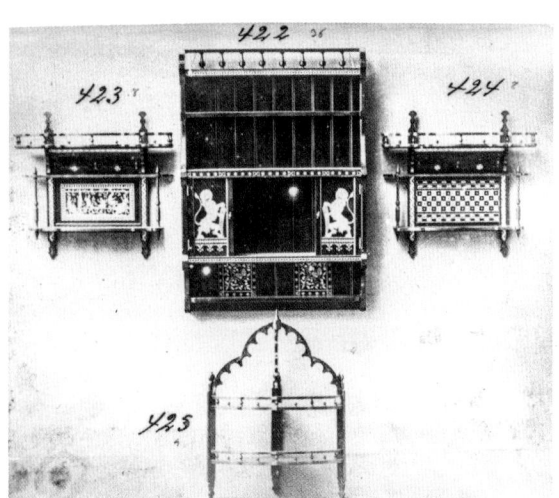

Hanging shelves and wall cabinet, from Album 1 [Furniture designed and sold by the New York firm of Kimbel and Cabus], ca. 1875

PEDESTAL, circa 1875

This ebonized square pedestal, shaped like a pavilion with openwork sides featuring carved, graphic flowerheads and foliage, exemplifies Kimbel and Cabus's interpretation of the Anglo-Japonesque style and demonstrates their ability to simultaneously work in a variety of styles to satisfy a range of tastes. Four compressed spring-like turned columns with differing carved foliate capitals rise from the balustraded square base to support the waisted pedestal top. The decision to make each capital different illustrates the firm's meticulous attention to detail, as well as its openness to whimsy. The latticework panels of conventionalized flowerheads and foliage, reminiscent of and perhaps inspired by those created by competitor firm Herter Brothers, form the aprons. A version of the pedestal, on which a tazza and vase are displayed, can be seen in the foreground of the saleroom illustration in the February 24, 1877 issue of the *American Architect and Building News* (see pp. 98-99). Among predominantly Modern Gothic style furnishings, the pedestal is a harbinger of changing taste as the Anglo-Japonesque style enjoyed increasing popularity during the late 1870s and early 1880s. It bears the firm's paper label under the base, a rare and notable feature, as most Kimbel and Cabus works are not labeled.

There are two variations of this form in the Kimbel and Cabus inventory photographs: one displays a less expensive decorative scheme using panels bearing a geometric checkerboard motif in place of the carved and pierced side panels; the other is raised on bracket feet.

In the period inventory photographs the number for the checkerboard version of this form is 442, and a graphite notation of 36 may indicate a price. The other version is number 384 with a graphite notation of 45.[1]

Ebonized wood
30 × 14 ½ × 14 ½ in.
(76.2 × 36.8 × 36.8 cm)

Collection of Barrie and Deedee Wigmore

1   Wood analysis of the pedestal on p. 155 was performed by Harry Alden of Alden Identification Service.

Pedestal (detail),
ca. 1875

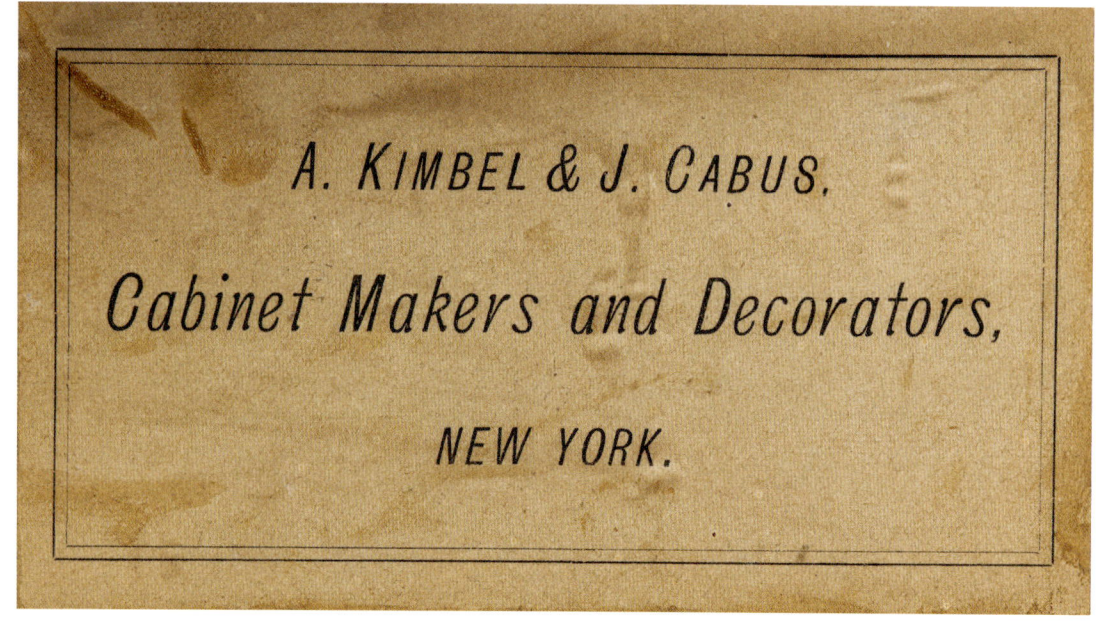

A. KIMBEL & J. CABUS.

Cabinet Makers and Decorators,

NEW YORK.

Label, ca. 1875

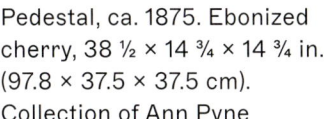

Pedestal, ca. 1875. Ebonized
cherry, 38 ½ × 14 ¾ × 14 ¾ in.
(97.8 × 37.5 × 37.5 cm).
Collection of Ann Pyne

Pedestals and screen, from
Album 1 [Furniture designed
and sold by the New York firm
of Kimbel and Cabus],
ca. 1875

HUMIDOR, circa 1875

The metal hardware hinges, drawer pulls, and escutcheons that Kimbel and Cabus employed on their furniture forms were produced by various makers, and were most likely obtained from New York City purveyors such as C. A. Stock (see the essay by Barbara Veith and Medill Higgins Harvey in this volume). Made from brass and nickel-plated silver with differing finishes, Kimbel and Cabus's hardware choices range from complex cast examples with detailed ornament to simple stamped forms with bold outlines. The firm must have provided the fabricator specifications in the case of this unusual and visually engaging casket-form humidor, for the metal mounts conform precisely to the shape of the piece, emphasizing its structure. The stamped diamonds and spiraling foliage with pointed leaf tips on the humidor's sides recall the abstracted patterns of British theorist and designer Christopher Dresser. The stylized trefoil hinges on the top, however, are more ornamental than structurally essential, and reference hinges seen on German architect Edwin Oppler's furniture designs for Marienburg Castle (see the essay by Melitta Jonas in this volume). This thoroughly Modern Gothic object, a humidity-controlled receptacle for cigars raised on four canted feet, would have been a fashionable accessory in a dining room or library. This humidor is depicted in the Kimbel and Cabus showroom image in the *American Architect and Building News* of 1877 (see pp. 98–99).*

American black walnut, brass-plated nickel
8 ⅛ × 18 × 10 ¼ in. (20.6 × 45.7 × 26 cm).

Brooklyn Museum, Purchase gift of Deedee and Barrie Wigmore, 2017.7

*   Wood analysis was performed by Harry Alden of Alden Identification Service.

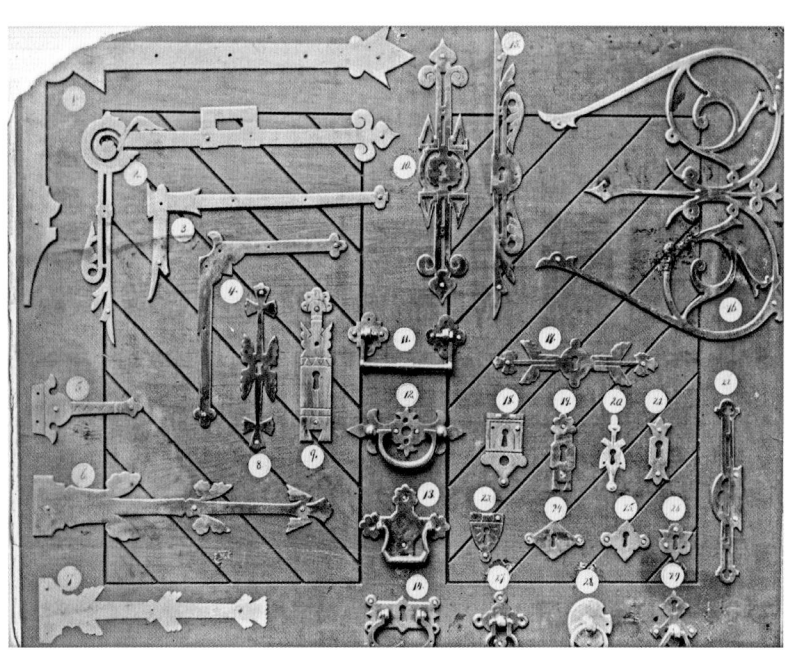

Hardware, C. A. Stock, New York, ca. 1875. Otto Heinigke Archive, Childs Gallery, Boston, MA

HANGING WALL CABINET, circa 1875

Evidently inspired by British architect Bruce James Talbert's cupboard design for British cabinetmaker Holland and Son's acclaimed display at the Paris *Exposition Universelle* of 1867, also illustrated as plate number 24 in Talbert's *Gothic Forms Applied to Furniture* published that same year, Kimbel and Cabus designed a pair of hanging wall cabinets, of which this is one example (see p. 161). In emulating Talbert's design, Kimbel and Cabus retained the overall rectilinear form with its shallow bottom shelf, the projecting central cupboard with double-doors and carved quatrefoils flanked by bisected columns with foliate capitals, and the top shelf with sloping sides terminating in carved owls. However, in place of Talbert's richly carved details and marquetry, the firm utilized less labor-intensive, and therefore more cost-effective, decorative motifs such as incised scrolls, bands of pyramidal projecting forms, carved zigzags, and elaborate cast metal strap hinges. In addition, the incised quatrefoils on the Kimbel and Cabus cabinet doors bear traces of polychrome decoration that at one time enriched the carved surfaces. In Vincent G. Stiepevich's painting *Victorian Interior* (1880), painted panels on a cabinet in the living room of James P. Kernochan, a New York money manager and a Kimbel and Cabus patron, hint at the scintillating effect of these colorful accents (see detail of the painting p. 160). The illustration of the firm's showroom in the *American Architect and Building News* in 1877 includes a version of this hanging cabinet on the wall (see pp. 98–99).*

White oak, paint, metal
49 ¾ × 29 × 11 ¼ in.
(126.4 × 73.7 × 28.6 cm)

Collection of Andrew VanStyn

*   Wood analysis was performed by Harry Alden of Alden Identification Service.

Vincent Stiepevich (American, born Italy, 1841–after 1910). *Victorian Interior*, 1880 (detail of painting, p. 85, fig. 62). Oil on paper, 10 × 14 in. (25.4 × 35.6 cm). Collection of Ann Pyne

Hanging wall cabinet
(detail), ca. 1875

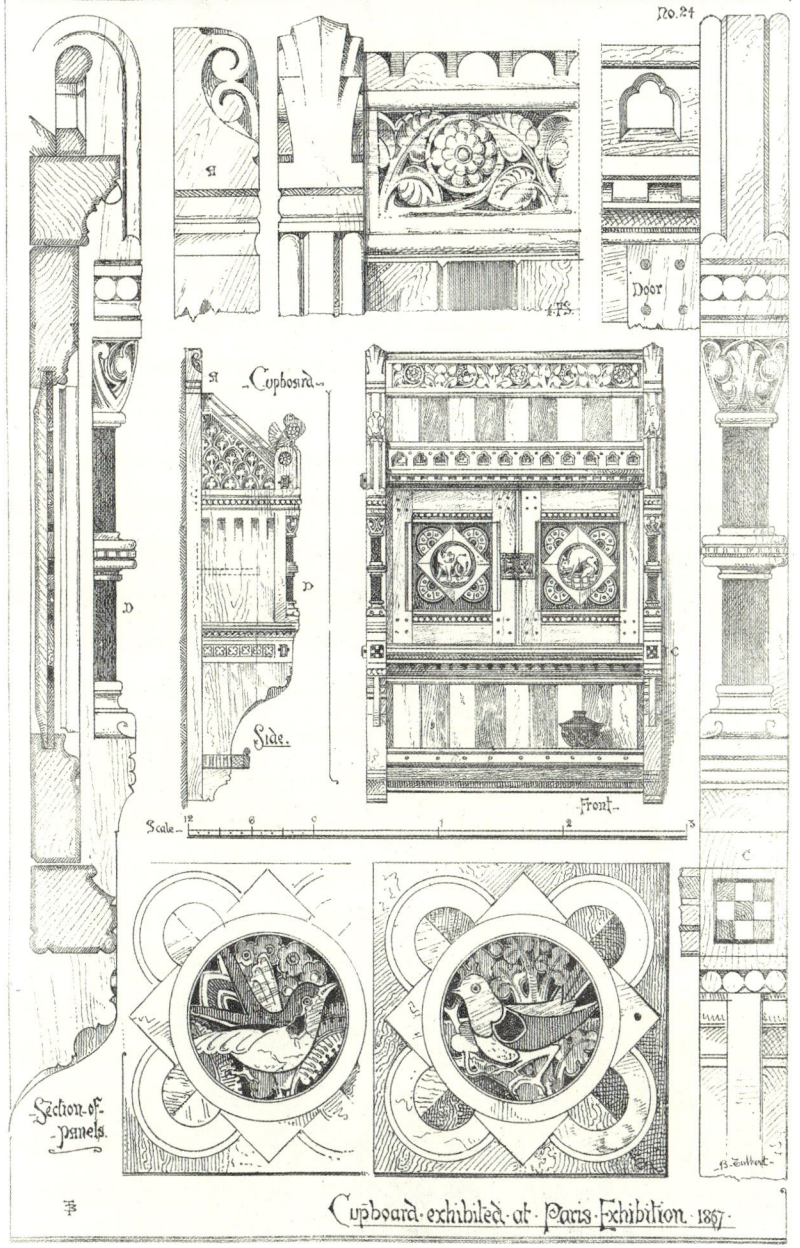

Bruce James Talbert, *Gothic
forms applied to Furniture,
Metalwork, and Decoration
for Domestic Purposes*
(Boston: J. R. Osgood, 1873),
plate 24

BED, HEAD AND FOOT BOARDS, circa 1875

In addition to rich case pieces and sumptuous upholstered seating furniture, Kimbel and Cabus offered "plain" furniture that was "within reach of all," according to their advertisements.[1] Because high-end objects were more likely to be kept, and thus endure over time, there are few known examples of their "plain" work. The labeled bedroom set—consisting of twin beds, a nightstand, washstand, and chest of drawers—of which this head and footboard are a part, is a rare survivor that provides some insight into the plainer aspect of the firm's production.[2] The restrained wood forms are incised and sharply carved with stylized flowerheads and pointed leaves, x-marks over circles, chiseled diamonds, reeded circular sunbursts, zigzags, and lines characteristic of Kimbel and Cabus's ornamental vocabulary. The panel-and-frame headboard boasts the most elaborate decorative scheme, consisting of a carved rising sun at the crest rail, with a pierced row of stylized flowers, flanked by incised flowerhead panels below and bedposts incised with stylized flowerheads and compressed turned cylindrical finials. In both form and decoration Kimbel and Cabus's bed resembles one by another maker illustrated and praised by critic Clarence Cook in *The House Beautiful* for exemplifying "how a bedstead may be simply treated and look pretty."[3]

Oak

Headboard: 58 ½ × 41 ⅞ × 2 ⅝ in. (148.6 × 106.4 × 6.7 cm)

Footboard: 31 ½ × 41 ⅞ × 2 ⅝ in. (80 × 106.4 × 6.7 cm)

Collection of Richard Pabst and Pamela Bradley

1   Advertisement in the *New York Observer and Chronicle* (May 14, 1868): 160.

2   The inside of the footboard is stenciled "450," an identification number. The nightstand and washstand bear the firm's rare paper labels.

3   Clarence Cook, *The House Beautiful* (New York: Scribner, Armstrong, 1878), p. 275.

Clarence Cook, *The House Beautiful: Essays on Beds and Tables, Stools and Candlesticks* (New York: Charles Scribner's Sons, 1881), p. 275

ÉTAGÈRES, circa 1875

Three versions of the same visually arresting étagère, two ebonized and one walnut (see pp. 8, 165, and 166), illustrate Kimbel and Cabus's inventive recombination of form and ornament to create a variety of wares for their customers. Designed for the display of art and books, these progressive forms were quintessential signifiers of the artistic home. The eccentrically shaped étagère consists of a broad lower body or carcass supported by a trestle base, with two vertical cabinets that flank two open shelves and support a narrower two-door upper cabinet with a turned balustrade at the top back. The étagère displays clean, rectilinear lines achieved through plank, panel, and frame construction; they are punctuated at intervals on the lower cabinet doors and sides by pointed projections and animated carved animal masks. Incised lines and geometric motifs—such as zigzags, "x"s and "o"s, multiple diamonds within larger diamonds, triangles within spheres, and stylized flowerheads and pointed leaves—emphasize the horizontal lines and enliven the form. On the ebonized versions incised motifs are gilt-enriched; however, one version (p. 8, fig. 1) is inset with British Minton and Company tiles depicting various birds, and the other version (p. 166) is decorated with printed-paper panels inspired by British designer Christopher Dresser's grotesques, as well as abstracted Anglo-Japonesque botanical motifs. By substituting printed-paper panels for tiles, Kimbel and Cabus presented a less expensive but equally stylish option for their customers. The walnut version of the étagère is inset with ceramic tiles by British maker W. B. Simpson and Sons (1833–present), and the incised motifs bear traces of polychrome decoration in blue and red (see p. 165). A critic writing for Harper's Bazar described objects "illuminated" by "mediaeval traceries of blue and scarlet" as being equally appealing to those in black and gold.[1] All three étagères display variations of the elaborate hardware, brass on the ebonized versions and nickel-plated metal on the walnut version, employed by Kimbel and Cabus on their most ornate forms.[*]

In period inventory photographs the étagère is identified as Number 244, and graphite notations of 90 and 160 may indicate prices for different versions.[2]

American black walnut, earthenware, metal, paint.
60 ½ × 41 ½ × 15 ¾ in. (153.7 × 105.4 × 40 cm)

Collection of Ann Pyne

Ebonized cherry, gilding, paper, metal
61 ³⁄₁₆ x 44 ½ × 15 ¾ in. (155.4 × 113 × 40 cm)

Collection of Helen Hersh and Charles Sporn

1 "New York Fashions, House Furnishing," *Harper's Bazar* 8 (July 3, 1875): 427.

2 In addition to these three étagères, there are at least three other versions of this form, and one variation, in private collections. There is also a closely related drop-front desk in the Munson-Williams-Proctor Arts Institute collection (92.34). A second version of the desk is in a private collection.

* Wood analysis was performed by Harry Alden of Alden Identification Service.

Étagère (detail), ca. 1875

Étagère (detail), ca. 1875

Étagère, from Album 1
[Furniture designed and
sold by the New York firm
of Kimbel and Cabus],
ca. 1875

DESK, circa 1875

Kimbel and Cabus's designs were informed not only by the work of the British architects and designers Talbert, Eastlake, and Dresser, but also by German architect Edwin Oppler and other members of the Hanoverian school of architecture. Oppler served as editor of the design journal *Die Kunst im Gewerbe* (*Industrial Art*), published between 1872 and 1878, which was a rich source of inspiration for the firm. Another notable source was *Die Gewerbehalle* (*The Workshop*), a design journal published between 1863 and 1884 under the direction of Professor Wilhelm Baumer of the Stuttgart Polytechnic and draftsman Julius Schnorr.

This monumental, tripartite drop-front desk, the most architectonic form depicted in the period inventory photographs, illustrates the creative ways in which Kimbel and Cabus drew from these different design sources to create astonishing new furniture forms. The rectilinear outline of the desk, achieved through plank, panel, and frame construction, is enlivened by elaborately pierced, carved, incised, and turned details. The upper section, evocative of a Swiss chalet or a cuckoo clock, displays a peaked "tiled" roof, a gable carved with scrolling foliage, arched openings below square panels pierced with circles, and a mirror-backed, baluster gallery; a design for a summer house published in *Die Gewerbehalle* in 1868 is a possible source for the unusual upper portion of the desk (see p. 170). A pair of delicately carved opposing stags flank a tree on the central drop-front, which opens to reveal the writing surface and interior storage compartments; a medieval-style cabinet stenciled with a similar stag motif illustrated in *Die Kunst im Gewerbe* (*Industrial Art*) in 1875 is likely a source for this part of the desk's design. Two open shelves with two more sloped "tiled" roofs, diamond-pierced sides, and turned balustrades at the front flank the drop-front. On the bottom section, vertical side cabinets with doors displaying carved squirrels flank a double-doored, glass-paned cabinet, below a trefoil alcove. The woodland creatures that ornament the desk evoke eighteenth and nineteenth-century Germanic vernacular "Black Forest" furniture, which frequently integrated carved animal figures into its forms.

In the period inventory photographs the desk is identified as number 380, and an ink notation of 135 may indicate the price.*

American black walnut, tulip poplar, metal
79 ½ × 42 × 14 ¼ in.
(201.9 × 106.7 × 36.2 cm)

Collection of Andrew VanStyn

*   Wood analysis was performed by Harry Alden of Alden Identification Service.

Desk with squirrels
(detail), ca. 1875

Desk with stags and squirrels
(detail), ca. 1875

*Gewerbehalle, Organ fuer d. Fortschritt in allen Zweigen
d. Kunstindustrie* 3 (1868): 40

Desk with stags (detail),
ca. 1875

Edwin Oppler, *Die Kunst im Gewerbe*
(*Industrial Art*) 4, issue 1 (1875): pl. 3, fig. 5

Desk, from Album 1 [Furniture
designed and sold by the New
York firm of Kimbel and Cabus],
ca. 1875

DESK, circa 1875

This imposing, tall, and broad drop-front desk typifies the substantial forms, or "massive work" endorsed by British architect and designer Bruce James Talbert (1838–1881) for the hall, dining room, or library of a Modern Gothic home, to which they contributed "severity, size and dignity."[1] Both functional and fashionable, the rectilinear desk has a panel-and-frame construction divided into four clearly delineated horizontal sections: a lower cabinet and drawer; a sloping drop-front that opens to reveal the writing surface and interior storage compartments; and an upper cabinet flanked by columns with foliate capitals and turned baluster finials that appear to pierce the sloping sides of the blind gallery at the top. Inset battens enhance visual interest, centering turquoise tiles on the upper and lower cabinet doors, and an incised shield on the desk front ensures the form is neither rigid nor ponderous. Incised foliate and geometric motifs, including blind trefoils carved in low relief at the top, further enrich the surface, evidence of the wealth of decorative techniques Kimbel and Cabus employed to enliven their designs. The brilliant Minton and Company tiles, depicting abstracted botanical motifs or scenes from British designers John Moyr Smith's *Shakespeare* series and C. O. Murray's *Spirit of the Flowers* series, exemplify the "new turquoise glaze tiles in Persian style" described in the *Cabinet Maker* as being adaptable to any style of furniture.[2] Together, the tiles and bold nickel-plated brass hardware create a dramatic contrast with the desk's rich black walnut surface. Elaborate hinges and escutcheons fulfill Talbert's dictum that "when metal work is used" it performs "some purpose . . . either strengthening, or as hinges or bands."[3]

In the period inventory photograph, the desk is identified as number 381 and a graphite notation of 85 may indicate the price.

Black walnut, nickel-plated brass, earthenware
68 ⅜ × 32 ⅛ × 21 ½ in.
(173.67 × 81.6 × 54.61 cm)

The Museum of Fine Arts, Houston, Museum purchase funded by the Interior Resource Centre Benefit Fund, 87.191

1   Bruce James Talbert, *Gothic Forms Applied to Furniture, Metal Work and Decoration for Domestic Purposes* (Birmingham: S. Birkbeck; London: the author, 1867–68), p. 3.

2   "Tiles," *Cabinet Maker* 6, whole no. 270 (July 24, 1875): 156. See pp. 70–71 for full quote.

3   Talbert (as in note 1).

Desk, from Album 1
[Furniture designed and
sold by the New York firm
of Kimbel and Cabus],
ca. 1875

DESK, circa 1875

A Modern Gothic interpretation of British medieval cabinet forms, this massive oak drop-front desk also references the eighteenth-century French *secrétaire à abattant*, as well as clean-lined Central European Biedermeier desk designs with which Anton Kimbel would have been familiar. Oak was, according to British architect and designer Charles Locke Eastlake, "by far the best wood to use both for appearance and durability," and considered an appropriate choice for Modern Gothic library and dining-room furniture.[1]

The rectilinear desk, achieved through panel and frame construction, is divided horizontally into four sections: lower cabinets and a drawer; a drop-front flanked by columns with foliate capitals that opens to reveal a writing surface and storage compartments; an upper drawer; and a blind gallery at the top. Incised bands of geometric ornament and abstracted botanical motifs emphasize the horizontal compartmentalization of the form. A central quatrefoil enclosed by scrolling foliage and spiraling tendrils carved in low relief creates visual interest on the drop-front that relieves the form's overall severity. Two carved owls, symbols of wisdom appropriate for a desk, perch on either side of the blind gallery at the top. Displaying a wealth of cast ornamental detail, the eccentrically shaped nickel-plated hinges, drawer pulls, and escutcheons are among the most elaborate examples utilized by Kimbel and Cabus and confirm this piece to be an expensive object. William F. Cochran, secretary and treasurer of the Smith Carpet Mills in Yonkers, New York and a notable philanthropist, owned a version of this desk, as can be seen in a photograph of his library at Duncraggan (see p. 83, fig. 59).

A variation on the form illustrates that it could be reinterpreted as a cabinet, with central doors in place of the desk. This version displays carved armorial trophies on the door panels, variations on the carved capitals and owls, and nickel-plated bracket hinges. Such modifications illustrate the ways in which Kimbel and Cabus altered and recombined elements to produce an almost infinite variety of offerings.[2]

The desk is identified as number 382 in the period inventory photograph, and graphite notations may indicate that two versions, priced at $195 and $215, were available.

Oak, nickel-plated metal (probably bronze)
65 × 32 × 18 ½ in. (165.1 × 81.3 × 47 cm)

Cooper-Hewitt, Smithsonian Design Museum, Museum purchase from Smithsonian Institution Collections Acquisitions Program and Walter Scholz Memorial Funds, 1997-42-1-a/e

1   Charles Locke Eastlake, *Hints on Household Taste* (Boston: J. R. Osgood, 1872), p. 129.

2   Wood analysis of the desk seen on p. 179 was performed by Harry Alden of Alden Identification Service.

Desk, from Album 1
[Furniture designed
and sold by the New
York firm of Kimbel
and Cabus], ca. 1875

Cabinet (detail), ca. 1875

Cabinet, ca. 1875. White oak, metal, 66 ¾ × 32 × 18 ½ in. (169.5 × 81.3 × 47 cm). The Nally-Stufano Collection

DESK, circa 1875

This delicate ebonized desk is unusual in Kimbel and Cabus's repertoire as it modernizes a French eighteenth-century *bonheur du jour*, or ladies' writing desk. It is one of three known variations of the form, including the example depicted in period inventory photographs.[1] This animated version exhibits arching lower front legs that curve down from the balustraded bottom shelf. The straight upper front and back legs support the desk carcass, which consists of a lower drawer, a compact, hinged writing surface that opens out, two small drawers above, and a top shelf accentuated by a balustrade of turned spindles. Incised, gilt-enriched lines and geometric motifs, as well as printed geometric borders, emphasize the desk's horizontal lines and contrast with the ebonized surface. Incised, gilded vegetal sprays on the sides enhance the verticality of the front legs. While its angular, attenuated, and ebonized form evinces affinities with Anglo-Japonesque aesthetics, the bold metal straps pierced with quatrefoils reinforce the desk's corners visually, if not structurally, and evoke the Modern Gothic style.

In the period inventory photograph, another small ebonized writing desk is identified as 410, and graphite notations of 50 and 55 may indicate prices.[*]

Ebonized cherry, hard maple, gilding, paper, metal
35 ¼ × 24 × 15 ½ in.
(89.5 × 61 × 39.4 cm)

Collection of Ann Pyne

1   There are at least two known versions of another small desk in private collections.
*   Wood analysis was performed by Harry Alden of Alden Identification Service.

410   411.

Desk and cabinet, from Album 1 [Furniture designed and sold by the New York firm of Kimbel and Cabus], ca. 1875

CABINET-SECRETARY, circa 1875

Distinguished by its striking form and dramatic ebonized surface enriched with abstract, gilded motifs, this cabinet-secretary exemplifies Kimbel and Cabus's most developed work in the Modern Gothic style. Plank, panel, and frame construction, commonly used for the firm's case pieces, convey the rectilinear lines. Architectonic elements such as the peaked gable, blind gallery, and alcove shelves with arched openings at the front and sides, coupled with rich ornament, create a powerful presence that belies the cabinet-secretary's relatively petite dimensions.

While it is a functional object with a drop-front writing surface, interior storage compartments, and lower cabinet, the cabinet-secretary's elaborate surface decoration and shelves for art objects signal that it was intended for ostentatious parlor display as much as it was for use. Bands of incised, gilded abstract botanical and geometric ornaments frame and emphasize the horizontal and diagonal lines. Elaborate cast metal hinges and escutcheons take a functional element to expressive heights, animating the drop-front desk and cabinet doors that are inset with colorful French tiles of Islamic inspiration. An inset marquetry panel with an abstracted botanical motif further enlivens the gable peak. Kimbel and Cabus made extensive use of colorful decorative ceramic tiles and, less often, in their most elaborate furniture, marquetry panels. The incised gilded wyvern, a two-legged winged dragon within a shield—an allusion to European heraldry and a symbol of valor and protection—provides a dramatic focal point at the center of the desk front. Close study of a surviving Kimbel and Cabus period inventory photograph, and an equally outstanding second version of this form, elucidates the subtle variations, from tile selection to incised motifs and wyvern presentation, that the firm employed to vary their wares for their clients.*

In the period inventory photograph, the cabinet-secretary is identified as number 324 and a graphite notation of 100 may indicate the price.

Painted cherry, copper, brass, gilding, leather, earthenware

60 × 35 × 14 in. (152.4 × 88.9 × 35.6 cm)

Brooklyn Museum, Bequest of DeLancey Thorn Grant in memory of her mother, Louis Floyd-Jones Thorn, by exchange, 1991.126

* Wood analysis of both cabinet-secretaries was performed by Harry Alden of Alden Identification Service.

Cabinet-Secretary
(detail), ca. 1875

Cabinet-Secretary
(detail), ca. 1875

Desks, from
Album 1 [Furniture
designed and sold
by the New York
firm of Kimbel and
Cabus], ca. 1875

Cabinet-Secretary
(detail), ca. 1875

Cabinet-Secretary
(detail), ca. 1875

Cabinet, ca. 1875.
Ebonized cherry,
metal, gilding, leather,
earthenware, 63
× 33 ¼ × 12 ½ in.
(160.0 × 84.5 ×
31.8 cm). The Nally-
Stufano Collection

CABINET, circa 1875

The rich assemblage of incised and gilded surface ornament and decorative tiles seen on this ebonized rectilinear cabinet emphasize its dual role as a showpiece in a drawing room or parlor and a functional storage object. The carcass of plank, panel, and frame construction, supported by four spiral-carved legs and a lower shelf or board stretcher, evokes a late-seventeenth to early-eighteenth-century British cabinet on a stand.[1] Incised and gilded zigzags, "x"s and "o"s, stylized flowerheads, shields, and pointed pyramidal projections emphasize the horizontal and vertical lines of the cabinet, while a turned balustrade at the top adds further visual interest, its spindles carved with eye-catching gilded zigzags. Gilt-enriched carved demilunes, consisting of carved geometric motifs of diamonds within a diamond within a square, scalloped borders, and everted pointed sprays, create a dazzling frame for the British Minton and Company tiles that are the focal point of the cabinet doors. The hand-painted tiles depict Medieval-inspired figures personifying "Music" and "Poetry," based on designs by Charles Rossiter (1827–1897) for Minton and Company. Because Kimbel and Cabus typically used transfer-printed tiles or less-expensive printed-paper panels in their case work, the presence of hand-painted tiles here gives the impression that a custom order was made for this imagery.[2] Cast spear-form hinges and escutcheons, among the more elaborate hardware employed by the firm, also indicate that this was a particularly expensive object.

The cabinet was handed down within the family of New York City banker and art and book collector George T. Bliss (1851–1901), and it was given to the Hudson River Museum by his daughter, the collector and philanthropist Susan Dwight Bliss (1882–1966). Although nothing further is presently known about when the family acquired the cabinet, it is fitting that it is now part of the museum's collection which is housed in "Glenview," the former home of stockbroker John Bond Trevor, another Kimbel and Cabus patron.

In the period inventory photographs a version of this cabinet is identified as number 331, and a graphite notation of 75 may indicate the price.

Ebonized wood, gilding, glazed tiles, brass
50 ⅜ × 27 × 13 ½ in.
(128 × 68.5 × 34.25 cm)

Hudson River Museum, Gift of Miss Susan D. Bliss, 61.11.24

1   There is at least one other known version of this form and a variation on it in a private collection.

2   Professional china painters in New York City, such as the renowned Edward Lycett (1833–1910), painted undecorated ceramic blanks to order. For example, in 1875 Lycett reported painting four six-by-eight-inch panels in brown and white over a gold ground depicting Medieval-inspired figures of "Wisdom," "Folly," "Poetry," and "Music," which we now know to have been inspired by Rossiter's designs (see p. 22, in the essay by Max Donnelly in this volume).

Cabinet and étagère, from
Album 1 [Furniture designed
and sold by the New York firm
of Kimbel and Cabus], ca. 1875

Cabinet
(detail),
ca. 1875

SIDEBOARD, circa 1875

This remarkable ebonized sideboard embellished with a multitude of incised, gilded geometric and abstracted botanical motifs embodies the eclectic synthesis of Western European with Asian-inspired and Middle Eastern-inspired forms and decoration characteristic of the Aesthetic Movement, which gained popularity during the late 1870s as interest in the Modern Gothic began to wane. The tripartite sideboard reveals Kimbel and Cabus's skillful adaptation to stylistic change, as well as their adept reconfiguration of various components to create new forms. It shares the same overall structure as a related sideboard in the period inventory photographs (see fig. below), but by adding a central niche with a "Moorish" arch between the two cabinet doors and an extra panel in the lower section, Kimbel and Cabus transformed the form's look and impact. Furthermore, they took the columns, turned balustrades, and owls from the upper section and rearranged them into a different configuration. The abstract floral tiles depicted in the period image have been exchanged for brilliant blue tiles with central cartouches enclosing pseudo-Kufic script. At the time, the pseudo-Kufic script and "Moorish" arch would have added worldly allure to the sideboard that, along with the art objects that would have adorned it, signaled the owner's worldliness and sophistication.[1]

In the period inventory photograph the related sideboard is identified as number 339, and a graphite column of numbers forming the equation 30+44+48=122 may indicate the price.

Ebonized cherry, gilding, porcelain, metal
61 ½ × 17 × 45 in.
(156.21 × 43.18 × 114.3 cm)

H. E. Bolles Fund, Museum of Fine Arts, Boston, 1999.93

1   See p. 60 fig. 24, p. 70 fig. 38, and p. 88 fig. 64 for other examples of the firm's work with Asian- and Middle Eastern-inspired forms and decoration.

Sideboard, from Album 1 [Furniture designed and sold by the New York firm of Kimbel and Cabus], ca. 1875

CABINET, circa 1875

This commanding ebonized cabinet with lavish decoration in varied media is one of the largest and most elaborate objects designed by Kimbel and Cabus. Five extant versions of the form are known, each displaying a different decorative program. Collectively they illustrate the firm's ability to satisfy a range of tastes and provide inventive and original objects for their most discerning customers (see p. 196).[1] Created with plank, panel, and frame construction, the broad tripartite form displays shaped sides and a hooded top that references British court-cabinets, as well as Edward William Godwin's and Bruce James Talbert's designs for dining and drawing-room furniture. The lower section consists of two cabinets inset with painted wood panels flanking a drawer and shelves; mirror-backed side shelves and a drop-front with a glazed drop-front door in the middle section, with two candlesticks flanking a painted panel above; fluted and spiral carved columns connect the middle section and the velvet-lined, coved hood at the top.[2] The cabinet is enriched with a plethora of incised and carved geometric and stylized botanical motifs that emphasize the structure of the form. In some versions, the incised motifs are gilt-enriched. According to the *London House Furnisher* report on "Modern Decorative Furniture," reprinted in the *Cabinet Maker* in June 1873, "a favorite decoration of the ebonized, or ebonized and gilt furniture is that of porcelain plaques . . . These are usually charged with emblematic figures. Panels display similar treatment with highly colored figures on gold grounds."(see p. 69, fig. 36).[2] The colorful depictions of Medieval-style huntsmen on the cabinet doors and the sprites flanking a brazier on the upper panel are painted on a gold ground that creates a luminous contrast with the ebonized surface and complements the elaborate brass hardware and the green-gold embossed velvet in the coved top. Kimbel and Cabus meticulously conceived each detail and element to complement and harmonize with each other, making the cabinet as much a work of art as the objects that would have been displayed within it.

In the period inventory photographs the cabinet is identified as number 262, and a graphite notation of 300 may indicate the price. Kimbel and Cabus's ink signature at the bottom suggests their proprietary interest in the design.

Ebonized cherry, gilt-plated copper alloy mounts, painted wood panels, transparent and mirrored glass, velvet
81 ½ × 52 × 20 in.
(207 × 132.1 × 50.8 cm)

The Baltimore Museum of Art, The Richard C. von Hess Foundation Acquisition Fund; partial gift of Michael and Anis Merson; and purchase with exchange funds from Bequest of Margaret Anna Abell; Bequest of Eleanor M. Anderson; Bequest of Alice Worthington Ball; Decorative Arts Fund; Gift of Elizabeth S. Ellis, from the Estate of Margaret Anna Abell; Gift of William Bose Marye; Bequest of Margaret D. Morriss; Gift of Abram Moses, in Memory of his Wife, Carrie Gutman Moses; Gift of Mrs. John W. Nicol, Jr.; Gift of Merrell L. Stout, Jr., in Memory of his Father, Dr. Merrell L. Stout, 1999.150

1   In addition to these two versions, there is one in the collection of the Hudson River Museum (73.39) and two further versions in private collections.

2   The two larger pieces of mirrored glass are silver mirrors. The two smaller pieces are tin-mercury amalgam mirrors.

3   "Modern Decorative Furniture," *Cabinet Maker*, whole no. 160 (June 14, 1873): 2.

Cabinet, ca. 1875. Ebonized cherry, gilt and painted decoration, coppered metal fittings, mirrors, red plush lining. 81 ⅞ × 52 ¾ × 19 ⅝ in. (207.9 × 134 cm × 49.8 cm). Victoria and Albert Museum, London, W.50-1984

Panel from a cabinet
depicting night, ca. 1875

Panel from a cabinet
depicting day, ca. 1875

SELECTED BIBLIOGRAPHY

AUTHORS' NOTE

Numerous nineteenth-century primary sources, ranging from archival materials to books, city directories, design drawings, ephemera, newspapers, periodicals, and photographs, were consulted in person and via the internet in preparation for this book. The selected bibliography includes published references to Kimbel and Cabus and its partners' families, as well as sources that provide substantive context for the firm's work. All other references, including city directory entries and newspaper articles, have been cited in the endnotes. Directory citations take into account the fact that many city directories were published mid-year. The bibliography is arranged in two sections, archival sources and published sources, and the latter section is further divided into two parts: nineteenth century, and twentieth and twenty-first centuries.

ARCHIVAL SOURCES

Album 1 [Furniture designed and sold by the New York firm of Kimbel and Cabus], ca. 1875, Smithsonian Libraries, Washington, D.C.

Andrew Dickson White (American, 1832–1918) papers, 1832–1919. Division of Rare and Manuscript Collections, Cornell University Library.

Centennial Exhibition Photograph and Ephemera Collection. Hagley Museum and Library, Wilmington, DE.

Design drawings. Estate of Wilhelm Kimbel (1868–1965), Kunstbibliothek, Staatliche Museen, Berlin, Stiftung Preussischer Kulturbesitz.

Design patents. U.S. Department of Commerce, Patent and Trademark Office, and National Archives, Washington, D.C.

Dun, R. G. & Co. Credit ledgers, R. G. Dun and Co. Collection. Baker Library, Harvard University Graduate School of Business Administration, Boston, MA.

Fifth Avenue Presbyterian Church, Fifth Avenue and 55th Street, New York, NY, church archives: church minutes, photographs, and records.

Hudson River Museum, Yonkers, NY, period photographs from the collection.

Kimbel Family Collection documents and photographs from Henrietta Mehlbach Richardson, courtesy of Elizabeth Richardson Elisher.

Kimbel family correspondence, curatorial files, American Wing, The Metropolitan Museum of Art, New York, NY.

New York State Census, New York, 1855, 1865; United States Federal Census, New York, 1840, 1850, 1860, 1870, 1880, and Products of Industry for New York, 1880.

U.S. Civil War draft records. National Archives and Records Administration (NARA).

PUBLISHED SOURCES: NINETEENTH CENTURY

"After the Centennial." *American Cabinet Maker* 14, whole no. 340 (November 25, 1876): 2.

American Cabinet Maker 6, whole no. 289 (December 4, 1875): 6.

"American Exhibitors." *American Cabinet Maker* 13, whole no. 318 (June 24, 1876): 8.

Artistic Houses, Being a Series of Interior Views of a Number of the Most Beautiful and Celebrated Homes in the United States. 2 vols. in 4 pts. New York: D. Appleton, 1883–84.

Bell, George, et al. *The Illustrated Catalogue of the Centennial Exhibition, Philadelphia, 1876* (John Filmer, 1876): 75.

"The Centennial." *American Cabinet Maker* 13, whole no. 316 (June 10, 1876): 7.

"The Centennial." *American Cabinet Maker* 13, whole no. 326 (August 19, 1876): 10.

"The Centennial." *American Cabinet Maker* 13, whole no. 332 (September 30, 1876): 7.

"The Centennial Awards." *Supplement to The American Cabinet Maker* published with *American Cabinet Maker* 13, whole no. 332 (September 30, 1876), after p. xvi.

"The Centennial." *Harper's Weekly* (December 2, 1876): 969–70.

"The Centennial Exhibition. III." *The Art Journal* 2 (1876): 225–32.

Clark, Colonel Emmons. *History of the Seventh Regiment of New York, 1806–1889.* Vol. 2 (New York: Seventh Regiment, 1890).

Cook, Clarence. "Beds and Tables, Stools and Candlesticks." *Scribner's Monthly* 12, no. 6 (April 1877): 820.

———. *The House Beautiful: Essays on Beds and Tables, Stools and Candlesticks.* New York: Scribner, Armstrong, 1878.

"Decorative Fine-Art Work at Philadelphia, American Furniture." *American Architect and Building News* 1 (December 23, 1876): 412.

"Decorative Interior. Messrs. Kimbel and Cabus (7 and 9 East Twentieth Street, New York)." *American Architect and Building News* 1 (November 25, 1876): 381, engraving following.

"Design at the Centennial." *American Cabinet Maker* 13, whole no. 336 (October 28, 1876): 11.

"Designing and Designers." *American Cabinet Maker* 13, whole no. 337 (November 4, 1876): 4.

Die Kunst im Gewerbe (Industrial Art). Edited by Edwin Oppler, vol. 1, issue I, 2 (1872); vol. 2, issue 3 (1873); vol. 3, issue 3 (1874); vol. 4, issue 1 (1875).

"Directory." Centennial Supplement to *American Cabinet Maker*: 3, presented with the issue of *American Cabinet Maker* 13, whole no. 319 (July 1, 1876): 3.

Dresser, Christopher. *Principles of Decorative Design*. London: Cassell, Petter and Galpin, 1873.

———. *Studies in Design*. London: Cassell, Petter and Galpin, 1874–76.

Eastlake, Charles Locke. *Hints on Household Taste in Furniture, Upholstery, and Other Details*. London: Longmans, Green, 1868.

Edwards and Critten, eds. *New York's Great Industries, Exchange and Commercial Review, Embracing Also Historical and Descriptive Sketch of the City, Its Leading Merchants and Manufacturers*. New York and Chicago: Historical Publishing Company, 1885. see p. 132.

Elliott, Charles Wyllys. "Art Applied to Life, Seen at the Centennial." *The Galaxy. A Magazine of Entertaining Reading* 22, no. 4 (October 1876): 494.

[Ferris, George Titus]. *Gems of the Centennial Exhibition: Consisting of Illustrated Descriptions of Objects of an Artistic Character, In the Exhibits of the United States, Great Britain, France, [. . .] at the Philadelphia International Exhibition of 1876*. New York: D. Appleton, 1877. see pp. 138–40.

"Furniture at the Centennial." *American Cabinet Maker* 6, whole no. 312 (May 13, 1876): 9.

"The Furniture Craze." *American Cabinet Maker* 15, whole no. 370 (June 23, 1877): 21.

"Furniture Exhibitors." *American Cabinet Maker* 13, whole no. 313 (May 20, 1876): 10.

"Gothic Revival." In "New York Trade News." *Cabinet Maker* 6, whole no. 257 (April 24, 1875): 9, 12.

"Household Furniture – The Gothic Style." *Harper's Bazar* (April 29, 1876): 277–78.

"Household Art, The Art of Furnishing." *Harper's Bazar* 10 (June 16, 1877): 370–71.

"The Illustrations." *American Architect and Building News* (March 24, 1883): 139–40.

"Individual Book Exhibits." In *Centennial Exhibition Number of the Publisher's Weekly* X, 1 (July 1, 1876): 13–18.

"Interior Designed by Messrs. Kimbel and Cabus, New York." *American Architect and Building News* 1 (September 23, 1876): 308, engraving following.

"Interior. Messrs. Kimbel and Cabus." (7 & 9 East Twentieth Street, New York, NY) *American Architect and Building News* 2, no. 61 (February 24, 1877): 60, engraving following.

"Interior Perspective of a Room. Messrs. Kimbel and Cabus, Decorators." *American Architect and Building News* 1 (July 22, 1876): 237.

M.E.W.S. "The Homes of America. 'Old Morrisania'." *Art Journal* 4 (1878): 81–85.

"Modern Gothic Ornaments." *American Cabinet Maker* 14, whole no. 341 (December 2, 1876): 2.

"New York Fashions—House Furnishings." *Harper's Bazar* 8 (July 3, 1875): 427.

"New York Interiors. Residence of W. H. DeForest, Esq." *Art Journal* 5 (1879): 141–42.

"New York Interiors. Residence of James P. Kernochan, Esq." *Art Journal* 5 (1879): 46–47.

"The New York Strikes." *Cabinet Maker* 3, no. 6 (June 15, 1872): 44.

"New York Trade News." *Cabinet Maker* 6, whole no. 262 (May 29, 1875): 28.

"New York Trade News." *American Cabinet Maker* 6, whole no. 289 (December 4, 1875): 6.

"Note." *Harper's New Monthly Magazine* 54, no. 31 (December 1876): 143.

"Our Separate Plate, American Art Furniture and Decoration." *Furniture Gazette* (October 7, 1876): 216.

"A Parlor View in a New York Dwelling House." *Gleason's Pictorial Drawing-Room Companion* 7, no. 19 (November 11, 1854): 300.

"Sayings and Doings." *Harper's Bazar* 9 (November 4, 1876): 711.

"The Seventh Regiment Armory." *Decorator and Furnisher* 6, no. 2 (May 1885): 44–46.

Spofford, Harriet Prescott. *Art Decoration Applied to Furniture* (New York: Harper and Brothers, 1878). see pp. 83–84, 86, 179.

———. "Medieval Furniture." *Harper's New Monthly Magazine* (November 1876): 809–29.

Talbert, Bruce J. *Examples of Ancient and Modern Furniture, Metal Work, Tapestries, and Decorations*. London: R. O. Rickatson, 1876.

———. *Gothic Forms Applied to Furniture, Metal Work and Decoration for Domestic Purposes*. Birmingham: S. Birbeck; London: the author, 1867–68.

United States Centennial Commission. *International Exhibition, 1876: Reports and Awards: Groups I–XXXVI*. Edited by Francis A. Walker. 6 vols. Philadelphia: J. B. Lippincott, 1877–78.

Whittemore, Henry, comp. *Homes on the Hudson: Historical, Illustrative, Descriptive*. Illustrated by Albert Bierstadt. New York: Artotype Publishing Company, [1895?]. see pp. 27–28, 36.

PUBLISHED SOURCES: TWENTIETH AND TWENTY-FIRST CENTURY

Aldrich, Megan. *Gothic Revival*. London: Phaidon, 1994.

Aldrich, Megan et al. *A. W. N. Pugin Master of Gothic Revival*. Edited by Paul Atterbury. New Haven: Published for the Bard Graduate Center for Studies in the Decorative Arts, New York, by Yale University Press, ca. 1995.

"Anthony F. Kimbel." *Art News* 68 (March 1969): 21.

Bishop, Robert. *Centuries and Styles of the American Chair, 1640–1970*. New York: E. P. Dutton, 1972.

———. *How to Know American Antique Furniture*. New York: Dutton, 1973.

Brislin, Alison Paige. "American Modern Gothic: Kimbel & Cabus, 1863–1882." Master's thesis, Sotheby's Institute of Art, 2009.

Burke, Doreen Bolger, Jonathan Freedman, Alice Cooney Frelinghuysen, David A. Hanks, Marilynn Johnson, James D. Kornwolf, Catherine Lynn, et al. *In Pursuit of Beauty: Americans and the Aesthetic Movement*. New York: Metropolitan Museum of Art, 1986.

Busch, Jason T., and Catherine Futter, eds. *Inventing the Modern World: Decorative Arts at the World's Fairs, 1851–1939*. New York: Skira Rizzoli, 2012.

Cooper, Helen A., ed. *Life, Liberty, and the Pursuit of Happiness: American Art from the Yale University Art Gallery*. New Haven: Yale University Art Gallery In association with Yale University Press, 2008.

Craven, Wayne. *Gilded Mansions: Grand Architecture and High Society*. New York: W. W. Norton, 2009.

D'Ambrosio, Anna Tobin, ed. *Masterpieces of American Furniture from the Munson-Williams-Proctor Institute*. Utica: Munson-Williams-Proctor Institute, 1999.

Davidson, Marshall B., ed. *The American Heritage History of Antiques from the Civil War to World War I*. New York: American Heritage Publishing Company, 1969.

The Detroit Institute of Arts. *The Quest for Unity: American Art Between World's Fairs, 1876–1893*. Detroit: Detroit Institute of Arts, 1983.

Donnelly, Max. "British Furniture at the Philadelphia Centennial Exhibition, 1876," *Furniture History* 37 (2001): 91–120.

Dubrow, Eileen, and Richard Dubrow. *American Furniture of the 19th Century, 1840–1880*. Exton, PA: Schiffer Publishing, 1983.

Edwards, Clive D. *Victorian Furniture, Technology and Design*. Manchester and New York: Manchester University Press, 1993.

Eidelberg, Martin. *E. Colonna*. Exhibition catalogue. Dayton Art Institute, October 28, 1983–January 2, 1984. Ohio: Dayton Art Institute, 1983.

Frelinghuysen, Alice Cooney, and Nicholas C. Vincent with Moira Gallagher. "Artistic Furniture of the Gilded Age" *The Metropolitan Museum of Art Bulletin* 73, no. 3 (Winter 2016).

Gere, Charlotte, and Michael Whiteway. *Nineteenth-century Design: From Pugin to Mackintosh*. New York: Abrams, 1994.

Gray, Nina, and Suzanne Smeaton. "Within Gilded Borders: The Frames of Stanford White," *American Art* 7, no. 2 (1993): 34.

Hanks, David A. "Kimbel and Cabus: Nineteenth-Century New York Cabinetmakers." *Art and Antiques* 3 (September–October 1980): 44–53.

Hanks, David A., and Donald C. Pierce. *The Virginia Carroll Crawford Collection: American Decorative Arts, 1825–1917*. Atlanta: High Museum of Art, 1983.

Harwood, Barry R. *The Furniture of George Hunzinger: Invention and Innovation in Nineteenth-Century America*. Brooklyn: Brooklyn Museum of Art, 1997.

Howe, Jennifer, ed. *Cincinnati Art-Carved Furniture and Interiors*. Athens, OH: Cincinnati Art Museum and Ohio University Press, 2003.

Howe, Katherine S., Alice Cooney Frelinghuysen, Catherine Hoover Voorsanger, Simon Jervis, Hans Ottomeyer, Mark Bascou, Ann Claggett Wood, and Sophia Riefstahl. *Herter Brothers: Furniture and Interiors for a Gilded Age*. New York: Harry N. Abrams in association with the Museum of Fine Arts, Houston, 1994.

Humphries, Lance, and Roberta A. Mayer. "Gilding an Antebellum Baltimore Townhouse: The Lost Mansion of John Work Garrett and Mary Elizabeth Garrett," *Nineteenth Century: The Magazine of The Victorian Society in America* 39, no. 1 (Spring 2019): 19.

Hunting, Mary A. "The Seventh Regiment Armory in New York City—Restoration of the Historic Site." *New York Magazine Antiques* (January 1999): 17–21.

Ingerman, Elizabeth. "Personal Experiences of an Old New York Cabinetmaker." *Magazine ANTIQUES* 84 (November 1963): 576–80.

Ketchum, William C., Jr., and the Museum of American Folk Art. *American Cabinetmakers: Marked American Furniture, 1640–1940*. New York: Crown Publishers, 1998.

MacDonald, Sally. "Gothic Forms Applied to Furniture: The Early Work of Bruce James Talbert," *Furniture History* 23 (1987): 39–66.

Madigan, Mary Jean Smith. *Eastlake-Influenced American Furniture, 1870–1890*. Yonkers, NY: Hudson River Museum, 1973.

———. "The Influence of Charles Locke Eastlake on American Furniture Manufacture, 1870–90," *Winterthur Porfolio* 10 (1975): 1–22.

———. "Eastlake-Influenced American Furniture, 1870–1890." *Connoisseur* 191 (January 1976): 58–63.

Nadel, Stanley. *Little Germany: Ethnicity, Religion, and Class in New York City, 1845–80*. Chicago: University of Illinois Press, 1990.

Parke-Bernet Galleries. *The Stock of the Well-Known Firm of Decorators, A. Kimbel and Son, Inc. [. . .] March 14 and 15 at 2 p.m.* New York: Parke-Bernet Galleries, 1941.

Pierce, Donald C. *Art and Enterprise: American Decorative Art, 1825–1917: The Virginia Carroll Crawford Collection*. Atlanta: High Museum of Art, 1999.

Rosenkranz, Joel, R. Ruthie Dibble, and Avis Berman. *The Art of Display: The American Pedestal, 1830–1910*. New York: Conner-Rosenkranz, 2018.

Shockley, Jay. *Landmarks Preservation Commission* (July 19, 1994). Designation List 259.

Thieme, Ulrich, and Felix Becker, eds. *Allgemeines Lexikon der bildenden Künstler von der Antike bis zur Gegenwart*. Vol. 20, *Kaufmann–Knilling*. Edited by Hans Vollmer. Leipzig: E. A. Seeman, 1927.

Tracy, Berry B., Marilynn Johnson, Marvin D. Schwartz, and Suzanne Boorsch. *Nineteenth-Century America: Furniture and Other Decorative Arts*. New York: Metropolitan Museum of Art, 1970.

Van Dyk, Stephen. "Focus On . . . A Unique Kimbel & Cabus Furniture Album," *19th Century* 28 (Spring 2008): 30–33.

Victoria and Albert Museum. *Art and Design in Europe and America, 1800–1900*. With an introduction by Simon Jervis. London: Herbert Press, 1987.

Voorsanger, Catherine. "Kimbel and Cabus: American Cabinet-Makers and Interior Decorators, 1863–1882." In *Encyclopedia of Interior Design*, edited by Joanna Banham, 675–78. London and Chicago: Fitzroy Dearborn Publishers, 1997.

———. "'Gorgeous Articles of Furniture': Cabinetmaking in the Empire City." In *Art and the Empire City: New York, 1825–1861*, edited by Catherine Hoover Voorsanger and John K. Howat, pp. 287–325. New York: Metropolitan Museum of Art, 2000.

Wolff, Wendy, ed. *Capitol Builder: The Shorthand Journals of Montgomery C. Meigs, 1853–1859, 1861, A Project to Commemorate the United States Capitol Bicentennial 1800–2000*. Washington, D.C.: Prepared under the direction of the Secretary of the Senate. U.S. Government Printing Office, 2001.

Zinnkann, Heidrun. *Mainzer Möbelschreiner der ersten Hälfte des 19. Jahrhunderts*. Frankfurt am Main: Historischen Museums, 1985.

Zukowski, Karen. *Creating the Artful Home: The Aesthetic Movement*. Salt Lake City: Gibbs Smith, 2006.

ACKNOWLEDGMENTS

With an eye for innovative design, Dr. Barry R. Harwood developed and shaped the Brooklyn Museum's decorative arts collection for thirty years. At the same time, he indelibly imprinted student minds with his high standards for research, scholarship, and writing as adjunct professor at the MA program in the History of Design and Curatorial Studies offered jointly by Parsons School of Design/The New School and Cooper Hewitt, Smithsonian Design Museum. Facing the prospect of completing Barry's long anticipated Kimbel and Cabus exhibition and publication after suddenly losing him required some bravery. Collaboration has been central to this undertaking, and I am profoundly grateful to Medill Higgins Harvey, Ruth Bigelow Wriston Associate Curator of American Decorative Arts and manager, The Henry R. Luce Center for the Study of American Art at the Metropolitan Museum of Art, for joining me as co-author and thought partner. Barry was professor and mentor to each of us at different times, and bringing his work to fruition has been deeply fulfilling. Medill has generously shared her meticulous research and thoughtful insights, and has fortified every dimension of this project as a colleague and a friend. I thank Anne Pasternak, Shelby White and Leon Levy Director, and David Berliner, president and chief operating officer, for their strong support of the exhibition and for trusting us to complete the project in Barry's honor.

Deedee and Barrie Wigmore have been vital to the realization of this project. We appreciate and acknowledge their long-standing interest in this topic as well as their pioneering collecting of Kimbel and Cabus furniture. We sincerely thank them for the generous support that has made this exhibition and publication possible.

We also recognize and thank the contributing authors whose essays provide illuminating context for our focused discussion of the Kimbel and Cabus partnership. Special thanks to Alice Cooney Frelinghuysen, Anthony W. and Lulu C. Wang Curator of American Decorative Arts at the Metropolitan Museum of Art, for vividly situating Kimbel and Cabus within the nineteenth-century New York City cabinetmaking industry. We also thank her for reviewing our work and generously sharing her insights, contacts, and research files. Much gratitude to Max Donnelly, curator of nineteenth-century furniture at the Victoria and Albert Museum, London, for evocatively and succinctly elucidating a complex topic: the development of the Modern Gothic style in England. We thank Berlin-based art historian Melitta Jonas for her engaging discussion of cabinetmaking in Mainz, Germany that sheds light on Anton Kimbel's formative years, as well as on the larger Kimbel family.

At the Brooklyn Museum, we thank Catherine Futter, interim director of curatorial affairs and senior curator, decorative arts, and Kevin L. Stayton, curator emeritus, for reviewing our work and sharing their knowledge with us.

There are nine institutional lenders, and we are grateful to them for remaining committed to the exhibition despite the extraordinarily challenging times. We thank the Baltimore Museum of Art; Cooper Hewitt, Smithsonian Design Museum, Smithsonian Libraries, Smithsonian Institution, New York and Washington, D.C.; Fleet Library at RISD, Providence, Rhode Island; Hudson River Museum, Yonkers, New York; Metropolitan Museum of Art; Mint Museum of Art, Charlotte, North Carolina; Museum of Fine

Arts, Boston; Museum of Fine Arts, Houston; and Toledo Museum of Art, Ohio.

We are also deeply grateful to our private lenders, many of whom have studied and appreciated Kimbel and Cabus's innovative work for years, for generously sharing their knowledge and graciously loaning their objects to the exhibition. We thank Joseph V. Garry; Helen Hersh and Charles Sporn; Wayne Mason; Richard Pabst; Susan W. Paine; David Parker, Associated Artists L.L.C.; Ann Pyne; Kevin L. Stayton; Andrew VanStyn; and Deedee and Barrie Wigmore.

We have undertaken several conservation projects in preparation for the exhibition and extend appreciation to Kevin O'Brien and Angela Romano-Vosburgh, Kevin O'Brien Studio, Philadelphia; Anne Anquetin and Diego Castro, Prelle/Passementerie Verrier, New York and Paris; Elena Basso, Nancy Britton, and Federica Pozzi, Metropolitan Museum of Art for undertaking the painstaking process of researching and reupholstering the Brooklyn Museum corner chair with a recreated period-appropriate fabric; we thank Harry Alden, Alden Identification Service, Chesapeake Beach, Maryland for identifying numerous wood samples. Special thanks to Ann Pyne and Andrew VanStyn for generously undertaking reupholstery projects for this exhibition.

We appreciate the church, library, museum, and other institutional staff who have facilitated collection visits, shared contacts, insights, and scholarship files. For their invaluable assistance we thank Virginia Anderson, Sarah Cho, Christine Downie, and Brittany Luberda, Baltimore Museum of Art; James Archer Abbott, Lewes Historical Society, Delaware; David Barquist and Miriam Cady, Philadelphia Museum of Art; David Burnhauser and Kirsten Reoch, Park Avenue Armory, New York; Benjamin Colman, Detroit Institute of Arts; Ariel Bordeaux and Claudia Covert, Fleet Library, RISD, Providence, Rhode Island; Anna D'Ambrosio, Munson-Williams-Proctor Arts Institute, Utica, New York; David Conradsen, Saint Louis Art Museum; Amy Miller Dehan, Cincinnati Art Museum; Ruthie Dibble, Chipstone Foundation, Milwaukee; Evan Fay Earle, Peter Corina, and Laura Linke, Division of Rare and Manuscripts Collections, Cornell University Library, Ithaca, New York; Nonie Gadsden and Thomas Michie, Museum of Fine Arts, Boston; Brian Gallagher, Mint Museum, Charlotte, North Carolina; Christine Gervais, Museum of Fine Arts, Houston; John Stuart Gordon, Yale University Art Gallery, New Haven, Connecticut; Dale Hansen and Kellie Picallo, Fifth Avenue Presbyterian Church, New York; Jana Hettmann, Kunstbibliothek, Staatliche Museen, Berlin; Amy Hopwood, Newark Museum of Art; Lauren Landi, Preservation Society of Newport County, Rhode Island; Joshua Lane, Winterthur Museum, Garden and Library, Delaware; Bonnie Lilienfeld and William Yeingst, National Museum of American History, Smithsonian Institution, Washington, D.C.; Aimee Lind, J. Paul Getty Trust, Los Angeles; Rosie Mills, Los Angeles County Museum of Art; Nicole Mullen, SFO Museum, San Francisco; Monica Obniski, High Museum of Art, Atlanta; Lauren Palmor, Fine Arts Museums of San Francisco; Angela Schad, Hagley Museum and Library, Wilmington, Delaware; Achim Stiegel, Kunstgewerbemuseum, Staatliche Museen, Berlin; Cindy Trope and Yao-Fen You, Cooper-Hewitt, Smithsonian Design Museum, Smithsonian Institution; Stephen Van Dyk, Elizabeth Broman, and Jennifer Cohlman Bracchi, Cooper-Hewitt, Smithsonian Design Library, Smithsonian Libraries; Laura Vookles and Alyssa Dreliszak, Hudson River Museum, Yonkers, New York; Christopher Wilk, Victoria and Albert Museum, London; Elizabeth Williams, RISD Museum, Providence, Rhode Island; Diane Wright, Toledo Museum of Art.

204

Many dealers and designers have generously shared their knowledge, research, and contacts with us, too. We especially thank David Bahssin, Joan Bogart, Meg Caldwell, Martin Cohen, Mimi Findlay, Roger Howlett, Paul Jeromak, Martin Levy, Ronald Mayne and DeBare Saunders, Alan Michaan, David Petrovsky, David Rago, Paul Reeves, Joel Rosenkranz, Federico Santi, Eric Silver, Bill Turner, and Ron Wagner and Timothy Van Dam.

We extend heartfelt thanks to the collectors who shared their passion for Kimbel and Cabus and welcomed research visits to their homes, and to the individuals who offered new perspectives or words of wisdom in support of the project: Ian Berke, Jay Cantor, Terry Carbone, P. J. Carlino, Elaine Cole and Nino Benigni, Brian Coleman, Ellen Denker, Elizabeth De Rosa, Jeannine Falino, David A. Hanks, Anissa Helou, Richard Iverson, Eve Kahn, Jezra Kaye, Carolyn Kelly, Joan Lippincott, Marjorie and Michael Loeb, Deborah Mills, Joe Napoli, Joan Parcher, Otis and Nancy Pearsall, Christina and Robert Prescott-Walker, Walter Ritchie, Alan Roberts, Stuart Slavid, Marco Polo Stufano, John Wadlington, Lori Zabar, Christina Ziegler-McPherson, and Karen Zukowski.

Very special thanks to Anton Kimbel's descendants Nicholas Farwell and Elizabeth Richardson Elisher, who shared her fascinating family archives and photographs with us.

Likewise, we are grateful to long-time Kimbel and Cabus scholar Wayne Mason for sharing his extensive research on the firm as well as samples of original upholstery, gimp, and cord from his collection. Our work has been immeasurably enriched by his generosity and insights.

At the Brooklyn Museum, I thank my colleagues in the Arts of the Americas and Europe for their encouragement and sage advice: Jane Dini, Catherine Futter, Margarita Karasoulas, Nancy Rosoff, Joseph Shaikewitz, Lisa Small, Shea Spiller, and Liz St. George.

I especially thank Nancy, Shea, and Susan Fisher, former director of collections and curatorial affairs, for their early support of my proposal. In addition, Shea has provided invaluable curatorial assistance, for which I am very grateful. I thank department volunteer Ralph Julius for his help. For attending to the countless aspects of exhibition and publication design, organization, logistics, and photography, I am deeply grateful to Walter Andersons, David Alvarez, Gwen Arriaga, Taylor Black, Lisa Bruno, Aisha de Avila-Shin, Nancy Currey, Harry DeBauche, Sarah DeSantis, Sara Devine, Jonathan Dorado, Bill Driscoll, Elyse Driscoll, Dolores Farrell, Richard Fett, Filippo Gentile, Jakki Godfrey, Joachim Hackl, Adjoa Jones de Almeida, McKenzie Keating, Jim Kelly, Beth Kushner, Tina March, Sharon Matt Atkins, Jocelyn Mosquera, Bob Nardi, Paloma Obregón, Terri O'Hara, Adam O'Reilly, Hope O'Reilly, Cindy Ortiz, Monica Park, J. J. Peytavi, Chad Phillips, Molly Seegers, Tom Smrtic, Paul Speh, Erika Umali, Maribel Vitagliani, Katie Welty, Christina White, Esther Woo, Andrea Yglesias, and Lauren Argentina Zelaya.

For shepherding the publication along under unusually challenging circumstances, I thank Audrey Walen for her attention to detail, her diplomacy, and her good humor. I also thank our fantastic ARTS intern Vanessa Chung, who helped in so many ways.

For working with us to create a fresh presentation of rich historical material, we thank Elisabeth Rochau-Shalem, Karen Angne, and Lucia Ott of Hirmer Verlag, as well as Jenifer Evans for her copy-editing.

For creating beautiful photographs despite complex logistics, we thank Gavin Ashworth as well as Jeff Antowiak and Mitro Hood.

And finally, my heartfelt thanks to my husband and son, Ian and Carl Ehling, for cheering me on every step of the way.

Barbara Veith

PHOTO CREDITS

COLOPHON

Published on the occasion of the exhibition *Modern Gothic: The Inventive Furniture of Kimbel and Cabus, 1863–82* organized by the Brooklyn Museum and held July 2, 2021–February 13, 2022.

Modern Gothic: The Inventive Furniture of Kimbel and Cabus, 1863–82 is organized by the Brooklyn Museum and curated by guest curator Barbara Veith in consultation with Medill H. Harvey, Ruth Bigelow Wriston Associate Curator of American Decorative Arts and Manager of the Henry R. Luce Center, The Metropolitan Museum of Art, and Shea Spiller, Curatorial Assistant, Arts of the Americas and Europe, Brooklyn Museum.

Leadership support for this exhibition is provided by Deedee and Barrie Wigmore.

Bibliographic information published by the Deutsche Nationalbibliothek
The Deutsche Nationalbibliothek lists this publication in the Deutsche Nationalbibliografie; detailed bibliographic data is available on the Internet at http://www.dnb.de.

First published in 2021 by the Brooklyn Museum and Hirmer Publishers

Brooklyn Museum
200 Eastern Parkway
Brooklyn, NY 11238-6052
www.brooklynmuseum.org

Brooklyn Museum

Hirmer Publishers
Bayerstraße 57–59
80335 Munich
www.hirmerpublishers.com

HIRMER

For the Brooklyn Museum:

Director of Publications, Interpretation, and Editorial Services: Audrey Walen
Director of Digital Collections and Services: Sarah DeSantis
Curatorial Assistant, Arts of the Americas and Europe: Shea Spiller
Special Intern: Vanessa Chung

For Hirmer Publishers:

Senior Editor: Elisabeth Rochau-Shalem
Project Manager: Karen Angne
Graphic design, typesetting and production: Lucia Ott

Editors: Barbara Veith, Medill Higgins Harvey
Authors: Max Donnelly, Alice Cooney Frelinghuysen, Medill Higgins Harvey, Melitta Jonas, Barbara Veith
Translation from German (Melitta Jonas essay): Russell Stockman, Quechee, Vermont
Copy-editing and proof-reading: Jenifer Evans, Lascabanes
Prepress and repro: REPROMAYER Medienproduktion GmbH, Reutlingen
Paper: Garda Ultramatt 150 g/sqm
Typefaces: ABC Marfa, GT Alpina
Printing and binding: Printer Trento S.r.l., Trento

Printed in Italy

ISBN: 978-3-7774-3658-6

Front cover: Cabinet-Secretary, circa 1875 (see pp. 182/183)
Back cover: "Showroom illustration for A. Kimbel & J. Cabus, 7 & 9 East 20th Str. New York," *American Architect and Building News* (February 24, 1877). Collection of Andrew VanStyn (see pp. 98/99)

Wood analysis by Harry Alden, Alden Identification Service, Chesapeake Beach, MD, 2020–21: pp. 70, 74, 96 n. 161, 100, 102, 106, 119 (top left), 124, 128, 134, 148, 150, 155, 156, 158, 165, 166, 168, 179, 180, 182, 187

Library of Congress Cataloging-in-Publication Data:

Names: Veith, Barbara, editor. | Donnelly, Max. Poetic and practical. | Frelinghuysen, Alice Cooney. Rich and tasteful enough. | Harvey, Medill Higgins. Kimbel and Cabus. | Jonas, Melitta. Kimbel dynasty. | Brooklyn Museum, organizer, host institution.
Title: Modern Gothic : the inventive furniture of Kimbel and Cabus, 1863–82 / editors Medill Higgins Harvey, Barbara Veith ; authors Max Donnelly, Alice Cooney Frelinghuysen, Medill Higgins Harvey, Melitta Jonas, Barbara Veith.
Other titles: Modern Gothic (Brooklyn Museum)
Description: Brooklyn, NY : Brooklyn Museum, 2021. | "Published on the occasion of the exhibition Modern Gothic: The Inventive Furniture of Kimbel and Cabus, 1863–82 organized by the Brooklyn Museum and held July 2, 2021–February 13, 2022"—Colophon. | Includes bibliographical references. |
Summary: "Modern Gothic: The Inventive Furniture of Kimbel and Cabus, 1863–82 traces the timeless American immigrant success story of Anton Kimbel and Joseph Cabus. The enterprising New York City design team pioneered an inventive take on Modern Gothic furniture of near-infinite variety, for a broad range of customers, and defined a significant aesthetic in the United States. The Brooklyn Museum, which retains the largest institutional holdings of Kimbel and Cabus's work, is the first to tell their story with new scholarship and fresh insight into this important yet little-explored partnership. A fully illustrated catalogue co-published with Hirmer Press will accompany the exhibition at the Brooklyn Museum that will be on view July 2, 2021–February 13, 2022 . The publication is co-authored by Barbara Veith, Guest Curator, Brooklyn Museum, and Medill Higgins Harvey, Associate Curator of American Decorative Arts and Manager, Henry R. Luce Center for the Study of American Art, Metropolitan Museum of Art, with additional contributions by Max Donnelly, Curator of Nineteenth-Century Furniture, Victoria and Albert Museum; Alice Cooney Frelinghuysen, Anthony W. and Lulu C. Wang Curator of American Decorative Arts, Metropolitan Museum of Art; and Dr. Melitta Jonas, Kunsthistorikerin, Berlin" — Provided by publisher.
Identifiers: LCCN 2021004465 | ISBN 9783777436586 (hardcover)
Subjects: LCSH: Kimbel and Cabus—Exhibitions. | Furniture, Victorian—United States—Exhibitions. | Gothic revival (Art)—United States—Exhibitions.
Classification: LCC NK2439.K55 A4 2021 | DDC 749.0973—dc23
LC record available at https://lccn.loc.gov/2021004465